WE ARE BORN

WE DO THE BEST WE CAN

THEN WE PASS ON

A PERSONAL SKETCHBOOK

VOL IV.... MINNESOTA, 1971-1984

.........ALBERT ALLEN POWERS..........

MINNESOTA

1971-1984

Copyright Albert A. Powers

All rights reserved. No portion of this book may be reproduced in any manner without the written permission of the author, except in brief quotations used in articles or book reviews.

----TO LOUISE----

She who has made the journey worthwhile.

----CONTENTS----

INTRODUCTION	1
ALEXANDRIA FLIGHT SERVICE	7
WEATHER	91
1410 BRYANT STREET	117
1501 RIDGEWAY DRIVE	157
FAMILY ADVENTURES	187
FIREWOOD 101	219
THE GREAT OUTDOORS-FISHING	234
THE GREAT OUTDOORS – TRAPPING	250
THE GREAT OUTDOORS – HUNTING	258
THE SEARCH FOR MYSELF	272
PARADISE MISSING	300
EPILOGUE	316

INTRODUCTION

On Saturday, October 9th, 1971, Louise and I were wrapping things up in Nome, Alaska. I was working as a Flight Service Specialist and the Federal Aviation Administration had reassigned me to Alexandria, Minnesota. I wrote a letter to my parents in Wood River, Illinois.

> Dear Folks,
>
> Right now everything is in a state of semi-confusion. We haven't received our travel orders yet but we've already had the Jeep and the household effects shipped out. The household stuff will go from Anchorage to Alexandria by truck. We'll pick up the Jeep in Anchorage and drive down the Alcan Highway.
>
> If all goes as planned, we'll fly out of here to Anchorage on Sunday, October 17. We plan to spend a couple of days in Anchorage getting the Jeep tuned up, Nugget's (my yellow Labrador) shots up to date, etc. Then we'll drive to Seattle. Louise still has some of her belongings there from when she was going to college. She also wants to visit some friends.

After Seattle, we'll drive to her home in Dickinson, North Dakota. Her parents have their 25th wedding anniversary on November 5th so we'll want to be there for that. Then we'll drive to Alexandria. I'm to report for duty on Monday, November 8th.

I'm sure you've never heard of Alexandria before. It's in Minnesota, about 125 miles northwest of Minneapolis-St. Paul. It's supposed to be kind of a resort area with lots of lakes for fishing. The population is around 7,500.

We're anxious to get there and get settled. We plan to buy a house. Hopefully we can get situated by Christmas. I hope to get checked out on the fishing so you and Dad can come up on your vacation next summer.

Don't know for sure when we'll be able to come home. Will try to get there for Thanksgiving. If not then, we'll try again around Christmas time. Everything will depend on my work schedule and how soon I'll be able to get checked out in the new job. We want to get home as soon as possible so all of you can meet Louise.

Built a big box to take Nugget on the airplane. He doesn't like the looks of it at all. Imagine we'll just have to stuff him in it and close the door. It will only take an hour and a half to get to Anchorage so he shouldn't have too long to suffer.

                              Allen and Louise

Thus it must have been around October 20th, 1971, when Louise and I departed Anchorage. We faced a long and arduous drive down the Alcan and on through British Columbia to Seattle. That was almost half a century ago. There are only a few memories that survive.

Louise drove part of the time on the gravel highway. I remember us cresting a small hill only to be confronted by the large grill of a semi-truck barreling north and taking up far too much of the road. Fortunately Louise was used to driving on gravel roads in rural North Dakota, where it was a common safety practice to keep to the right hand shoulder when driving up a hill. There could not have been much more than six inches between our vehicle and the speeding semi. It was heart thumping.

Then Louise was struggling with intestinal discomfort. "I forgot to tell you," she informed me, "driving makes me gassy." As it turned out, driving was not the cause. More about that later.

I had talked in the last book about our bitterly cold winter in Nome, when the temperature had plunged to forty-eight degrees below zero. The engine hoses in the Jeep had rotted from the cold and I had had to replace them. Now it turned out that the tires had also rotted and the gravel surface of the Alcan was tearing them up. We experienced numerous flat tires. I replaced all four tires plus the spare when we reached Seattle.

For some reason the only place I remember overnighting was at Burwash Landing in the Yukon Territory of Canada. The entire building smelled of kerosene. It was from the heaters that were used to warm the rooms. It brought back memories. I had first smelled the kerosene as an Air Force navigator and we were flying into radar sites across far northern Canada and Alaska. I also remember that at Burwash Landing there was no problem with our dog, Nugget, staying in the room with us.

The only other memory was while we were driving through British Columbia. On our right was a rocky chasm that dropped sharply to a river several hundred feet below. There was no guard rail and a howling wind was buffeting the Jeep back and forth. To make matters worse the steering was mushy. We had packed too much weight in the back of the vehicle, causing the rear end to squat down and the front tires to rise slightly. There was not enough weight on the front tires to give them a good grip on the road.

I rearranged things when we picked up Louise's belongings in Seattle. They added even more weight, enough to bust a couple of the rear springs as it turned out, but now the load was more evenly distributed. We pushed on to Chehalis, Washington, south of Seattle and stayed a night with Ellen's family. Ellen had been one of Louise's roommates in Nome. Her mom and dad had visited Nome shortly before our wedding and Ellen's mom had baked a wedding cake for us.

Then it was time to head east. Our route out of Chehalis took us through mountainous backroads until we could hook up with Interstate 90 and proceed on towards Spokane. I remember that we needed to drive through a mountain pass going into Idaho. It was snowing and most travel was not advised. Semi-trucks were cautioned to put chains on their tires. Louise and I hesitated a bit. Should we try it then or wait until the road conditions improved? We opted to push on. It was not all that bad compared to what we were used to in Alaska. The Jeep's four-wheel drive worked well.

Interstate 90 intersected with Interstate 94 in Billings, Montana. Interstate 94 passed through Louise's hometown of Dickinson, North Dakota and continued on to our final destination of Alexandria, Minnesota.

We reached Dickinson in time to join in the celebration of the 25th anniversary of the wedding of Louise's parents, George and Martha Kubischta. Oh my, I was thrown into kind of a whirlwind of activity. I had been a bit nervous about meeting Louise's family. They were good Catholics and I was an agnostic. Would they look upon me with suspicion? Fortunately they did not, then or at any time in the future. I was welcomed into the family.

The anniversary celebration was held in a large ballroom. There was music from a polka band, with dancing and drinking and visiting. It was not long before Louise's dad, George, cornered me. He was trying to be helpful. He pointed out two or three dozen people and explained in great detail how they were related to him and Martha. I could not keep up with his wide knowledge of his family genealogy. By the time he was into the sixth or seventh generation of his family tree my brain had seized up and I was hopelessly lost. In my own family I had barely known anything about aunts and uncles and first cousins, let alone an extended family tree. But George had a passion for genealogy and he passed that interest on to Louise and me. I looked into it for a few years then dropped out. Louise picked up the trail and over the years has accumulated several volumes of family information.

The anniversary was on November 5th, 1971, and I was due to report for work on the 8th. It was a one-day drive of about 400 miles from Dickinson to Alexandria. We finished the long odyssey from Nome in typical Powers fashion. Eighty miles short of our destination I foolishly ran out of gas. I had to hike a mile and a half to the little farm town of Barnesville to get some fuel. We checked into a motel in Alexandria some time after dark on Sunday, November 7th.

ALEXANDRIA FLIGHT SERVICE

I could not wait. Louise and I had checked into a motel on the edge of the airport. As soon as she was settled I drove to the Flight Service Station. It was a small, white, stucco-sided building. I walked up the three wide concrete steps to the front door.

I entered and stood behind the pilot briefing counter. One man was on duty. I introduced myself. The first question he asked me was what church I went to. When I replied that I did not go to church at all his eyes widened in surprise. I was just as surprised that he had even asked the question. What difference did it make in whether or not I would be a competent Flight Service Specialist and a decent person to work with? I was to find out that in Alexandria religion was everything, and that those of us not involved in religion were looked upon with suspicious eyes.

It came as kind of a shock. In my first book, about growing up in Illinois, I had written about what for me had been a negative experience with extremist religion. The Rev, as I had called him, had been one of those evangelistic ministers who had condemned anything the least bit intellectual, who had thundered that those of us who were not like him were evil bastards who would roast in the fires of hell. I had been more than happy to get away from him. Surely life must have something better to offer.

The intervening years, from age thirteen to thirty-one, had been relatively free of religion. I had become interested in agnosticism while I was in high school. I thought it made ultimate sense. There was no way we could either prove or disprove the existence of a divinity. Mostly, though, I'd had to hide who I was, to keep it locked up inside. I had no desire to argue about religion. Now I was thrown back into the world of extremist religion and I did not feel at all comfortable. There was too much bigotry and hypocrisy and willful ignorance associated with it. I had questions and I had doubts about the validity of this radical brand of religion.

The conflict between me and religious zealots was just as discouraging and depressing now as it had been twenty years earlier, and I the weaker to deal with it. The rotating shift work drained me, both physically and emotionally. I kept my thoughts to myself while I was at work. Louise was the only person I could talk to.

My initial experience working with bush pilots in Nome had provided a good start in Flight Service. Now there was much more to learn. In Nome I had never briefed jet pilots or worked with students. And in Nome I had not been required to take weather observations. That would be a whole new field of study, one that I would enjoy.

The first order of business, just as it had been in Nome, was to pass an area examination. That meant memorizing every airport, common radio frequency, and navigational aid associated with the Alexandria Flight Service Station. It was a large order. In addition I was to begin on-the-job (OJT) training at the various work positions – inflight, preflight, teletype, etc.

I was promoted from a GS-9 to a GS-10 pay grade. It meant an increase in base salary to around $17,000 per year. In addition, there was extra pay for working evenings, Sundays, holidays, and overtime. Now we had ten or twelve specialists to man the station as compared to the seven or eight at Nome. We were open for business twenty-four hours a day, 365 days a year. But the relief from the rotating shift work that I had hoped for did not occur. If anything it became even worse. We worked what was called a "Cincinnati watch," appropriately named, or so I heard, after the schedule a group of Specialists in Cincinnati, Ohio had devised. It amounted to a different shift every day followed by three days off.

We began the work week with a four P.M. to midnight shift. This was followed by a ten A.M. to six P.M., an eight to four, a seven to three, a six to two, and to complete the cycle, a midnight to eight. Some of the specialists liked this schedule because it meant getting off at eight o'clock on a Saturday morning and not having to return until four P.M. the following Monday. To them it was like a three day weekend.

I suffered under that Cincinnati watch. After a few weeks I was utterly exhausted. I had nightmares about imaginary college failures and pilots crashing in flames. I felt so bad that I worried about emotional illness. My body clock was messed up. I did not know when to sleep, when to eat, or when to go to the bathroom. It was like being in a constant state of jet lag. It took at least two days for me to recuperate from the mid-watch that ended our work week. Then I had only one day to get ready for the next week. In twenty-eight years I never got used to working mid-watches. I could sleep for four hours or for fourteen hours and wake up feeling like I had been drugged. It amazes me, when I think back on it, that exhaustion was never much of a subject we talked about. I often wondered if it affected other Specialists as much as it did me.

The muscle tension was terrible. My shoulders were hunched and my neck was stiff. I went to a chiropractor in hopes of getting some relief. It did not seem to help much.

Looking back, I have to wonder whether the rotating shift work explained all the tension. There seemed more to it. I made mention of it on more than one occasion in the notes I kept. The thought sometimes came to mind that every pilot we talked to on the telephone or the radio, or briefed in person at Flight Service, could shortly thereafter crash and die, that even though the chances were minimal they were still there. I realized that it was a gloomy way of looking at things. Surely we saved more lives than we lost.

The worst case scenario would have been that the victim's family sued the FAA for millions of dollars, claiming negligence on our part. Even though we as government employees could not be held personally liable there would have been an emotional price to pay. We would have been required to testify in court. A judge or a jury could have found us to be negligent. The prospect was frightening. How would we ever live it down? It would remain with us for the rest of our lives.

I will have to say that in more than twenty-eight years of working in Flight Service I never heard of such a thing happening, of Flight Service being sued. I do not believe the same could be said of the Center or Tower options, who often were called into question when a big airliner crashed and there were several dozen fatalities. I can think of two or three pilots I briefed on the telephone who a short time later did crash and die but there was no mention of my being at fault.

Still, there was that constant, underlying stress, no matter how small it was. Flight Service was one of those jobs where we held people's lives in our hands. Bad things could happen in aviation. Every radio contact had the potential to turn into an emergency situation. Student pilots became lost. Company pilots worked their way around thunderstorms. Airplanes iced up. They encountered severe turbulence. Pilots could do dumb things; they took chances when there was no need to. The underlying stress was not something we Specialists talked about.

I wondered in my case whether the stress could have been related to my years of flying as an Air Force navigator, to the fundamental danger that is associated with aviation. I recalled that there had always been an underlying tension when we were airborne, especially flying radar missions in the Constellations. We could not trust them. I remembered my very first flight in the Connies. It had taken place off Cape Cod, Massachusetts, and an engine fire had lit up the entire night sky. There had been many more engine fires, many emergencies. We had lost three airplanes and fifty crewmen. Could the stress I now felt working in Flight Service be a form of Post-Traumatic Stress disorder (PTSD) as a result of my time in the Air Force? There was little mention of the seriousness of PTSD at the time.

Thankfully, within a year we voted to change the schedule. Instead of working one mid-watch at a time we worked six in a row about every two months. It still took a toll on the body and the emotions but it was better than that dreadful Cincinnati watch.

I remember the summer when Louise thought she would help me through the stretch of six mid-watches. She and the children would visit her family in North Dakota and leave the house all to me and the dog so I could sleep undisturbed. It turned out that a quiet house was terrible. I could not sleep. There were no noisy children at play, no screaming and laughing, no banging doors, no vacuum cleaner. It was not natural. It was, in fact, downright disturbing. I was a mess by the time my family returned. Louise expressed concern about my emotional condition.

There was a great difference, too, between the workload in the summer months, when vacationers flocked to the area, and the workload in the winter months. Our traffic count - the number of pilots we talked to on the radio, the number of weather briefings, and so forth – described almost a perfect bell curve, with the maximum traffic in July and the minimum in January. Summer was stressful.

The larger air traffic facilities had a break room and a cafeteria. At Alexandria our old and tiny Flight Service building had no separate place to eat, was drafty, had one small bathroom, cold floors, and window air conditioners. To its credit it did have large windows so that we had a good view of most of the airport. We usually packed a brown paper bag lunch and ate at our work positions. We were often so overwhelmed by work during the summer months that we could not take time for a lunch break. We would gobble down our sandwiches between phone calls, or talking to pilots on the radio, as I am doing in the above photo. It invariably led to heartburn. There were days when we had no time at all to eat lunch. We would carry our food back home with us. Our nerves would be wound so tightly by the end of the day that it would have taken an entire pitcher of martinis to calm us down, and I was not a drinker.

Working at a small Flight Service Station allowed us to witness and to participate somewhat vicariously in some of the Walter Mitty dreams of greatness. High school teenagers pumped gas in order to earn flying lessons. The pilots were like gods to them. There were men experiencing mid-life crises. A local TV personality quit his job and attempted to start a charter business. It failed, and his marriage along with it. The ultimate dream was to become an airline pilot. I remember three from Alexandria who made it.

There was quite a variety of airplanes that passed through the Alexandria airport. The runways had been constructed during WWII. They were long enough and solid enough to handle even some of the larger airline-type airplanes. Little single engine aircraft, I called them bug smashers, formed the bulk of our traffic. Larger twin-engine planes and small passenger jets made up maybe twenty per cent of the traffic count. I remember a Boeing 727 landing a couple of times when the Vice President paid a visit to Alexandria. Military C-130 cargo planes out of an Air National Guard unit in Minneapolis were occasional arrivals. We worked closely with Army helicopters from Camp Ripley, north of Minneapolis.

The oddest plane of all was an old Ford Trimotor that was parked on the ramp in front of Flight Service for a couple of days. God, it was an odd and clumsy looking piece of machinery. The body and wings were constructed of shiny aluminum corrugated sheet-metal. No wonder it had been nicknamed "The Tin Goose." There was a propeller on each wing and one on the nose. I climbed inside to have a look. The cabin was incredibly narrow, with barely enough room to walk between the two single rows of seats. The plane had been produced sometime in the 1920s or '30s. It had been beautifully restored.

People hung around the Station and the airport. They were fascinated by airplanes and pilots. The airport became a part of the community. Teachers booked field trips to learn about flying and about weather. School principals called to check the forecast. Was snow moving in and should they cancel classes for the day? Local pilot groups asked us to speak at their meetings. Summer Sundays were a particularly enjoyable time for family visits. I looked out of the Flight Service window one Sunday afternoon to see a young father and mother pushing a baby carriage down the runway. I called the Airport Manager to chase them away. There were rumors about occasional midnight drag races on the remote end of one of the runways.

I felt professional working with the pilots and that feeling was often reciprocated. It was a good feeling when they sometimes asked for me by name. There was some teaching involved in so far as student pilots were concerned. Flight Service was usually their first contact with Air Traffic Control and the FAA. I took pleasure in working with them. Of course there was little teaching involved with commercial and airline pilots. It is more likely they could have taught us.

The professionalism led to an accommodation. I was given a Special Achievement Award for the period November 1, 1973 through November 1, 1974. The Flight Service Chief praised me for accomplishing the job in a superior manner. He especially made note of the fact that the Alexandria Airport Manager had expressed his appreciation for my good service, and that he was speaking on behalf of his entire staff and students. Of course the award made me feel good. Apparently I was doing something right in my life. Positive feedback is always appreciated. The cash award of $200 that accompanied the prize was also much welcomed.

There were requirements for constant training and retraining. It was a vital part of the job. We needed to remain sharp, to keep up with procedural changes and new equipment. I was appointed the Station training officer, mainly because nobody else wanted to do it. I made up monthly quizzes. We completed refresher courses and practiced our lost aircraft procedures. Most specialists groaned at the constant repetitiveness but training was a necessary evil.

I particularly enjoyed working with Special VFR (SVFR) clearances. (Visual Flight Rules rather than flying by cockpit instruments). It made me feel more like an Air Traffic Controller than a mere Specialist. I was responsible for keeping traffic separated.

SVFR conditions applied when the ceiling was below 1,000 feet and/or the surface visibility at the airport was less than three miles. VFR aircraft then needed a clearance to enter or to depart the airport "control zone," an imaginary boundary generally three miles in diameter around the airport. Technically, the Air Traffic Control Center in Minneapolis was in control of the zone but we had a letter of agreement whereby we could request the zone for a specified period of time if the Center was not working other traffic either landing or departing Alexandria. We became really proficient at clearing traffic. We generally worked with one airplane at a time but there were occasions when two small aircraft would arrive or depart together. This was legal so long as they kept visual separation.

I remember one occasion when two Canadian pilots flying little bug smashers were stuck in Alexandria due to fog. Their destination was Winnipeg via Fargo and Grand Forks, North Dakota. The weather northwest of Alexandria was marginal but above the legal requirements for VFR flight. The pilots figured they could follow Interstate 94 until the weather improved. They were in a hurry to depart and requested SVFR clearance as they taxied out. It was legal for them to depart as a flight of two so long as they remained in visual contact with each other while they were in the control zone.

I dialed the Minneapolis Center controller via a direct telephone line and got the zone. The clearance I gave them would have read something like – "ATC clears Canadian aircraft such and such and such and such (two airplanes) to depart the Alexandria control zone to the northwest. Maintain VFR. Maintain visual separation. Report when clear of the zone."

One of the pilots read back the clearance word for word and the pilots applied takeoff power to their little bugs. I watched them as they became airborne. They were soon out of sight and a couple of minutes later they reported clear of the zone. It was one of those times when I hoped for the best. The weather was marginal and the pilots were pushing their luck. It was not uncommon when the weather conditions were iffy for light aircraft to fly low and navigate by following roads. Another term for VFR flight, remaining clear of the clouds, was "Vee Follow Roads" and for IFR, using cockpit instruments while in the clouds, "I Follow Roads."

I could visualize the two Canadian pilots finding themselves almost immediately over the Interstate and turning northwest towards Fargo, 100 miles up the road. A few minutes after they departed all the lights on the west side of Alexandria suddenly went out. One of the airplanes had been flying so low, probably not much more than fifty feet above the ground, that it had clipped a power line strung over the highway. It apparently had caused no major damage to the airplane because I heard no more from the pilots. It had been the pilot's lucky day. Probably if the power line had been a few inches higher or lower it would have caused the aircraft to crash.

There are special memories, even after almost half a century, of coming up with unique ways to help pilots. One day when the weather was low I heard an unusual clicking noise on one of our radio frequencies. It sounded as if someone was clicking his transmitter. I had just given an aircraft a SVFR clearance to land. "By the way," the pilot told me, "I have visual contact with another aircraft out here who looks like he wants to land. Apparently his radio is out of service." I surmised that the other aircraft was the source of the clicking noise.

I don't know, there were probably some Flight Service Specialists who would have ignored the situation. But I was mindful of the paragraph in our regulations that called upon us to use professional judgement when we encountered unusual situations not covered by the book. I was also mindful of the Air Force pilots and the Alaskan bush pilots I had worked with when they had sometimes stretched the rules a bit in order to complete a mission. They had exercised professional judgement.

"Unknown aircraft east of Alexandria," I called out on the radio, "if you can hear Alexandria radio click your mike button two times."

"Click, Click."

"Roger, understand you can receive but not transmit. If that is correct, click your mike button three times."

"Click, click, click."

"Roger, understand you can receive but not transmit. Are you requesting a Special VFR clearance to enter the control zone and land at Alexandria? If you are, click your mike button two times."

"Click, click."

"Roger, standby for clearance."

I called Minneapolis Center and received permission to use the zone for twenty minutes.

"Unknown aircraft east of Alexandria, I have a clearance for you. Click you mike button twice if you are ready to copy."

"Click, click."

"ATC (Air Traffic Control) clears unknown aircraft east of Alexandria to enter the control zone. Maintain VFR. Report entering the zone. If you copied the clearance key your mike button three times."

"Click, click, click."

"Roger, understand you copied the clearance. Click your mike button three times when you enter the zone."

A couple of minutes later – "Click, click, click."

The aircraft made a safe landing and the pilot came into Flight Service to thank me. He was beginning to run low on fuel, he said. If the situation had gotten desperate enough he would have had no choice except to land without a clearance. That was something he had wanted to avoid.

I had used professional judgement to issue a clearance in an unusual and entirely unorthodox way. There was nothing in the rules about it. There is an expression for it. It is called "Thinking outside the box." Years later national evaluators tossed out the provision for using professional judgement. They favored doing everything strictly by the book. They did not want us to do any thinking on our own. It became a bone of contention for me and is one of the reasons I decided to retire earlier than I would have liked to.

I developed the impression that those who did everything by the book were afraid to stick their necks out, were afraid to accept responsibility for their actions, were afraid to think outside the box. If a pilot was struggling and needed advice he was on his own. If anything went wrong, if the aircraft crashed, the briefer could always claim he had done everything by the book. It seemed the very opposite of how professionalism should be defined. The professional would bend over backwards trying to help, would use what he had learned from years of experience, so long as it did not compromise safety.

I observed, too, that many of those who did things strictly by the book were terrified about dealing with emergencies. Let's say a low time VFR pilot is about to fly into IFR weather and radios for help. The by-the-booker will get out the emergency checklist and start getting background information. Where did the aircraft depart from, what is its destination, how many people are on board, how much fuel is remaining, what is his heading, and on and on. It is all vital information but it takes time to get it. And no matter what the book says it should not have first priority in this situation. The first order of business is to advise the pilot to make a 180-degree turn before he ever enters the low weather. Then collect the background information and help the pilot find an alternate destination or a nearby airport where he can safely land.

Even more dramatic, let's say a pilot called in desperation to say that he had twenty minutes of fuel remaining and needed a heading to the nearest airport. There were no GPS readouts in those days to show him. He had to rely on air traffic controllers. Our choice was to waste ten of those precious minutes getting background information or to figure out an immediate heading to an airport and obtain the background information later. I remember saying things like – "Cessna one two three Mike Charlie, turn left now heading two two five. Report established on a heading of two two five. You are approximately fifteen miles northeast of the Fergus Falls airport." When the pilot reported on the heading I would then say things like – "Roger, continue heading two two five. How many people are on board and how much fuel is remaining?"

Thus I would take action first and get the background information later, after I had the pilot safely headed towards an airport. Safety and professionalism had a higher priority than following a checklist. Fortunately I never had to work an emergency while a quality control person or a national evaluator was watching. They would have gone berserk.

I don't know, we were all different, and we all had different experiences. I had been an Air Force navigator. I had logged more than 3,000 hours of flying time. One of the other Flight Service Specialists had been a radioman in the Navy. A couple more had been starving pilots and another had worked in an Air Force control tower. Another had been a policeman. A standardized, by-the-book way of doing things certainly had value so far as aviation safety was concerned. But it could also be used as a crutch for those who did not want to deal with emergencies. I looked at some of my fellow employees. I looked at the national evaluators. Had they ever been in an aircraft weighted down with ice? Had they watched a flight engineer race down the aisle to peer out a window at an engine fire? Hell, I had to think that nearly half of the Air Force missions I had flown had involved some kind of emergency. We'd had to man up and deal with it.

I continued to polish my pilot weather briefing technique. I remembered that the ABC's of good writing were Accuracy, Brevity, and Clarity. I surmised these characteristics should apply to the spoken word as well. After all, why would anybody call it a "briefing" if we made no attempt to keep it brief?

But brevity was not something that was universally practiced by all Fight Service Specialists. I remember one Flight Service Chief in particular. He would occasionally come out of his office and into operations to help us out when things became hectic and the telephones were ringing off their hooks. He was strictly old school in his weather briefing technique. He read everything verbatim from the teletype sheets and used a checklist to make sure he covered every detail of information. It was not at all unusual for him to take ten or fifteen minutes to complete even the simplest briefing. I could imagine the pilots' eyes glazing over long before our Chief had finished. It was doubtful they had a clear picture of the weather.

I observed one specialist who could deliver an entirely professional weather briefing in four or five minutes. He did it by <u>summarizing</u>, by verbally painting a weather picture rather than reading dozens of reports. He could churn out an amazing amount of work in a short time.

The technique was simple and one which I made frequent use of the rest of my career. Most of our little bug smasher airplanes seldom flew above 10,000 feet. There was a reason for it. Protracted flight above 10,000 feet in unpressurized airplanes required that oxygen be available to prevent hypoxia and the associated mental confusion or loss of consciousness. When all the reported and forecast clouds were at 15,000 or 20,000 feet, why the hell was there even a need to talk about them? All we needed to say was – "There is high pressure enroute. No clouds are reported or forecast below 10,000 feet."

There it is – a complete weather picture in less than ten seconds. Add the current and forecast weather at departure and destination, the forecast winds aloft, plus other aeronautical data, such as a navigation aid that was out of service, or a restricted area to avoid, and the briefing was complete in just a few minutes.

Or conversely – "There is low pressure enroute. All stations are reporting IFR. The forecast is for little change until early tomorrow morning. VFR flight is not recommended." Usually that was enough information for the pilot to make a decision. Why waste another ten minutes, unless it was something the pilot wanted to do, talking about the weather conditions when the pilot had already decided not to go?

I remember there was one pilot who made frequent VFR charter flights from Fergus Falls, near Fargo, to Minneapolis. He must have known every fence post along the route of flight. I probably briefed him several hundred times over the span of the thirteen years I worked in

Alexandria. We came to trust each other's judgement. He would call on the telephone and make a simple request. "All I want to know is one thing. Can I go VFR or not? If I answered "no" that would be the end of the conversation and I would log it as a complete weather briefing. Otherwise, I would give him all the information.

Years later, when the idiot national evaluators took over, this kind of briefing would have driven them berserk. I had not done things by the book. I had not wasted fifteen minutes of the pilot's time or my time explaining in great detail why VFR flight was not recommended. The evaluators would have condemned me back to the classroom for remedial training.

Mention of Fergus Falls has caused my mind to wander for a moment. For a few months there had been an ad in Alexandria's little *Echo Press* newspaper. Somebody in Fergus Falls was selling beef at an incredibly low price. The public rushed to take advantage of the bargains. Then there was an announcement by the Ottertail County sheriff's department. The people selling the beef had been arrested. They were cattle rustlers. They had stolen the animals in Kansas or Texas or some place like that and had marketed the meat in this remote little town in Minnesota.

Of course weather briefings were not always as simple as the picture I have painted. There were times when they were downright complex and aviation safety became more of a concern. Sometimes there was marginal or IFR conditions for part of the flight and decent weather for the remainder. Sometimes the weather was either deteriorating or improving. This took a more detailed look but could still be painted somewhat with words. Professional judgement needed to be used to ensure safety.

The final say was, of course, the pilot's. Some wanted everything read to them. Others preferred the summarized version. In my defense I will have to say that the positive feedback I received from numerous pilots over the years gave me the feeling that I was doing a good job. Before they hung up, they would complement me for a clear and concise weather briefing. Some wanted to know my name so they could ask for me. That was not something the FAA allowed us to do.

We were not trained meteorologists but if we wanted to be good at our jobs and promote aviation safety we needed to learn more than just to read weather reports and forecasts verbatim. We needed to get some idea of what was going on in the atmosphere. We needed to learn how to read weather charts.

Surface charts of course show highs and lows and frontal activity on the surface. We see them all the time on TV. The standard atmospheric pressure is measured at 29.92 inches of mercury. It is also measured at 1013 millibars (mb), a metric unit of pressure. A 700 mb chart, for example, shows weather conditions at about 10,000 feet; 500mb, 18,000 feet; and 300mb, 30,000 feet. They provide data on what is happening in the atmosphere.

The 500 mb chart became one of my favorites. I would look at the position of a high or a low on the surface and compare it to its position on the 500 mb chart. If it did not show up at 18,000 feet that usually meant it was shallow and weak. If the position aloft was directly above the surface location that meant there was little movement. It was called a "stacked" low. If the position aloft was quite a bit east of that on the surface it indicated rapid movement to the east.

Of course there was much more to it than the simple example I gave above. There were many more meteorological charts than those I have mentioned. Unfortunately what we learned about charts was mostly by word of mouth among us or by individual study. The FAA provided little additional training. Some specialists were interested in the charts and others were not. I was somewhere in the middle.

I do not remember ever working an actual lost aircraft while I was stationed in Nome. Bush pilots tended not to get lost. But at Alexandria we worked with so many lost aircraft that every journeyman became quite proficient at it. It was a year-round problem but the summers were especially busy. Student pilots flooded out of the Minneapolis area and the flight school at the University of North Dakota in Grand forks. They were completing the cross-country portion of their training. Invariably three or four or five would get lost every weekend day and call for help. They were trying to navigate by map reading and by using radio aids to navigation that were called VORs - Very High Frequency (VHF) Omni-Directional Range. They did not fully understand the VORs and I had learned in the Air Force that map reading can be surprisingly difficult for the uninitiated.

The student pilots would be frightened and unable to think clearly. Since I had been an old Air Force navigator myself and had worked my way out of many a shaky situation, I would try to encourage the students to relax by making light of the situation. I told them that they were not entirely lost, that we could be assured they were somewhere over the State of Minnesota. Hopefully that brought a smile to their faces.

We used a combination of Direction Finder (DF) that homed in on the aircraft's radio, VORs, and NDBs (Non-Directional Beacon) to pinpoint the lost aircrafts' positions and to guide them to the airport of their choice. I thought the NDBs were interesting, though I do not remember other Flight Service Specialists making much use of them. I had used them to navigate across much of frozen Canada when I had been an Air Force navigator. What was most intriguing was that many commercial radio stations could be used as NDBs. Pilots could tune into a football game and the aircraft's receiver would provide a direction to the radio station.

I tried to teach the students some little tricks of the trade. It they were lost and near a town I told them they could buzz down and read the name of the town from its water tower, then proceed from there. It was one of the lessons I had learned in the Air Force navigation training school.

Sometimes pilots would request a practice DF steer to the Alexandria airport. Our DF locked onto the aircraft's radio transmitter and gave us a heading to the airport. We used the DF a lot, especially when locating lost aircraft.

One sunny summer afternoon a young Piper Cherokee pilot took three of his friends out for a joy ride. An hour or so later he radioed for a practice DF steer back to the Alexandria airport. I had to deny the request because I was busy working with other aircraft. "Okay, then," he responded, "how about the real thing. I'm lost." I located him east of the airport and brought him in. He had been showing his friends the sights and had not paid attention to navigation.

We used the DF to guide airplanes directly over the airport. One of us would be communicating with the pilot by radio, giving him corrections to his heading. When the airplane was getting near the airport the other specialists would stand outside Flight Service and look for it. We wanted to confirm the accuracy of the DF. We were surprised at how difficult it was to spot a small airplane against either clouds or a clear sky. We often heard the engine noise before we saw the aircraft.

I was working alone one spring evening when I received a call from a lost aircraft. He was on a VFR flight plan from Watertown, South Dakota, to Fargo, North Dakota. He had deviated east of course to get around some low weather. His airplane was experiencing electrical problems. None of his navigation aids, including his gyro-stabilized compass, were functioning properly and his radio communications with me were intermittent. I was able to receive a short DF strobe which indicated that the aircraft was southwest of Alexandria.

All the stations in the area were reporting IFR conditions. Alexandria's ceiling was eight hundred feet broken, which meant there were some gaps in the clouds. The surface visibility was a good seven miles, more than enough for VFR flight. I felt that under the circumstances our best option was to bring the airplane to Alexandria. He had plenty of fuel and I could get him a SVFR (Special VFR) clearance.

As it seemed to happen so often, especially in aviation, what at first appeared to be a fairly simple problem slowly deteriorated into something far more serious. The airplane's directional gyro would not hold a heading and his backup magnetic compass was bouncing back and forth all over the place. We finally resorted to simple commands, such as "turn fifteen degrees right" or "ten degrees left" and the pilot would approximate the heading. My goal was to get him within sight of the Alexandria airport.

Fortunately, as the pilot tacked his way towards Alexandria his radio transmissions became stronger and the DF bearings more reliable. Things were looking up.

But another problem became increasingly more serious as the situation dragged on. I had hoped to get the airplane on the ground fairly quickly but that was not happening. With his electrical problems I had not been able to get a cross bearing on him and determine how far out he was. He had been farther out than I had initially thought. Now half an hour had gone by.

I could see by looking out the window that the weather at Alexandria was deteriorating. The visibility was decreasing and when that happens the ceiling often lowers also. But I had no time to step outside and take a hasty weather observation. I was beginning to sweat.

The pilot confirmed that as he got closer to the airport the ceiling and the visibility were lower. I turned the runway lights up to the maximum brightness and crossed my fingers. I kept checking the DF bearing to make sure the aircraft was not straying too far off course. Finally, thankfully, the pilot reported the airport in sight.

Because of the lowering weather conditions I wanted to get the pilot on the ground ASAP. I recommended a straight-in approach to runway 4, even though that meant landing with a slight tailwind. Pilots prefer landing into a headwind, which reduces their groundspeed. The pilot, however, elected to fly a normal pattern and land on runway 22. He parked the plane and walked into Flight Service.

"You were right," he told me, "I should have come straight in on runway 4. The ceiling was down to 400 feet as I approached the airport. It had dropped to 200 feet by the time I flew the pattern and was on final approach for 22. I barely made it in even after I had the airport in sight."

There were some situations that not only turned out well but in the end were mildly humorous. The incident I remember most vividly took place on a beautiful VFR summer day. I was working the radio position when I received a call from a pilot northwest of Alexandria. He said he was in radio contact with a young lady on air-to-air frequency 122.9. She was lost and needed help. I instructed the pilot to have her come up on our Flight Service frequency 123.6.

I established radio contact with our lost pilot and, after obtaining preliminary information, determined by cross referencing the DF bearing and a VOR navigation aid reading that she was near Fergus Falls, forty miles northwest of Alexandria. She said she wanted to land at Alexandria. She had plenty of fuel. I gave her a DF steer to the airport. Everything went smoothly and in less than half an hour she was on the ground.

The pilot parked her Cessna 152 on the ramp and walked into Flight Service. She asked if she could telephone her instructor in St. Cloud, sixty miles southeast of Alexandria. After a few minutes of conversation she handed the phone over and said her instructor wanted to talk to one of us.

I watched as another specialist took the call. I noticed the visible expression of amazement that came over his face. What the heck was going on? The instructor said that under no circumstances were we to allow the student pilot back into the airplane. He would arrange for someone to drive him to Alexandria. Then he would fly her and the airplane back to St. Cloud.

What had happened was this. The young student pilot had only recently soloed. She did not yet have the training or experience for cross country navigation. The instructor had released her for a strictly local flight in the St. Cloud area. Ideally she would not have strayed much more than five or ten miles from the airport. Something had gone wrong and she had lost her bearing. She had kept flying rather than asking for help right away. When I found her she had strayed *100 miles* to the northwest of St. Cloud. It must surely have been one of the most far reaching local flights in student pilot history.

Student pilots sometimes had difficulty seeing an airport in the winter, even if they were right over it. Everything was white. The runways, even though they had been plowed, would be covered with a layer of packed snow. For some reason the airport at Park Rapids seemed to challenge pilots in the winter, even though the VOR radio aid was located right on the airport. We had a student pilot on a cross-country flight from Grand Forks to Park Rapids. I had guided him to two or three passes over the airport without him seeing it. I had a microphone in one hand and a telephone in the other. I was relaying information from the airport operator, who was standing outside and watching from the ground, to the young pilot. "Tell the pilot to look at his one o'clock position for about one mile." Finally - "Tell him he's right over the airport – look straight down." The aircraft made a safe landing.

Radio communications in general aviation usually followed the same format I had learned as an Air Force navigator. We used the phonetic alphabet. "A" was alpha, "k" was kilo, "z" was zulu, and so forth. In the numbers 1-10, nine was always pronounced "niner." It was a system that had been worked out over many years to promote clarity and to minimize misunderstanding at a time when radio communications were often fuzzy and garbled due to atmospheric conditions.

In the 1970s citizens band (CB) radio had become widely popular. It was a form of short range, person-to-person communications. It did not require a license. CB slang expressions showed up in popular TV shows and in movies. They were also extensively used by truckers. "Good Buddy" was the person they were talking to. "That's a big ten-four" meant that they acknowledged a message. "Smokey Bear" was a police officer. Remember that there were no cellular telephones in those days. People could install CB radios in their personal vehicles and use them to call for help in an emergency.

It was inevitable that some of the CB slang would spill over into aviation talk. Particularly annoying was the substitution of the letter "o" for the number zero. "My ETA is oh five hundred," instead of "zero five hundred." "My telephone number is four one four oh two two oh," instead of four one four zero two two zero." We used to chide them – "Please do not say oh when you mean zero. Oh is what you say when someone gooses you."

We must have been responsible for fifty or more Minnesota airports. Many of them were tiny. Some were little more than a windsock in a farmer's pasture, with a barn or a machine shed serving as a hangar. The windsocks were important. It was safer for pilots to land or take off into the wind rather than to deal with a tailwind. The head wind increased the speed at which the air was flowing over the airplane's surfaces, thus providing more lift. At the same time, a headwind reduced ground speed so that aircraft did not need as much runway to land on or depart from. Crosswinds could be problematic. Most of the little airports had only a single, grass runway. Each airplane was rated for how much of a crosswind it could safely tolerate.

These were seldom more than fifteen or twenty miles an hour.

So a pilot landing at one of these little airfields would look down at the windsock. Its orientation would indicate the direction of the wind. If it was hanging limp the wind speed was less than three knots. Slightly extended was around six knots; mostly extended, around twelve knots; and fully extended around 15-20 knots or more. Remember that ten knots is about 11 ½ MPH.

We were encouraged to visit these little airports, to get a visual picture in our minds of what they looked like, and to spend time with the pilots who flew out of them. When things were slow on a winter day, and two or three of us were working, the Chief would give his permission for one of us to take the government car and go for a drive. It was a pleasant break from the normal work day. We were able to talk to the pilots, to get a sense of the problems they had to deal with, and how we could better serve them.

Those little airports were unique. They mostly were composed of short, sod runways that had to be mowed in the summer and remained closed all winter when snow moved in. I remember sending out a notice on more than one occasion advising pilots to be careful of gopher mounds.

Some of the pilots flew out of the private airports and the farm fields by choice. They wanted minimum contact with the FAA. They wanted to be independent and were wary of government oversight. The only problem was that if they did wreck their airplane, and they had not checked the weather or had any contact with the FAA, they could have a problem with both the FAA and their insurance company. The FAA could suspend or pull their pilot's license; their insurance company could refuse to pay the repair bill.

Then there were those rare few, mostly low-time and inexperienced pilots, who actually bristled against the rules. They would heed no advice or words of warning. A disproportionate number of them died. One had to wonder why. There must have been some kind of a psychological problem.

Things went well with management and with the pilots but the rotating shift work kept dragging me down. I was constantly exhausted. The summer traffic was brutal.

One summer evening I was working alone, as was common. It must have been round eight P.M. and the specialist working the ten A.M. to six P.M. shift had long departed. The telephones were going unanswered. I needed to step outside and take a weather observation. I had no time to sort through the many teletype reports. Two pilots were calling on the radio. Pilots in flight had priority so I was talking to one and had asked the other to standby.

I quickly finished with the first pilot but the second one was being a pest. First he wanted this weather report and then the frequency of that navigation aid and then a forecast someplace else. There was nothing coherent to his requests. He was wasting my time while the work piled up behind me.

Finally, I snapped. I'd had my fill. I was exhausted and grouchy to begin with. I turned off the microphone and let out a string of curses that would have burned the ears of the saltiest sailor. That was when I heard a soft cough. I turned and saw a lady standing ten feet away, behind the briefing counter. I had not heard her enter the building. "Oh, my god," I apologized. "Please excuse me. I thought I was by myself. I had no idea you were standing there." I was embarrassed as hell. "That's okay," she replied. "My husband is a plumber. I hear him talking like that all the time." She was there to check her pilot husband's ETA (Estimated Time of Arrival).

At Alexandria there was for many years, and still may be, an active sky diving chapter. To my way of thinking, people who purposely jump out of a perfectly functioning airplane are a breed apart. I'm not talking about those who jump one time just for the thrill of it and then hang it up. I'm talking about the ones who jump hundreds of times, year after year. Spiritually, I think they march to the same drummer as the Alaskan bush pilots. They skirt the edges, taking risks, always in danger of falling off.

We had first-time skydivers land in lakes, on rooftops, and dangling from power lines. We had them limping off the airport with sprained ankles and carried off with broken bones. And the mixture of aircraft wanting to enter the pattern while parachutes floated down sometimes provided a heart thumping diversion. Of course the skydivers were required to file a notice with us before they jumped and we were required to warn aircraft of the activity.

Most of the skydiving activity took place during daylight but there were occasional night jumps where they attached a light to their parachute harness. I remember stepping out into the darkness one evening and watching as spots of light floated down. I could not see the jumpers or their parachutes but I could hear them yelling in wild exaltation.

People enjoyed watching the skydivers. Many of the parachutes were colorful, with multiple hues and patterns. When they popped open my little daughter compared them to flowers blossoming. And these were not the old military parachutes of WWII fame. They were flatter, more modern, and highly maneuverable. We watched them swirl around like maple tree seeds whirly-birding to the ground.

When people continue to take risks sooner or later some tragedy is bound to occur. I wasn't at work when it happened in Alexandria. I am glad I was not there to witness it.

It took place on a clear, summer Sunday afternoon. An instructor and a student were going up for the student's first jump. The doctor who performed our annual flight physical examinations was at the controls of the single-engine airplane. Brenda, the young wife of our airport manager, and her visiting parents were watching from the steps of the Airport Operations building, next door to Flight Service.

The instructor and the student jumped out of the airplane together, the instructor to yell directions to the student as they descended. They were directly over the airport. The student's parachute opened; the instructor's did not. The student landed safely. The instructor's body hit on the tarmac by the gas pumps, not more than fifty feet from where Brenda and her parents were sitting. Witnesses said the body bounced several feet into the air. I had to wonder whether the instructor was screaming in wild-eyed terror or mute with fear. It must have been a hell of a way to die. They said that Brenda became hysterical. What had been intended as an enjoyable afternoon had ended in unspeakable tragedy.

There were many aircraft accidents and many lives lost. A lot of them were weather related, particularly during the summer. We called it "get-home-itis." Minnesota, with all its lakes and resorts and cottages, was a huge summer vacation destination. Wealthy pilots would fly up from Illinois and Iowa and Nebraska to spend a holiday weekend at their "cottage," which to most of us was more akin to a mansion than a humble home. They needed to return to work immediately after the weekend. They would take crazy chances when the weather turned bad. Fog seemed to be the main factor. Strictly VFR pilots with no real experience flying on instruments would attempt to climb on top of the fog. Their brains would be scrambled by vertigo and they would crash. It happened several times.

A person who has never experienced vertigo may not understand the problem. It is an inner ear phenomenon. In the case of aviation it is also known as spatial disorientation. A pilot flying in the clouds has no reference to the horizon. Is his left wing lower than his right, is he turning or climbing? He has no way of knowing without being able to see the horizon. Everything starts spinning and he gets nauseous. He loses complete control of the aircraft. It has happened thousands of times.

The solution is to place an artificial horizon in the cockpit instrument panel. It will indicate whether the aircraft is in straight and level flight or otherwise. But it takes some interpretation. There is a learning curve that involves additional training and experience. Pilots practice flying "under the hood." They strap a device to their head that limits their vision to only the cockpit instrument panel. All outside visual references are taken away.

Beginning pilots are usually not comfortable using an artificial horizon. Experienced pilots who have flown many thousands of hours on instruments are so used to it that they hardly pay any attention. It is the difference between flying VFR (Visual Flight Rules) with visual reference to the earth and IFR (Instrument Flight Rules) using an artificial horizon.

I no longer remember how many of these summer vacationers we lost in the thirteen years I worked at Alexandria. There were probably at least six or eight crashes, with fifteen or twenty fatalities.

We used to say that some of the most dangerous pilots were doctors and dentists with low time IFR experience and flying a Beechcraft Bonanza. They had the money to buy the more powerful airplane than the typical little bug smasher, and they were intelligent enough to learn things quickly, but they were always in a hurry. They would have rushed through all their training in the minimum amount of time. They had the rating to fly IFR but lacked experience.

They would get themselves into solid IFR flying conditions and encounter more problems than they could handle.

A noted surgeon from New Jersey had a summer place on one of the Alexandria lakes. He would fly his twin-engine Piper Aztec to Alexandria for a few days of rest and recuperation. Thus it happened that he had worked all day, then piled his wife and five children into the airplane before heading for Alexandria. He did not file a flight plan but expected to arrive around midnight. As he passed over Minneapolis he checked the Alexandria weather and found that it was deteriorating. The wise thing would have been to land at Minneapolis, refuel, recheck the weather, and decide whether or not to proceed. Instead he chose to press on. Fatigue could have been a factor in opting not to get more fuel.

The weather was IFR when he arrived over Alexandria. He shot an approach but could not find the airport. Now he was in big trouble. He did not have enough fuel to fly the hundred miles back to Minneapolis or the hundred miles farther northwest to Fargo. Fergus Falls, forty miles northwest, had reported a slight improvement in weather. Our specialist tried to help the pilot with DF steers. The pilot, now critically low on fuel, decided to try for it. He crashed a mile short of the Fergus Falls runway. All seven people on board died. It was a hell of a tragedy and it did not have to happen at all.

Another pilot was based in Montana. He had a brother who lived in Green Bay, WI. The brother passed away and the pilot was desperate to get to Green Bay for the funeral. He loaded his wife and daughter into his airplane and took off.

He was a VFR-only pilot and he had good weather all the way from Montana to Fergus Falls, where he landed to refuel. The weather all the rest of the way to Green Bay was IFR with low ceilings and visibilities. He called and got a complete weather briefing from Robin, one of our specialists. She told him that VFR flight was definitely not recommended. The pilot thought he could get by if he flew low along Interstate 94. *Robin begged him not to try it.*

Forty-five minutes later, two farmers standing in a field north of Alexandria heard a loud, whining noise and a terrific crash. They rushed over to where the airplane had left a crater in the ground. The pilot and his wife and daughter had perished. He had been in a panic to get to a funeral. Now there would be three more. Was it worth it?

I don't know. Death is a part of many jobs – of police and medical people and social workers and air traffic controllers. But there is always a question when someone dies – did I do enough? And there was always the underlying stress in Flight Service – will I be the last person this pilot ever talks to?

One summer a twin Cessna was hauling machine parts to a manufacturing plant in Alexandria. It was shortly after midnight and the weather was low IFR. The pilot attempted an approach and crashed in a swamp a quarter mile short of the runway. It took rescuers two hours to locate the wreckage. Both the pilot and co-pilot had been seriously injured. I could only imagine how awful it must have been lying helpless and alone and in pain in that mosquito infested swamp.

One last story and I will get off the gloomy subject of aircraft fatalities. In my twenty-eight years of working in Flight Service I lost only one pilot. The majority of journeymen were luckier. They never lost any.

He was young and inexperienced, strictly a VFR pilot flying a little single-engine Cessna. I doubt that he had logged more than a hundred hours of flying time. He flew in daylight hours and decent weather from northern Michigan to Eau Claire, Wisconsin, where he stopped to refuel late in the afternoon. He had already put in a long day of flying. His destination was Morris, Minnesota, thirty miles southwest of Alexandria. The specialist at the Eau Claire Flight Service Station advised him not to try the rest of the trip VFR. A low pressure system with IFR conditions was moving into the Morris area. The pilot filed a flight plan and elected to press on anyway.

I was working the evening shift at Alexandria, from 4 P.M. to midnight. Morris was one of our airports. I looked worriedly at the single inbound strip and hoped the pilot had had enough sense to check the weather and know what he was heading into. Fergus Falls, a few miles north of Morris, was already reporting IFR. Near dark, I looked to the west of Alexandria and could see low clouds in the distance.

I paced the floor with worry. I had a VFR pilot heading into IFR weather. We never knew how these things were going to turn out. Hopefully the pilot would see the weather ahead of him before it got too dark. I could breathe a sigh of relief if he decided to turn around and land elsewhere.

It was just after dark when the weak radio call came in. I could barely hear it. The pilot was in trouble. I noticed his bearing on the Direction Finder strobe. He was due south of Alexandria. I remember the sound of his voice to this day, forty years later. The pilot said he had flown all day, was tired, and had encountered some clouds. He asked for help. I did what I had been trained to do since my earliest days in Flight Service. I advised the pilot to immediately turn back east and get the hell out of the weather. That was the only communication I had with him and I'm not certain he even received it.

I sent out a teletype message, asking if anyone else had spoken to the aircraft. The specialist at Eau Claire replied that he had advised against flight. The specialist at Redwood Falls Flight Service, south of Alexandria, responded that he had barely heard the pilot calling me and that he had also picked up a DF bearing. Eventually we had to notify Search and Rescue. A search was conducted over the next three or four days but no wreckage was located.

A farmer spotted the airplane about ten days after the crash. It was hanging in some trees at the back part of his acreage. Of course the pilot had not survived. It was unfortunately another case where the pilot was flying tired and unable to think clearly. And it was another case of get-home-itis. Why do we Americans push ourselves so damned hard?

The experience was momentary but it will remain vivid in my memory for the rest of my life. It was one of those things that cannot be unforgotten. It cannot be un-experienced.

Alexandria was the home of Bellanca aircraft. The factory was next door to the Flight Service Station. Pilots loved the superb flying qualities of the Bellanca Viking and Super Viking. They were single-engine, four-seat, high performance, retractable gear airplanes. They cruised at around 200 MPH. They were fabric-covered and the wings were constructed of wood.

Their manufacturing heyday was in the late 1960s and all of the 1970s. But as the years went by improvements were added, the weight increased, and the price went up. I think it was sometime in the 1980s when the plant closed.

Vern Praska was the test pilot. He flew each airplane as it came off the assembly line, testing it to make sure it was airworthy. One of the Viking's characteristics was a safety feature that precluded landing with the gear up instead of down. If the aircraft neared stall speed and the gear had not been lowered, a loud gear warning horn would go off. This feature was a pain in the neck for Vern because part of his checklist was to conduct numerous stalls at altitude. The horn would blast the cockpit with noise. Vern would silence the horn by tripping the circuit breaker. It was not the smartest thing to do. Vern had to remember to reset the circuit breaker before landing. Otherwise that critical safety feature was inoperative.

It had to happen sooner or later. One winter day Vern landed on one of Alexandria's snow-covered runways. I looked out to see that for some reason the airplane had come to a full stop on the runway. It was cocked at a funny angle, the propeller looked bent, and Vern was walking away. Vern had forgotten to reactivate the warning horn, and even though it was extremely rare, he had forgotten to lower the gear. He had landed gear up. I asked him what it was like. "You know, Al," he answered, "it felt like sliding down the runway in a big cardboard box." The damage to the aircraft was minimal, nobody had been hurt, and Vern kept his job.

I watched another landing that was somewhat more eventful. A Beech Musketeer was on short final for runway 13 at Alexandria. There was a strong crosswind and as the aircraft neared touchdown the low-time pilot lost control. The plane veered to the right, off the runway, and plowed through three feet of accumulated snow. All I could see was a white plume with the Musketeer obscured somewhere within it.

The single-engine aircraft came sliding fifty feet in front of Flight Service and buried itself nose first in a huge drift. It was one of those brief visions that burns itself into a person's memory, for as the plane came sliding by I can remember seeing four sets of eyeballs, huge as saucers, staring out at me. The three passengers and the pilot deplaned, and as they stood there in a tight knot they had the sickly look of people who had just survived death or were facing the firing squad. I imagine that if we had checked we would have uncovered evidence of uncontrolled bladder and bowel movements.

We never knew what pilots were going to do. We controlled the airport runway lights. We would normally turn them off at midnight in order to conserve energy and save the city some money. The information was published in official documents and pilots were required to be aware of it. If they wanted to land after midnight all they had to do was call us on the radio and we would turn on the lights.

One night I was working another mid-watch, from midnight to eight. A few minutes before two o'clock, I stepped outside to take an hourly weather observation. It was mostly dark, with only the pale light from a crescent moon. I was startled to hear an aircraft engine running. I peered into the darkness and could barely make out a little airplane just setting down on one of the runways. What the hell! What was he doing? I'd had no radio contact with him and the runway lights were turned off.

The aircraft came taxiing in and parked on the ramp a few feet away. A cheerful young pilot hopped out and approached me. He was flying a Super Cub and he had decided on the spur of the moment to bring it to Alexandria for maintenance work. His radio was out and he needed to get it repaired. He'd had just enough ambient light to find the runway. I had to wonder what he would have done otherwise. He had no radio to call for help.

I suspected something was amiss. I stepped closer and checked his breath. Perhaps he had been drinking. But that did not appear to be the case. Drugs were not in popular use at the time. It seemed the pilot was just young and foolish.

Harold Chandler was the airport manager - or Fixed Base Operator (FBO), as was his official title - for most of the thirteen years I worked at Alexandria. The airport was his baby. When airplanes pulled up to the fuel pumps to take on gas, Harold would run, not walk, to refuel them. He was probably in his mid-sixties. He supplemented his salary by piloting VFR charter flights.

I no longer remember when Harold retired. It must have been a year or two later when I talked to him. I asked him how retirement was going. He said it was terrible, that he did not know what to do with his time. As it turned out, the airport had been everything to him. He'd had no other interests to fall back on when he had retired. Harold lived on for many more years. He had been a popular airport manager. When he passed, the airport was renamed after him. It is now called Chandler Field.

One of Harold's specialties was hand propping airplanes to get them started. It made me nervous to watch him do it. Aircraft were equipped with engine starters but sometimes the starter was not working. When that happened the pilot could turn the propeller by hand and get the engine to fire. Today the FAA has banned the procedure unless someone is sitting at the aircraft controls with his feet on the brakes.

But in Harold's day, he would adjust the engine controls, set the parking brake, and step outside the airplane by himself to turn the propeller by hand. Oh my, when the engine fired up Harold would be standing not more than a couple of feet away from the rapidly turning propeller. If he had lost his balance and stumbled into it, or if the brake had failed, the propeller would have been chopped him to pieces. More than one pilot had perished over the years by hand propping an airplane.

I remember watching another pilot who damned near did die. He must not have set the parking brake properly and the airplane got away from him. It spun in a couple of circles before the propeller chewed into the side of a twin Cessna parked nearby and the engine died. The pilot was lucky. He had been standing there entirely unprotected.

We had an agricultural spray plane working out of the Alexandria airport for a couple of years. I remember it as a Piper PA-25 Pawnee. All the grass was dead where the aircraft was parked, a result of the herbicide spray. I could not help but wonder what effect the liquid and the fumes from the herbicide would have on the pilot's health. I remember that Connie Chandler, Harold's son, was an airline pilot who also flew part time as a spray pilot. Connie crashed a spray plane and died. It must have been a crushing blow to Harold and his wife, Edith. Connie had been their only child.

We became extremely familiar with pilots who hauled freight and mail in light aircraft in the middle of the night. Those were the days, the 1970s and '80s, when photographic film was widely used. Today everything is digital. Exposed film was mailed in for processing. It was common for the film to be sent by air. The pilots flew VFR, often in the worst kind of weather. They would sometimes sleep on the couch in the chief's office while waiting for the weather to improve. It was a hell of a way for pilots to earn a living but a good way to build up flying hours if their goal was to eventually fly for the airlines.

In extremely windy conditions it was a common practice for wing walkers to hang onto a light aircraft's wings and walk it from the runway to the ramp. Otherwise a strong crosswind could blow the fragile aircraft over. A Piper

Super Cub landed on runway 22 at Alexandria. I remember watching it. The wind was blowing so hard down the runway that the little craft kept going airborne. The low-time pilot could not keep it on the ground so that he could taxi in. Finally the pilot put down on the grass next to the runway and wing walkers helped him to the ramp.

It was uncommon but not unheard of for airplanes to make an emergency landing on a highway. Pilots were taught during initial training that if the engine quit or they were forced by other mechanical problems to make an emergency landing they should look for a road or a flat field or a clearing among the trees. I was working alone one early summer evening when a pilot called in. He was flying a little north of Fergus Falls.

"Alexandria radio, this is November such and such. My engine has just quit. I'll be making a landing on State Highway 32, just north of County P."

"Roger, November such and such. Do you require assistance/"

"Negative, Alexandria radio. I'll call you when I can get to a telephone." (Remember, we had no cell phones in the 1970s.)

"Roger, November such and such. The local surface winds are such and such and the altimeter is so and so."

And just in case something might go wrong I called the Ottertail County police and told them what was going on. As it turned out, the pilot landed without incident.

The FAA required us to notify the General Aviation District Office (GADO) in Minneapolis in regard to any aircraft accidents or incidents. They would investigate, and if the pilot was found to be operating in violation of FAA regulations he could be fined or lose his license.

But when I called GADO about the airplane landing on the highway the inspector didn't even want the information. It's not an incident, he told me, as long as nobody gets hurt and the aircraft is not damaged. He told me that there is nothing we can do about an engine that quits and there is nothing illegal about landing on a highway. I vaguely recall one or two other times when I was working and airplanes landed on Minnesota highways.

Forced landings on a highway are relatively safe. The surface is smooth. The main concern is power lines. Landing in open fields is something else. The field may look perfectly flat from the air. What remains hidden is the old rotting fence, or the shallow ditch, or the pile of rocks.

I was working near dusk when a local aircraft with four aboard approached from the southeast. I gave the pilot an airport advisory, which amounted to winds and altimeter and any traffic, and waited for his arrival. Everything seemed routine until the pilot suddenly announced that his engine had quit four miles east of Alexandria and he was putting down in a field just north of Interstate 94. He made a landing in a plowed field. No one was hurt but there was some damage to the airplane. The nose gear had buckled and the propeller was bent when it hit the dirt. This was officially an incident and GADO had to be notified.

Running out of fuel happened more often than it should have. Too many pilots pushed the envelope. Running out of gas when we are driving an automobile is one thing; running out of gas when we are thousands of feet in the air is something else. An aircraft flying from Ohio to Little Falls in eastern Minnesota ran out of fuel short of his destination and made a forced landing. Another airplane flying from Little Falls to Rapid City, South Dakota, crashed with dry tanks. In this latter case there were fatalities.

One winter night the pilot of a Beechcraft 95 Travel Air got into a drunken argument with his girlfriend. The BE95 was a sweet little twin-engine bug smasher with autopilot and all the latest navigational aids. The pilot hopped into his airplane. He departed from Brainerd, Minnesota, and headed west. He was not heard from again.

The concerned girlfriend notified the authorities. Neither Alexandria Flight Service in Minnesota nor Grand Forks Flight Service in North Dakota had talked to the pilot. Fargo Tower radar showed a westbound aircraft passing over their site at around midnight. They had not talked to it. A widespread search and rescue found nothing.

The aircraft was located the following spring on the side of a butte in far western North Dakota, not all that far from where my wife, Louise, had grown up. The body was still inside. Theory had it that the pilot had put the airplane on autopilot, had passed out or fallen asleep, and the airplane had flown on until it ran out of fuel and crashed. The distance from departure to crash site was over 400 miles.

There never seemed to be a whole lot of fatalities at one time. The most I can remember was the seven family members who perished at Fergus Falls. But sometimes I wonder, if we counted them all over twenty-eight years, how many were there? Certainly a hundred or more.

We talked to some on the radio or the telephone. Some we read about in the newspaper. Mostly, though, they were faceless and without a life story to tell. We felt sorry for them but sometimes we were also upset with them. Damnit all, in almost every case they pushed themselves beyond their own capabilities, or beyond the capabilities of their aircraft. They often got themselves into weather they could not handle. Too often they were in a hurry to return to work after a weekend. As I have said, we called it "get-home-itis." There were times we strongly recommended, even begged, that they not try it. Still they did. There is a reason why aviation is viewed as a hazard by insurance companies. They have the statistics to prove it.

I have to balance this gloomy picture with a more positive observation. I must have briefed thousands of pilots over the years who made the wise choice to wait for better weather. I remember them sitting around Flight Service for hours or even days at a time. They used to recite, usually with a certain amount of light humor and a smile, the aphorism that – "If you have time to spare, go by air."

At nights and on weekends we worked unsupervised. We were in charge. It was a good experience for us. We had to make decisions. I enjoyed the wide variety of duties. I thought it made our job more interesting. In addition to our regular workload of working with pilots and taking weather observations, we had to take care of administrative duties. We had to write up accident reports and coordinate searches for aircraft who had failed to close their flight plans, to tell us that they had safely arrived at their destination. Was the airplane safely in a hangar or tied down at a private airstrip or had it crashed somewhere? We were told that our responsibility was to find the airplane and not necessarily the pilot. If the airplane was okay then the pilot had to be also. Sometimes these searches went nationwide.

We received a teletype report searching for a Beechcraft Baron on a flight from Denver to Dallas. The pilot had not filed a flight plan but his wife became worried when he did not call her from Dallas. The tail number of that airplane seemed somehow familiar to me. I thought I may have spoken to the pilot the day before. I searched through the flight strips from the previous day and sure enough I came across a radio contact I had logged with the pilot. He had reported that he was landing at the Detroit Lakes airport, north of Alexandria. I called the airport and the Baron was still parked there. The nationwide search was called off and the wife was notified.

We had located the airplane and not the pilot. We had not needed to talk to him at all, to find out what the hell was going on. It was a long way from Dallas to Detroit Lakes. It turned out that a girlfriend was involved. It was a situation that the pilot and his wife would have to resolve. We can only imagine what she had to say.

We never knew what to expect when we had to call the home of a pilot who had not closed his VFR light plan. It happened a lot. More often than not the pilot's destination was a tiny local airport or his own private strip with no telephone available. He would button up the airplane, tie it down, and maybe stop by his favorite watering hole on his way home, completely forgetting that he needed to telephone us and close his flight plan.

Usually his wife was not alarmed. She knew her husband's habits. She would have him contact us. Sometimes a wife or a live-in girlfriend would be concerned. Other times they would become almost hysterical.

We were under a time constraint. We needed to begin a communications search within thirty minutes after the estimated time of arrival. It there was no answer at home we needed to call the airport operator or the local police and have them search the airport and its hangars for the airplane. As was noted above, there was no requirement that we actually talked to the pilot, so long as we located the aircraft. The search would be expanded if we had not located the airplane within an hour. Eventually it could go nationwide.

All of us spent many long hours pacing the floor, waiting for the telephone call that an airplane had been located. It was rare that things did not eventually work out well, though it sometimes took hours to resolve the situation. I have a faint memory of a time or two when everything went horribly wrong, when the pilot had not survived. They were not events that I personally was involved in.

A North Central Airlines plane slid off the runway during a winter landing at Brainerd. Nobody was hurt and there was minimal damage to the aircraft. I needed to file an accident report. I tried to talk to the pilots by telephone, as was the protocol with general aviation pilots. Oh no, the airline pilots were whisked into isolation before I could get a chance to talk to them. They would not talk to anyone without an attorney or a company representative present.

Over the years there had been some minor conflict between Flight Service and Center Controllers. In short, some of the Center people were arrogant bastards. They thought they were our superiors and could order us around. I remember one particular incident in Alexandria. An aircraft under Minneapolis Center's control had landed at a small airport and had forgotten to cancel his clearance. The Controller called me on our direct telephone line and told me to call the airport and verify that the plane had landed. I was alone at the time and I was busy working with other aircraft. I told the Controller he would have to make the call himself. His response was to *order* me to make the call. That put us in a pissing contest. I told him to have his supervisor call my supervisor and straighten things out. But I did not attempt to locate the overdue aircraft.

Later, I talked it over with my Station Chief. He agreed that Center Controllers should not think they could order us around. They could request our help in locating overdue aircraft and if we had time we would try to honor the request. But the actual responsibility for Center's late arrivals was the Controller's, not ours.

Center and Tower controllers were represented by the Professional Air Traffic Controllers Organization (PATCO). It was a trade union that operated from its founding in 1968 until its decertification in 1981. That was the year the Controllers went nuts and staged an illegal nationwide strike. They were represented by a lawyer by the name of F. Lee Bailey. They made crazy demands – a 32-hour work week, a $10,000 a year pay raise for everyone, and increased retirement benefits. They were already earning a boatload of money. Greed and arrogance and the lust for power seemed to deprive them of their sanity. They threatened to shut down air commerce in the United States if their demands were not met. President Reagan fired more than 11,000 of them.

It was one hell of a situation. The strike and its aftermath undermined the bargaining power of American workers and their labor unions. They have not recovered even now, in 2020. And air travel was significantly reduced for several years while the FAA hired and trained new controllers. Supervisors and administrative personnel filled in as much as they could. We in Flight Service, who belonged to a different union than PATCO and had not gone on strike, took on as much of the work load as we legally could. The extra work translated into lots of overtime pay. There was poor morale and increased burnout in the Centers and in the Towers for many years.

As I mentioned in an earlier book, if I had chosen the Center or the Tower option when I had first come to work for the FAA, I would now have been forty-one years old, with a family to support, and no job. I had lucked out when I had opted for Flight Service. I knew one person from my Flight Service training class who did not fare as well. He had transferred to the Tower option and was working in

Fargo, North Dakota. He had bowed to peer pressure, participated in the strike, and was one of those fired. Years later I ran across another one of my old Flight Service classmates. He also had also transferred to the Tower option and was working in Green Bay, Wisconsin. But he had refused to go on strike and had kept his job.

The little labor union that represented Flight Service was called NAATS – National Association of Air Traffic Specialists. My feeling, though it may not be accurate, was that PATCO did not deem us worthy enough to be a part of their union. I went for a couple of years without joining and then opted to start paying my monthly dues. The FAA had a policy of negotiating with unions in regard to work schedules, vacation requests, and so forth. Our NAATS representative at Alexandria had been able to get rid of the Cincinnati watch and to straighten out summer leave requests.

Thus NAATS gave us some voice in our work environment. I remember hearing stories of the non-union days when the Station Chief could be a dictator. Some of the older specialists said they could plan their vacation, maybe make reservations, and the Chief would cancel the request at the very last second if another specialist called in sick. That was not allowed to happen under our union contract. The Chief was required to call in someone to work for overtime pay.

Life at Alexandria Flight Service was not entirely about pilots and weather. There are little stories that we remember. We brought our lunches mostly in brown bags. In a back room we had a refrigerator where we could stow our food and a toaster oven for making grilled cheese sandwiches. It must have been some time in the late 1970s when we upgraded from the toaster oven to a brand new microwave oven. It took some getting used to. I tried to make a grilled cheese sandwich with it. What came out was a soggy mess. It was completely inedible.

Some months later I was working an evening shift by myself. Around 7:30 hunger pangs set in and I decided to warm up my pork chop. The timer was not digital as they are today. It was a manual timer that wound down. A bell dinged when the cooking was done. I set the timer for four minutes and walked back into operations. I had grown up in southern Illinois on pork chops, green beans with bacon, mashed potatoes, and blackberry cobbler. My mouth was watering thinking about that pork chop.

Wouldn't you know it, I hadn't been back in operations more than a couple of minutes when everything went to hell. The telephone rang and two pilots called in on the radio. It took a good fifteen minutes to get it all straightened out. I was sitting at the inflight position taking a well-deserved break (WDB) when it slowly dawned on me that something wasn't right. I SMELLED SMOKE!

I rushed to the back room. Smoke was billowing from the microwave. The timer had stuck. My beautiful pork chop! It had been reduced to a blackened piece of charcoal about the size of a fifty cent coin. But I'll be damned if I still didn't have to try it. Maybe saliva would soften it. Maybe there was some hint of flavor left. I bit into it but it was as hard as coal. I'm lucky I did not break a tooth.

We were on occasion plagued by gulls and geese on or near the runways, especially where the airport bordered Lake Winona. The airport manager would hop in a vehicle and chase them away. I remember that State and Federal officials were a bit stuffy about allowing anyone to shoot the birds. There were a couple of times, I think at night, when a landing aircraft ran into them. There was little damage to the airplanes but a few geese did not survive. One of the Specialists retrieved them and took them home for his wife to cook.

Everybody who has worked for the public knows that the workload is unpredictable – either we are buried with business or there is nothing to do. To that extent, one would surmise that business at three o'clock on a mid-winter morning in northern Minnesota would amount to practically nothing. But Murphy's Law, whereby "Anything that can go wrong, will go wrong," seemed to apply even then.

It happened on more than one occasion. Alexandria Flight Service was housed in an older, somewhat rundown building. There was a single tiny bathroom with only a toilet bowel and a small sink. It was located maybe twenty feet from operations. I would be sitting on the pot at three o'clock in the morning, a cigarette in one hand and a magazine in the other, my trousers and my underwear down around my ankles, nothing having gone on for hours, when wouldn't you know it, the telephone would ring in the other room or a pilot would call on the radio. There would be a mad flurry of activity as I tried to finish my job, flush, pull up my pants, wash my hands, and dash back to operations. Damn those pilots anyway.

Mid-watches in Nome had not been so bad from one perspective. I had never been entirely alone. There had always been a National Weather Service person working on the first floor of Flight Service while I paced on the second floor. And later, in Green Bay, two or three specialists plus a supervisor worked the mid-watches.

But at Alexandria we were totally alone until the specialist who worked the six A.M. to two P.M. shift showed up. I was always worn out and wired on caffeine. My nerves were frazzled. The darkness outside the brightly lit interior of Flight Service seemed to press in tightly, to become almost claustrophobic. My imagination turned to thoughts of robbers and murderers and random mayhem.

The airport was a mile from town. There were no routine police patrols. In fact, I do not ever remember a cop stopping by even for a visit, day or night. I felt isolated and alone. If someone were to walk through the door with a knife or a gun in his hand I would be a goner.

We could not see the main entrance door from operations. It had a bell that tinkled when someone opened it. If I were sitting alone in operations at two- or three o'clock in the morning and the door bell sounded my heart would start thumping. It invariably scared the hell out of me. I would jump up and get ready to meet whatever danger was approaching from around the corner. Nobody routinely locked that door. I have to admit, though, that there were a few times when my nerves were so much on edge that I had to lock it, at least until the sun was up and I could see who was sneaking up on me. Of course no one ever did.

I fantasized even further. I came up with various plans of action to save my butt. My favorite was to flee to the crawl space that ran under half the building. It could be accessed from the basement that ran under the other half. The basement was where we stored the teletype paper and the records from our daily operations. It was lighted while the crawl space was obscured in darkness. I figured the crawl space would be a good place for me to hide from assassins.

It may have been that it was another specialist who got me started on this trip into the imagination. He said that for a time years before he had brought a gun with him when he had worked at night. He had a sister who was fighting with her husband and the brother-in-law had talked of doing bodily harm to the family.

I darned near did not survive one night without having a heart attack. It was in the middle of winter, around ten-thirty at night. I was all alone. I had not seen or talked to anyone for hours. I had all the inside lights brightly lit and could not see a thing outside in the inky darkness. Bright lights seemed to help keep the goblins at bay.

I was intent on something I was reading. Suddenly there was a loud pounding on one of the large plate glass windows not six feet away from where I was sitting. I looked up and my heart almost stopped. A masked man was beating on the window. He was dressed all in black and standing in three feet of snow.

Now it was suddenly no longer a matter of my overactive imagination. My worst fears were about to come true. It could be just a matter of minutes before my life blood was draining out of me. Goodbye cruel world! Goodbye sweet family! I was so paralyzed with fear that I could not move. All thoughts of escaping to the crawl space were erased as my mind went completely blank. So this was what it felt like when a person was about to die!

The masked man stumbled away from the window and to the side door where he collapsed. I had confided my night terrors to several of my fellow workers. Was one of them now playing a dirty trick on me? Had he collapsed with laughter? Did I dare go outside or was it a ruse to get me outside where I could be attacked and my body dragged away? Maybe I should lock the door and call the cops.

Finally I got control of myself. Fantasy was one thing; reality was another. I needed to find out what was going on. I opened the glass door just a crack. "Help me," the masked man moaned. "I was snowmobiling on the airport and I crashed." I dragged him inside the building and dialed emergency 911.

By the time the EMTs (Emergency Medical Technician) arrived the man was sitting up and fairly coherent. It turned out that he was a neighborhood teenager who had foolishly been riding by himself at night. It was bitterly cold and windy. At the time there was so security fence surrounding the airport. People could walk or drive onto the airport at any point. The boy had staggered a half mile down the runway and to Flight Service, where he had collapsed. He was darned lucky that the crash had not injured him to the point that he had laid in the snow and frozen to death. The medics transported him to the hospital for overnight observation. He was released the next morning.

As was usual in any job, I suppose, we had a cast of individual and diverse personalities who worked as Air Traffic Control Specialists (ATCS) at Alexandria. After thirty-five years I no longer remember all their names. One of them always made me smile with the way he greeted me. "I don't care what low opinion others have of you, Powers," he would say. "I still think you're all right."

We had our share of characters. The one who stood out beyond all the others was a fellow by the name of Jim. Big and bold and blessed with a booming voice, Jim cut his own swath through life. The first time my two small children met him they fled in terror. He called them "rug rats." But it wasn't long before they were wrapping their arms around his knees and begging for attention. He was a lot of bark but no bite. Children seem to see through that kind of thing quicker and easier than adults. Most of us cringed the first few months we were around Jim but when he transferred out five years later he left a gap in our lives. I often think of him.

Jim seemed to make up his own rules as he went along but the irony was that Jim was more attuned to aviation safety than many of the other specialists I worked with. He was an experienced pilot with twin engine time. Everybody knew that flying an airplane with two engines took more training and more experience than flying a little single-engine bug smasher. Jim's professional philosophy was that everything took a back seat to safety, and that a good way to promote safety was to keep things simple where possible. What, for example, was the difference to a student pilot between ceilings that were 10,000 feet high and those that were at 18,000 feet? Both were good flying conditions. There wasn't much need to dig through reams of teletype paper to confirm it. But when ceilings and visibilities were marginal, Jim's ears pricked up and he paid more attention. He wanted the latest reports and lots of details.

As I mentioned above, I at first had doubts about Jim. But after I got to know him I often said that if I were a pilot and in an emergency, Jim, even with his unorthodox ways, was someone I would trust to get me safely on the ground. Next in line would be Dick, the specialist I had met the first time I had walked into the station. The two could not have had more opposite personalities. I considered Dick to be the ultimate professional. He knew the book by heart. He kept up with changes in equipment and procedures. He remained on top of changes in the hourly weather. I would absolutely have trusted Dick's professional judgement.

Jim, on the other hand, avoided work whenever possible. He was ever on the alert for shortcuts. He questioned everything. It seemed that his mind never stopped working. He and our young airport manager devised an entirely new IFR approach to the Alexandria airport. It was not an FAA approved procedure but it was something that the manager and Jim practiced to make certain it was safe. They tucked it away for use in an emergency. FAA inspectors would have gone nuts if they had gotten word of it.

As I said, Jim had a quick mind and pilot experience. In an emergency he would have quickly analyzed the situation – a mechanical problem or pilot error, the pilot's qualifications, weather conditions, the amount of fuel remaining – and come up with a reasonable solution. The rest of us, without pilot experience, would have stumbled our way through while leaning heavily on the book for guidance. Jim would have solved in five minutes what would have taken the rest of us fifteen or twenty minutes, and time is of the essence in an emergency situation. In a way, Jim, with his experience, could put himself into the pilot's position while the rest of us could not.

One cold and blustery winter evening Jim was scheduled to give a presentation to a group of pilots in Wadena, an old railroad town forty miles northeast of Alexandria. These pilot meetings were more-or-less regular events at several of our airports. Jim drove a government car to the event. The highways were drifting over with blowing snow. Jim was expected to be back in Alexandria no later than midnight. When he did not show up the specialist on duty telephoned Wadena to confirm that Jim had indeed been at the meeting. Sure enough, we were told, he had made his presentation and had departed around ten-thirty.

Well, it was winter and we were worried. What if he'd had an accident on the icy roads and was lying in a ditch somewhere? We contacted the state and local police and hospitals in the area. Nobody knew anything about Jim. His wife, Doris, was sick with worry. An all-night vigil began. We would not have been the least bit surprised if Jim had been found some time after dawn, where the car had hit an icy patch and slid into a farmer's field. Rescuers would find Jim's body, frozen like a popsicle.

Around ten the next morning we received a phone call. It was Jim. And this is just the kind of character he was – "Don't pay the ransom," he told us. "I've escaped and I'm on my way home." Well, the truth of the matter was that Jim had lived in Wadena during his high school years. His father had worked for the railroad. Jim had met an old high school buddy at the pilot meeting and afterwards the two of them had gone out for a few drinks. They'd ended up at the friend's house around two o'clock in the morning, where the friend had passed out on the couch and Jim had fallen asleep on the living room floor. In the morning, the friend's wife had been so irate that she had left them to sleep while she went to work.

There were two consequences. First, Doris met Jim at the front door with her bags packed. She was furious. "I'm flying to California to spend some time with my sister," she informed Jim, "and I have the credit cards with me." The second consequence was that the FAA suspended Jim for two weeks without pay. It had been an awfully expensive night out.

Another Specialist, let's call him Joe, had a similar experience with his teenage son. It was on another cold and bitter winter night. The son had a girlfriend and was often out until midnight. Acting like a normal teenager, he never hung up his coat when he returned home. He would throw it in a heap on the floor. Joe had nagged him for years – "Hang up your coat!"

Joe, being the conscientious father that he was, never slept soundly until his son was safely home. He would get out of bed at midnight or two A.M. and look for his son's coat. If he saw the coat lying on the floor he would know that everything was okay.

On the night in question Joe checked several times and his son was not home. Finally, at 2:30 in the morning he was worried enough to call the girlfriend's house. The parents told Joe his son had left before midnight. Joe paced and paced. Had his son been involved in an accident? Was he lying in a ditch somewhere freezing to death? Joe called the police. No accidents had been reported. Joe woke up the rest of the family.

Someone finally had the presence of mind to check the son's bedroom. And there the son laid, sound asleep, not a worry in the world. For the first time in his life he had hung up his coat.

I remember that Joe dreamed of running a strawberry farm. He owned eight or ten acres on the north side of town, just past the county fairgrounds. He studied and he researched. He planted acres of berries. Soon he added sweet corn and other vegetables. Customers would come to the farm and pick their own produce. He had family to run the farm while he was working at Flight Service.

It must have been seven or eight years later when I asked Joe: "You dreamed of running a strawberry farm. You worked hard and you succeeded. What do you think of it now?" He was quiet for a moment, lost in reflective thought. Then he shook his head from side to side and responded. "You know, Al, I had not thought about it until just now when you asked me, but I HATE IT!" As it turned out, it was mostly the customers who were the problem. They groaned and they complained and they tried to cheat him. Another problem was the brutal hours. He had to be open for business early every summer morning, seven days a week.

Another specialist had the emotional maturity of about a high school sophomore. If he got upset at something we said he would slam his pencil to the floor. It was like a child throwing a tantrum. Of course the rest of us soon cured him of the habit. If he said something we did not appreciate we would slam our pencil to the floor!

There was one specialist who was particularly difficult to get along with. He felt as though he could subject everyone around him, including the pilots, and including FAA management, to the tyranny of his moods, of his anger. He was best described as a contrarian, someone who disagreed with everyone just for the hell of it, who enjoyed provoking an argument. We felt especially bad for his poor wife and children. They must have suffered from his verbal abuse. Sometimes there are relationships that need to be abandoned due to sheer exhaustion. We learned that it was a waste of time even trying to get along with this jerk.

Another character was Sam, one of the local pilots. He owned a Holiday Inn motel out on the Interstate. Sam was always in a hurry. One day he rushed into Flight Service for a quick weather briefing to St. Louis. He did no flight planning and did not file a flight plan. Then he scurried out to his twin-engine Piper Aztec and was soon airborne. About ten minutes later he radioed in. "Say," he asked us, "what would be a good heading for St. Louis?" His destination was 400 miles away and he had not taken the time to plot a course. We got out the charts and quickly did his flight planning for him before he faded out of radio range.

One of our fellow workers died. I remember that on mid-watches he had completed a correspondence course on automobile mechanics. He was at home, underneath his car, installing a new muffler. He had driven the vehicle up on a pair of cheap ramps he had ordered through the mail. The ramps collapsed and the car settled on his chest. The way I heard it, there were no broken bones but the specialist could not breathe. He had suffocated.

Oh my, it was of course tragic. I had never looked inside a casket or attended a funeral in my life. I did not know if I could handle it. I felt emotionally unprepared. I trembled with nervousness. What a baby! Louise chastised me. Funeral rites had been a natural part of her Catholic upbringing. I needed to grow up. In a way, making my emotional way through the visitation and the funeral was a rite of passage.

It is of course difficult to attend a funeral without thinking about – well, death. There is a mystery to the whole thing. Where a person once existed there is nothing. It is a difficult reality to grasp. How can one go from love and laughter and life to utter nothingness? How can one go from a physical presence to nothingness? I wondered what went through a person's mind if he was lucid enough to know that his life had been reduced to a matter of minutes. Was there a final acceptance, a letting go? Was there a relief that the struggle was over?

For a few years Flight Service hired summer aids. There are only two that I remember. One girl was a high school senior and the other girl was in college. Summer was our busy time and we could use the extra help. One of our routine jobs was to post the weather reports that came in via teletype. We tore the sheets of paper apart. Hourly surface observations were under one clip, terminal forecasts under another clip, area forecasts under another, and so forth. It took a lot of time to keep everything up to date, but it was an easy job for the summer aids to learn.

I look back in anger and frustration at the shoddy way our summer aids were treated. I found out later that the younger one had been sexually harassed by one of our married specialists. There was no protocol in those days for handling sexual harassment. The girl really had no one to turn to and she quit before the summer was over. The prevailing attitude seemed to be that unwanted sexual advances were normal, that boys will be boys. I thought there should come a time when boys grow up and become responsible men. Today all government employees must go through training on how to recognize and deal with sexual harassment. Those caught doing it can be fired. To my mind it is a vast improvement.

I heard only rumors about the other summer aid. Apparently she did finish her college degree, then returned to Alexandria to figure out what to do with the rest of her life. She worked one last time as a summer aid. She had some thoughts of continuing her education, of going for a master's degree at the University of Nevada, Las Vegas. Apparently some of the religious extremists in Flight Service talked her out of it. To them Las Vegas was Sin City and surely she would lose her soul if she moved there. Of course not one of them had any education beyond high school. They had no clue as to what they were talking about. They had nothing that qualified them to counsel her. I heard that she gave up on her education, that she ended up working in a local dentist's office. It angered me to think of her life going to waste rather than her having the opportunity to go out and explore the world, to learn and to grow, to broaden her knowledge. Religion extremists took that away from her. It was frustrating. It was damned near evil.

Government employees are not supposed to accept gifts from the public. It is a policy I entirely agree with. But one Saturday near Christmas, with no supervisor around to interfere with him, one of our local pilots walked into Flight Service and deposited a case of some very nice bourbon on the pilot weather briefing counter. There were twelve bottles in all. "Merry Christmas," he announced. "This is to show my appreciation for all the good work you do." "Oh, no," we responded, quite vigorously, "We cannot accept it. We could get into trouble if we do." "I don't care," was his answer. "I'm walking out and leaving the bottles here. You can take them or you can throw them into the trash." Well, the religious people would not accept the booze. Somehow the rest was distributed among the few who did imbibe. I came away with two bottles even though I do not drink. I am allergic to alcohol.

Our chief was an old German, set in his ways, nice but conservative to the core. He still sported a flattop haircut, a style that had been in vogue in the 1950s. Now it was the late 1970s. The style seemed to fit his personality. One Monday morning he showed up with his hair in curls! It was difficult for us to hold back our chuckles. The story was that his daughter, who was attending hairdresser school in Minneapolis, had been home for the weekend. She had used her father as a guinea pig. The things we do for our children.

Bob was another specialist. He was diminutive in stature and in personality – a nice but meek person. He was soft-spoken, stood about five feet four inches tall, and weighed in soaking wet at probably a hundred and twenty pounds. His wife was a few inches taller and outweighed Bob by a good hundred pounds. She loved to bake. Her specialty was oatmeal raisin cookies.

These were no ordinary cookies. Each one was about the size of a medium cow pie and absolutely mouth-smacking delicious. They were soft and warm. We used to boast that each one contained enough calories to fuel a twenty-mile hike. Bob's wife packed all his lunches and about once every two weeks she would toss in three or four of those cookies. The problem was that they were too much for Bob to handle. He was not used to eating that much. But he did not want to disappoint his wife, or who knows, maybe he was afraid of her. Maybe she had baked those cookies just for him and he had damned well better eat them. At any rate, Bob would hand them out to the rest of us, almost begging us to take them. He did not have to search too far for willing customers.

There was one time when Bob's meekness almost got him into trouble. He was working by himself on an evening shift. A pilot walked into Flight Service, got a weather briefing to Mason City, Iowa, filed a VFR flight plan, hopped into his little single engine Cessna, and soon was airborne. Bob had other work to catch up on so it was a few minutes before he had a chance to sit down at the teletype machine. He needed to forward the inbound information to Mason City Flight Service.

It was then that Bob discovered something was missing. The pilot had forgotten to calculate an estimated time enroute (ETE) and without it Bob did not have an ETA. Bob got back on the radio but the pilot was already out of range or had switched to another frequency. He did not answer Bob's call.

Okay, Bob thought, it's not a big problem. I'll just figure it out myself. It's a little over 200 miles to Mason City, the airplane travels at about 120 MPH, so I'll pad the time a bit and say it will take two hours of flight time. Bob fired off a teletype message with the ETA. Nevertheless, Bob was a worrier and a fidgeter. What if he had miscalculated the ETA? What if something went wrong? What if the pilot encountered unexpected strong head winds? It could become a worst case scenario and Bob would be blamed.

Sure enough, two and a half hours passed and Mason City sent a teletype message. The airplane had not arrived. The procedure was to give a pilot an extra half hour beyond his ETA before we began looking for him. Now Bob began to sweat and to pace the floor. He had lied. What was he to do now? Well, we know how lies work – one lie leads to another and then to another. Bob sent a new message to Mason City to extend the ETA another half hour. If the airplane had crashed how would Bob have explained the delay in looking for it? Of course he could not have. The FAA would surely have fired him.

Fortunately, Mason City soon sent another teletype message that the airplane had safely landed. It was a lesson learned for Bob and for the rest of us. Do not try to lie your way out of trouble. And perhaps it was an example of the meek having as many adventures (or misadventures?) in life as the bold.

Then there was the story about the student pilot filing his first flight plan over the telephone. He was being extremely slow and careful. "Item number one – type of flight, VFR. Item number two – aircraft tail number, November one two three four Quebec. Item number three – airspeed ninety knots. Item number 4 – departing Morris."

About this time the Flight Service Specialist became impatient. At this rate it would take a half hour to file one simple flight plan. "Can you go a little faster?" she asked. "Uh, okay," the student responded, "move that airspeed up to ninety-five knots."

One time I was sent to Minneapolis for a week of refresher training. I booked a room in a motel in Bloomington. The Flight Service Station was located across the field from the main terminal of the Minneapolis-St. Paul International airport. We had been in class two or three days when an older Specialist from Minneapolis called in sick. One of his fellow workers thought he knew the cause: "He's an old man and he's feeble. He must have had his semi-annual sex last night." The entire class erupted in laughter.

I do not remember that we had a coffee pot at Alexandria. I think we brought our own. I remember packing a thermos of coffee with my lunch, especially on a mid-watch. I had trouble with the thermos bottles. The ones I bought were cheap and lined with glass. I kept dropping and breaking them. I remember walking into work one midnight. The specialist I was relieving held the door open for me. I had a brand new thermos bottle under my arm. It was a replacement for one I had broken only the day before. That damned bottle slipped out of my arm, bounced off the concrete step, and the inner glass shattered into a thousand pieces. I did not know whether to laugh or to cry. What wrong had I done that the gods were so against me? But that was it. There would be no more cheap thermos bottles for me. I shelled out the money for a heavy duty, unbreakable, Stanley thermos bottle. I still have it today, forty years later.

One summer we had a local lady who was participating in the Powder Puff Derby. This annual transcontinental air race for women pilots had been inaugurated in 1947 and ran through 1977. Humorist Will Rogers had coined the name. At any rate, our pilot had been stuck in Alexandria for a couple of days. The weather was marginal and she would call every half hour or so for a complete update.

She had worn out all the other specialists. They were beginning to get grouchy. I, on the other hand, had just returned from vacation and was fresh. I was polite and patient with her. She asked for my name and I foolishly gave it to her. It was a mistake. She continued to call every half hour, only now she asked "Is Al there?" It provided the ammunition my fellow workers could use to tease me.

I will take time now for a bit of a longer and more detailed story that is mostly true. It is based on an actual event. I call it "The Boilermaker."

****

THE BOILERMAKER

At Alexandria we were visited one summer by an odd and unsettling dreamer. Looking back now, from the vantage point of forty years, I suspect our little airport was no more than a random waypoint on an odyssey of fancy, on a strange Walter Mitty-like excursion where each grand delusion lasted for months, fantasies that were spun not entirely from the imagination but were based on other people's lives, where each pause in an unplanned travelogue provided a new and thrilling identity to explore, until he was forced from the field by a harsh and unforgiving taskmaster called reality. He appeared, it almost seemed, from out of the mists of the imagination, played out his flight of fancy, and then was gone.

It was a mid-summer day and he had most likely been northwest bound on Interstate 94 out of Minneapolis. He probably had had no particular destination in mind. Perhaps he had pulled into the rest stop a few miles southeast of Alexandria. Maybe it was there that he had spotted the low-flying airplanes taking off and landing at the airport. Then, like a honey hunter following bees to the hive, or the functioning of a compass needle, he had homed in on us.

His rusted-out Ford sedan had drifted down our dusty access road and had pulled up to the curb midway between the Flight Service Station, where I was employed as an Air Traffic Control Specialist, and the Airport Operations building. Perhaps he had sat behind the steering wheel for a while, where he could watch the beehive of activity – people coming and going, aircraft taxiing in and out, a line boy busy refueling airplanes. It would not have been surprising if he had felt the fantasy developing even then, the excitement rising, a whole new world opening up before his eyes. It would take a few days to assay it all, to discover where the rich lode of imagination lay, to find his path into fantasyland.

In my mind I can envision him leaving his car and standing at the edge of things. He would have had a bottle of soda in one hand and a candy bar in the other. He would have said nothing, asked no questions, just watched and listened, patiently absorbing it all. He would have seen sky divers and spray planes, passengers and politicians and plebeians. And at the center would have stood the mighty gods – the pilots – making decisions that others accepted without hesitation, imperial in their demeanor and in their status. Thus began his new role.

It's hard to say when we first took notice of him. Probably he had been there for some days, hanging around the fringes, a part of the crowd, until he emerged almost as if from the subconscious, and came into focus. He had been a boilermaker in the Navy, he told us, and he had recently worked as a security guard in Minneapolis. He was waiting for a welfare check to arrive at the post office. Could we spare him fifty cents for a candy bar? He hadn't eaten all day.

He stood around five feet ten, dressed always in a white T-shirt and blue jeans, plain black oxford shoes, and white socks. Everything looked like it was government-issue. His hair was cut short, like a military or a prison or a mental ward haircut. He weighed around 220 pounds. He had a large belly and fat arms. There was an aura of brute strength about him. I felt a nervous sense of feral ferociousness.

I don't know, is it just me, or is it an alpha male thing? I have an almost subconscious habit of evaluating men who are strangers to me. Do they pose a physical threat or an emotional threat? Could I win in a hand-to-hand scuffle with them? In the case of the boilermaker, I could imagine a short and losing struggle, a scene where he was easily able to overpower me. I felt a twinge of fear.

I remember one midnight watch, on duty by myself, when he walked into Flight Service at two o'clock in the morning. He stood close to me. He stunk like a goat – like sour, unwashed sweat. He made me nervous. I wanted him gone. He seemed to sense my apprehension. He asked for money. I opened my wallet and gave him what I had. It was only a couple of dollars and he could see that my wallet was empty. Much to my relief he left. I was grateful that he did not make a habit of showing up in the middle of the night. Rumor had it that he spent his days at the airport, mooching money for candy bars and soda, and at night slept in his car.

For weeks he shuttled back and forth between the Flight Service building and the Airport Operations shack. We discovered during conversations with the airport manager that the boilermaker would hang around operations until he was more or less asked to leave, then retreat to Flight Service where he would again overstay his welcome.

His plans gradually came into focus. He would, he confided in us, become a professional pilot. He added that he would accomplish this not after the years of training and experience that were normally necessary, but before the summer was over. He had already learned most of what he needed to know, just by listening to the pilots talking. It did not seem all that difficult. All that was lacking were a few hours of actual flying and he would be checked out. It would be easy. (Isn't that the way it is for most of us? What's the use of fantasizing if it involves blood, sweat, tears, and years of hard work? In our dreams, at least, fame and fortune should come easily.)

There wasn't much of a curtain between fact and fantasy in the boilermaker's mind. Once the vision was fleshed out it was as good as accomplished. Now he already stood on an equal footing with the real pilots. At times he became even more than a peer, he became an instructor to less experienced pilots. "If it were me," he might say, for example, "I would not cancel the flight because of some icing. I would fly right through it."

His downfall was probably initiated not so much as a result of the advice he freely offered to pilots, who were amused by it, but mostly due to his impact on paying passengers, who in general could not distinguish between an aileron and an antenna, or a cumulonimbus cloud and low stratus, and who had to rely on the professional judgement and the experience of the charter pilot to get them safely to their destination. "I'm sorry," the pilot might say, "but we will have to cancel the flight to Minneapolis. Federal aviation regulations will not allow me to fly into areas of forecast or reported severe icing." The passengers would retrieve their luggage, disappointed but accepting the pilot's judgement. That was when our boilermaker would appear among them and announce that if he were the pilot he would have flown right through the icing. Needless to say his unsolicited and uninformed opinions did not sit well with either the pilots or airport management.

It probably would have been a kindness to have told him point blank: "Look, we don't mean to hurt your feelings bur you have to go. You're causing problems. If you don't leave we'll have to call the police and have them remove you." But no one had the heart to do it.

In the latter part of August someone finally came up with a solution. The boilermaker needed to be shown the difference between fantasy and reality. It was one of the hottest and most turbulent days of the year. A young instructor pilot took the boilermaker up for his first airplane ride. It was in a small, two-seater aerobatic plane. The boilermaker went up as a passenger and in his fantasy fully expected to return as a qualified pilot. He was given a free, thirty-minute demonstration of almost every aerobatic maneuver known to mankind. He returned white as a sheet, his clothes soaked with perspiration, vomit everywhere. He got into his car, departed the airport, and was never seen again.

I have to wonder what happened to him. Did common sense and reality return him to normalcy? Or was he finally so overwhelmed by living in an alternate world that he became a lifelong patient in a psychiatric ward? Or did he remain entirely unchanged, moving from one fantasy to another? At his next stop did he tell them that he had been a boilermaker in the Navy, a security guard in Minneapolis, and a pilot in Alexandria?

A couple of years later the young pilot who had given our boilermaker his first and last ride was killed while flying north of St. Joseph, Missouri. He had been performing aerobatics.

****

There is another memory of the way things were in the 1970s. Smoking was still popular. I remember that I smoked the Winston brand of filtered cigarettes. The person who had the contract to clean Flight Service was a man by the name of Bill. His specialty was cleaning the large plate glass windows that were covered with a film from the cigarette smoke. He found that hot water worked better than any commercial cleaning product. But holy cow, if the cigarettes were doing that to the windows what the heck were they doing to our lungs? I remembered viewing a cadaver's lungs in a university physiology course I had taken. The lungs were black from smoking cigarettes instead of a normal and healthy pink.

The introduction of ELTs (Emergency Locator Transmitters) in the 1970s had been a huge leap forward in locating downed aircraft. They were supposed to automatically transmit a loud, wailing sound on emergency radio frequencies when an airplane crashed. Aircraft flying overhead, and later, satellites in orbit, could pinpoint the location of the crash. Most general aviation aircraft were required by regulation to have an ELT installed. But like many advances in technology the ELTs were not deployed without some early miscues. It took a few years to work out some of the wrinkles.

When I was stationed in Nome, Alaska, I remember hearing about two aircraft that had crashed shortly after takeoff from Northway, Alaska. Both had an ELT but neither ELT had activated. One aircraft was found by normal Search and Rescue (SAR) teams. The other was spotted by hunters a couple of years later in a dense forest seven miles from the airport.

At Alexandria we had many missteps with the ELTs. The Bellanca aircraft factory, located next door, was required to install ELTs in all their new airplanes. Extra ELTs sat on shelves in the stockroom, ready for installation. The ELTs would unexpectedly go off while still in their shipping cartons. Their loud wail would drown out radio communications. We soon discovered that our Direction Finder (DF) would point towards the blaring ELT. A quick telephone call to the factory would result in a scramble to locate the errant transmitter and disarm it.

Sometimes the ELTs would go off in a parked aircraft. It was difficult to determine which one. It happened so often that our electronics technicians invented a device that would pinpoint the location. Other ELTs would activate on a bumpy landing. Those were relatively easy to track down.

One pilot brought an ELT to airport operations. He wanted to show it to other pilots. Returning to his car he casually tossed the unit into the back seat. It went off and our DF tracked him as he ran errands all over town. We called the airport manager, got the name of the pilot, called him and had him deactivate it. He had no idea it was blaring. He would have needed to tune a radio to the proper frequency in order to hear it.

We tried to be helpful to the pilots. Sometimes as they were nearing Alexandria they would ask us to make a local telephone call so that someone would drive out to the airport and pick them up. There was one pilot who owned a car wash in town. He lived elsewhere but often flew in early in the morning. It was around five A.M. one Sunday morning when I was winding down a mid-watch. Another specialist would arrive at six to share the work. The pilot was about ten miles out when he requested that I call his brother to pick him up. I dialed the number and passed along the message. "Who the hell is this?" an extremely angry voice responded. Oops! I had dialed the wrong number.

Then there was the inbound evangelist who had his pilot radio me, demanding in an arrogant tone that I notify people to come out to the airport to meet them. It pissed me off. Who the hell did he think he was – a big time celebrity, or God's chosen messenger? I told him I was busy. He would have to make his own phone call. The pilot mentioned something about talking to my supervisor. I ignored him. Nothing ever came of it.

A holdover from the 1950s was something called the Scheduled Weather Broadcast (SWB). We had first been introduced to it during training at the FAA Academy in Oklahoma City. Each hour, twenty-four hours a day, 365 days a year, every Flight Service throughout the country was required to broadcast local surface weather reports over local radio frequencies and over the VORs (Visual Omni Range radio navigation aids). The idea was that airborne pilots would monitor the broadcasts to keep abreast of the weather and for landing information.

Well, maybe it had been a good program in the old days when many private pilots could not afford to buy two-way radios, but by the time I began working in the very early 1970s the procedure was already outdated. It was a rare pilot who did not have two-way radio communications. In fact in twenty-eight years I do not ever remember encountering one. When pilots were out flying and they wanted to check the weather they would call us on the radio. The problem was that the big shots in Washington had not kept up to date with general aviation. They were more interested in and more influenced by the airlines.

The main problem was that the VORs transmitted a continuous three-letter identification in Morse code. For example, the three-letter identifier for the Alexandria VOR is AXN, which in Morse code is dit dah, dah dit dit dah, dah dit. I remember that as an Air Force navigator I had not needed to memorize the Morse code. The correct code for each VOR was clearly marked on our navigation charts. Such was also the case for general aviation.

Pilots did not want to listen to a constant barrage of dits and dahs. They would turn off the volume on the VORs, thus negating any chance of even hearing a scheduled weather broadcast. They did not care. Nobody listened to the broadcasts.

I made those damned broadcasts for probably twenty years and had only one confirmed report of a pilot actually listening to them. I was shocked when he radioed in and said he had listened to the broadcast but had missed one report. Could I repeat it? I took note of the fact that he was communicating with me over a two-way radio. He had not needed to listen on the VOR. The fact of the matter was that about the only people who did listen were the evaluators from the FAA Regional Offices.

There was grumbling from the very beginning of my FAA career. Specialists were questioning if there was really a need for the broadcasts. What was the purpose? If it was three o'clock in the morning in the middle of January and there was a blizzard blowing, who the hell would even be listening? A very few of my fellow workers argued that even if one in a thousand pilots ever listened to the broadcasts we should continue making them, that it was a matter of aviation safety.

The grumbling eventually gave way to outright protests. We certainly had no problem doing the reports if pilots needed them, but it was apparent they did not. The decision makers at FAA headquarters in Washington, D.C. refused to budge. They supposedly had the big picture while we poor saps in the field did not know what we were doing. They continued to argue that the SWBs were critical for flight safety. They were stuck in the 1950s.

Finally, in the 1980s, somebody in the FAA decided to do a national survey. At the end of each broadcast we were required to ask – "If anyone is monitoring this broadcast, please respond." Nobody did. Finally, after years of hesitation the broadcasts were cancelled.

It was a case of leaders in Washington being far out of touch with changes that had taken place in the field. Many of those in Washington had not worked in the field for twenty years or more. They may have thought they had the big picture but what they had was outdated. We were to find out as the years went by that it was a much more serious problem than just being out of touch. We were to learn that the cream does not always rise to the top. Too many of our Flight Service and Air Traffic people in Washington barely had a high school education. The Peter Principle seemed to apply. They were eventually promoted to a position that they obviously were not qualified for, where they were incompetent, and then left there to rot.

There was a recent (2019) article in the *New York Times Magazine* about airport codes, the usually three-letter identifiers the FAA assigns to airports. The author complained that they look like acronyms, that technically they are abbreviations, and that sometimes it is difficult to figure out what word they are abbreviating. OKC makes sense for Oklahoma City but who the heck would associate Hartford, Connecticut with BDL? Little could the author have known that some FAA bureaucrat with a high school education may have made the official assignment. He or she may have given it some thought or they may have penciled it in between bites of a tuna sandwich.

People may suppose that a small Flight Service Station would be socially isolated from the national scene. That did not seem to be the case in Alexandria. I swear that every national politician running for office, every religious evangelist hoping to make a name for himself, every big name singer at the county fair, made his or her way through Flight Service. I spent an evening with former Vice President Hubert Humphrey as he and his pilot were waiting for the weather to improve. I shook hands with current Vice President Walter Mondale, with Senator Bob Dole, and with country singer Charlie Pride.

As far as the traveling evangelists were concerned, they were no different than any amateur actor or musician trying to become a star. It makes me smile when I think of it. Musicians would start off performing in cheap dives and work their way up. I witnessed evangelists who launched their careers by hiring little single engine bug smashers to fly them from one tiny rural church to another. Then, as their name spread, they would move up to a larger, twin-engine airplane, and, if they eventually moved up to the really big stage, where they could perform before a TV audience, which rarely happened, then they would use the bushels of tax-free money they collected to buy their own private jet.

The important thing was that they were not satisfied to be stuck in a small church. They wanted to become famous. They may have justified it to a certain extent by claiming that if they reached a larger audience they could save more souls, but strip away all the sham and it was apparent they were mostly doing it for themselves. It was a giant ego trip.

The Secret Service visited a couple of times to coordinate with our local police before the arrival of a big-name politician. I remember one agent in a dark pant suit and white blouse. She showed us an Uzi submachine gun she had strapped to the small of her back. Her jacket kept it out of sight.

I have one final memory of my work in Alexandria. The Airport Operations building was located just a few feet from Flight Service. We made frequent short trips there when we needed something from their vending machines – candy, chips, soda, cigarettes. There was an old black and white framed picture hanging on the wall. It showed an ancient biplane entangled in the bare branches of a leafless tree, where it had obviously crashed. Printed underneath were words I was never to forget. *Flying is hours and hours of extreme boredom interrupted by brief moments of shear panic.* Nothing truer could have been said about Flight Service on a mid-watch in the middle of January.

WEATHER

In Nome we'd had a National Weather Service office that had taken care of all the weather observations - the surface observations, the radiosonde launchings, and so forth. In Alexandria the surface weather observations were a responsibility of the Flight Service Specialists. It was one of my favorite parts of the job. I had to learn the various types of clouds and how to estimate their height above the ground. I needed to learn about fog and the conditions under which it was formed. I had to keep a wary eye out for the development of thunderstorms. All of this was, of course, undertaken in the context of working with pilots and keeping them safe. Today much of what we did has been replaced by automated weather observing sites.

Becoming a certified aviation weather observer added a new and interesting dimension to the total aviation experience. It provided an increased awareness of the envelope in which pilots operated – wind speed and direction, temperature and dew point, low and middle and high clouds, fog and haze and other restrictions to visibility – all were critical factors in aviation.

As it turned out the specialist I had met the first time I had walked through the door of Alexandria Flight Service was also a neighbor who lived across the street from the house

Louise and I bought. I could not have asked for a better Flight Service mentor. Dick set high standards. He was thoroughly professional in all the work he did. He kind of took me under his wing when it came to taking weather observations and I leaned on his expertise.

Let me put this into the proper context right away. Weather observations are absolutely critical to aviation safety. Marginal weather conditions at the destination airport meant a pilot had a serious decision to make. Should he continue on or look for an alternate airport where the weather is better? If he were to continue on and unable to land at his primary airport would he have enough fuel to go elsewhere? I remember when planning fuel needs in the Air Force we were required to have enough fuel to make it to the primary destination, plus enough extra gas to get to an alternate airport, and an extra forty-five minutes of fuel beyond that. There were times when we had to dip into the forty-five minutes of reserve fuel, when weather prevented us from landing at both the primary and alternate airports.

I'm not certain that our little VFR puddle jumpers operated under any such fuel restrictions. I never heard any mention of it. But certainly they had to be keenly aware of how much fuel they were burning, how much remained in their tanks, and what was happening with the weather. More than one general aviation airplane ran out of fuel and crashed. There were also many harrowing stories of airplanes landing with five or ten minutes of fuel remaining, or even more dramatic, of the engine quitting as the airplane touched down.

Surface visibility was an extremely important factor in aviation. It became problematic when it dropped below three miles and critical when it was less than a mile. Dick pointed out all the visibility markers we relied upon. A copse of trees was seven miles northwest. The lights at the rest stop on Interstate 94 were four miles southeast. There were various other markers at three miles, two miles, one mile, a half mile, and three-eighths of a mile. I remember standing outside in fog on more than one occasion trying to get a sense of the visibility. It was more difficult at night but I came to feel comfortable in providing pilots with accurate surface visibility data.

In the spring and summer of 1980 flight and surface visibility was slightly reduced by another event, the explosion of Mount St. Helens in Washington State, 1,600 miles away. Volcanic ash spewed high into the atmosphere and was carried east by the prevailing winds.

Ceiling height was another critical factor. It began to become problematic below 1,000 feet. There were various ways to estimate or to measure it. Probably the most reliable was through pilot reports, which were strongly encouraged. We were told to end weather briefings with the words – "Pilot reports are requested." I tried to be a little more informal, while a little more emphatic. I would say something like – "If you have time to call in a pilot report we would greatly appreciate it. We rely on them a lot." It gave pilots a feeling of teamwork, of cooperation, of pilot and specialist working together.

The way it worked in reality was the following. A pilot departing an airport would report something like - "Base of the first layer twelve hundred, tops two thousand five hundred, base of the second layer seven thousand, negative icing in the clouds." Or a landing pilot would call in that he had broken out of the clouds at one thousand two hundred. Pilots would also call in other critical information, such as turbulence, icing, flight visibility, and freezing levels. This was valuable feedback for us and important information to pass along to other pilots.

Freezing level was one of many important considerations. Carburetors could ice up and cut off the flow of fuel. Of course when that happened the engine would stop running. The trick was to apply carburetor heat.

There were abbreviations associated with pilot reports. ICGICIP meant there was a report of icing in the clouds in precipitation. BRAG indicated that braking action on the runway was good, BRAP equaled braking action poor, and BRAN was braking action nil.

We eventually had a clash with FAA management over braking action reports. They did not want us to relay the information to inbound pilots if the information was more than, if I recall correctly, an hour old. What the hell, if the temperature was still below freezing, nobody had worked on the runway, and it was ten o'clock at night, why not tell a pilot that two or three hours ago the braking action had been reported as nil? We could at least give the pilot a heads up that he or she should use caution to not slide off the runway. But the legal idiots at FAA headquarters were always so cautious of lawsuits that they forgot about aviation safety, about lives. They painted a worse-case scenario of being sued. People could die so long as our asses were covered in court.

Another means of estimating a ceiling was with the use of a weather balloon. We filled them with a measured amount of hydrogen. They ascended, if I remember correctly, at a rate of 500 feet per minute. We used a stopwatch to measure the time between when we launched the balloon and it entered the clouds. Two minutes would equal a thousand feet and so forth. This use of balloons was primitive but normally quite accurate.

There were limitations to the use of balloons. For one thing they could not be used at night, for the obvious reason that we could not see them. And there was a problem with wind. Sometimes it blew so hard that the balloon would be some distance away before it entered the clouds. I used binoculars to track it. I remember with some amusement that there was a philosophical question as to whether the use of binoculars was valid or not. Some thought it should strictly be a matter of eyesight. I thought I was being perfectly logical when I argued that it did not matter how we did it so long as we had an accurate measurement of when the balloon disappeared into the clouds.

At night we used a ceiling light. It shone straight up and created a spot on the clouds. We used a handheld instrument to measure the angle of the spot and referred to a chart to give us the height. The light was not all that powerful. It worked fairly well with low ceilings, which was the most important, but the spot became more difficult to discern as the ceiling got higher.

Then there was the more challenging way to estimate the height of clouds – by eyeballing them. It is amazing how difficult it is for the novice to look at clouds and try to guess how high they are. But we learn that there are clues. For one thing, if we look at clouds then find out how high they actually are, through pilot reports, for example, we get the feedback we need to fine tune our senses.

There is another means by which we can learn to estimate. It is called a cloud chart. It has pictures of twenty-seven different classifications of clouds. Each cloud type has its own nomenclature, its own personality, its own prescribed place in the atmosphere. They are divided into three categories of nine each – low, middle, and high clouds. "Low" clouds are defined as those whose bases are below 6,500 feet above the surface. "Middle" clouds range from 6,500 to 20,000, and "high" clouds between 20,000 and 40,000. Thus if we can determine the cloud type and whether it is a low, middle, or high cloud we can have a starting point for determining its approximate height.

Low clouds are divided generally among stratus and cumulus. Stratus clouds form in flat layers. Cumulus clouds are puffy like cauliflower. Stratocumulus is a combination of the two – flat bottoms with puffy tops.

Cumulus clouds have a vertical component that is caused by thermal convection, that is, when heat "lifts" moisture in the form of water vapor. If there is enough of a vertical component then the clouds are called "towering cumulus." There is no real defining point at which a cumulus cloud becomes a towering cumulus; it is subjective. I remember standing outside on very hot summer days when I was going through Air Force Navigator School in Waco, Texas. I could watch the tops of cumulus clouds building by the minute. The bases were probably around 6,000 feet and the tops 18,000 to 20,000. They would certainly have been classified as towering cumulus. Light aircraft attempting to fly through them would have been bounced around by moderate to severe turbulence. These clouds often would dissipate by sunset. As the evening air cooled down there was not enough heat and moisture to support them.

But if the heat and moisture persisted, towering cumulus could continue to grow into cumulonimbus clouds – thunderstorms with a distinctive anvil top. The tops could reach 60,000 feet or higher and destroy any airplane ever built.

Middle clouds were referred to as "alto" clouds – altostratus and altocumulus. Dick showed me how altocumulus castellanus clouds resembled castles with turrets.

The feathery, wispy clouds that some people called horsetails were all a form of high cirrus clouds, formed of ice crystals. Although the official classification of high clouds given above is from 20,000 to 40,000 feet, I'd estimate that the cirrus clouds around Alexandria ranged from about 18,000 feet in the coldest part of the winter to about 30,000 feet in the hottest summer months. This again was mostly a subjective call. It was rare to receive a pilot report on cirrus clouds and certainly our little puddle jumpers did not fly high enough to encounter them.

One of the main things about the cirrus clouds was that they were sometimes an early indicator of an approaching weather system. They were worth paying attention to. The old adage - "Red sky at night, sailor's delight." - usually was a fairly accurate indicator of fair weather moving in. "Red sky in the morning, sailor's warning." Often meant lower weather was approaching.

There were other little tweaks we could use. When weather conditions were stable the dew point at sunset was often an accurate indicator of the overnight low temperature. Then there was something called the "greenhouse effect." It is a warming of the atmosphere. It our case it took place when clouds obstructed heat from escaping the earth. Instead of the earth cooling off on a clear night it would remain noticeably warmer when clouds were present. There were times when clouds moved in at night and the surface temperature increased due to the greenhouse effect.

It had no real meaning for most pilots when I included SUN DMLY VSBL in the remarks section of an aviation weather observation. The remark was there for the use of National Weather Service meteorologists. It more closely detailed the makeup of the cloud layer. Was it thick or was it thin? The sun or sometimes the moon could be seen through a thin layer. A thin layer was more related to the early development of a weather system.

I was to learn years later when I was doing outdoor photography that a thin layer of clouds, where the sun was dimly visible, provided just about the ideal lighting. Bright light had too much contrast for the film or the digital sensor to handle. Gloomy light obscured details. Sunlight that was filtered by thin clouds was most often just about right.

Virga was sheets of rain that hung out of clouds but did not touch the ground. A form of precipitation called snow pellets were cloudy or opaque; ice pellets were clear. Quite often in the summer, when the air was stagnant, prefrontal haze would form from dust and smoke particles in the air. A good rain would clear them out.

I remember that when all else failed, when we had no pilot reports of the height of the clouds, and when they were too high for a balloon or a ceiling light to be of any use, we had one final option to fall back on. That was the weather report at St. Cloud, sixty miles to the southeast. The station was staffed by meteorologists from the National Weather Service. Surely they must know what the hell they were doing. If they estimated the clouds at 12,000 feet, and we were also looking at altocumulus clouds over us, then that would give us a good approximation.

This assumption soon went to hell in a handbasket. Our maintenance people took care of the teletype equipment at St. Cloud. They made regular visits. If things were slow at Alexandria we could ride along and spend some time talking to our NWS counterparts. Maybe we could learn something from them. I mentioned how we relied on their weather report. It caused them to laugh. As it turned out, they relied on our weather report because they figured we had pilot reports to back us up.

I cannot leave this section without talking about what is for me one of the most interesting and dramatic cloud types. It is called a *cumulonimbus mammatus*. It is associated with severe thunderstorm activity. The mammary clouds hang down like pouches or breasts bulging from the layer of clouds. If anything is a warning to aviators and the public in general to beware of severe weather conditions it is surely these clouds.

I talked about these mammatus clouds with one of the charter pilots who worked out of Airport Operations next door. It seemed that forever thereafter if he saw a cloud with a bulge in it he would inform me that he had seen one of those "mamma" clouds.

One of the enjoyable things about being a husband and a father was in teaching my family about the clouds. Louise found it interesting and the children loved it. One day our little daughter, Jenifer, who was five years old and in kindergarten, was outside during recess. She was standing beside the teacher's aide who was supervising the playground. "Look at those beautiful cumulonimbus

100

mammatus clouds!" she said. The aide was both flabbergasted and amused that such words could come from a little girl's mouth. "Where does your father work?" she asked Jenifer. "At the airport," Jenifer replied. "Oh, well, that explains it."

When severe thunderstorms rolled through there was always the potential for funnel clouds and tornados to develop. I never saw one myself or remember one being reported. The most severe storm we experienced happened one hot and humid summer afternoon.

Cumulonimbus rain clouds could often be seen many miles distant. On this particular day we spotted a giant cloud perched almost due west of us. We were guessing at the distance. Some thought it was thirty or forty miles away. I thought it could be fifty or sixty. We had a direct telephone line to the Fergus Falls airport, forty miles west of us. I picked up the phone and talked to them. They could also see the huge cloud. They estimated it to be forty or fifty miles *west of them*. That would make it eighty or ninety miles west of Alexandria.

We watched over the next couple of hours as the storm roared ever nearer. We issued special weather reports to warn pilots of the hazard. That is something we did with all thunderstorm activity. I called home to warn Louise. She and the children took shelter in the basement.

We watched through the large windows in Flight Service as the storm bore down on us. The sky turned an ugly and menacing darkish green. Then the winds hit with full force. Airplanes were ripped from their tie-down ropes. One flipped entirely over our little Flight Service building and landed on my supervisor's pickup truck parked in front. Another ended up in the metal tower that supported the airport rotating beacon light.

We stood thunderstruck as everything outside erupted in fury. The large windows in Flight Service *bulged inward*. What the hell were we doing standing in front of them? Shattered glass could have cut us to shreds. I glanced down at the wind speed indicator. I had not noticed it before but there was a peg at 100 knots, which is 115 MPH. The needle was pegged for a few seconds before it swung back to a more normal reading. We learned that these were called straight line winds.

I called home. There was no major damage to our house. I found one of the wind driven roof turbines I had installed to ventilate the attic in a field about 200 yards away. The heavy wooden patio table had been flipped onto the lawn.

The only MAYDAY broadcast I heard in the twenty-eight plus years I worked in Flight Service took place one bitterly cold winter day when I was working the radio position at Alexandria. I think the temperature was about twenty below. The radio communication was short and to the point.

"MAYDAY, MAYDAY, MAYDAY! Alexandria radio, this is November one two three four Alpha. My engine has quit. I have oil on my windshield and I'm going down!"

"Roger, November one two three four Alpha, this is Alexandria radio. I copy your mayday. What is your location?"

"I'm south of Brainerd. I just passed over an airport. I'll try to turn back and land there."

"Roger, November three four Alpha. The local surface winds are three two zero at eight knots, the altimeter setting is three zero zero two. How many people are on board?"

There was no response and there was not much more we could do for the pilot. We called the State Police to alert them to a possible downed aircraft, although "south of Brainerd" was not a very specific location.

Fortunately the pilot did land safely. He called us from the airport at Little Falls, Minnesota. An oil seal had burst in the engine. That sometimes happened in extremely cold weather. The pilot was damned lucky that day. The emergency had taken place over an airport.

I have a mental vision of another winter event. There was a barn on the west side of Highway 29, between Alexandria and Glenwood. It had caught on fire one bitter winter night. When I drove past the next day the entire structure was coated with a thick layer of ice and long icicles hung from every edge. If I recall correctly there was a newspaper picture of one of the firemen, his facemask and helmet covered with frost. Being a firefighter in Minnesota in the middle of the winter was no picnic.

Blizzards were another weather phenomenon we had to cope with in west central Minnesota. It was probably about the second or third winter we were in Alexandria when a blizzard moved in and dumped three feet of packed snow. Drifts were six to eight feet deep. I was stranded at home for three days. Two specialists were stranded at Flight Service. They survived on cigarettes and candy bars and soda from the vending machine next door. They slept on the cots we kept for such emergencies. One of them had a bright idea. He filed for twenty-four hours of pay each day, since technically that is what he had served. But of course the FAA would not allow it. They paid each specialist for working twelve hours each day.

People went nuts during blizzards. They died. One young couple called our neighbor girl to babysit for them during a blizzard. They thought it would be challenging and great fun to go snowmobiling when the temperature was near zero, the wind howling at sixty to eighty miles an hour, and the visibility reduced to nothing. Fortunately our neighbor girl declined. She probably saved their lives.

Snowmobilers did crazy things every winter. There were a number of reports of riders running into barbed wire fences. It must have taken a goodly amount of surgical thread to sew them back together. I remember reading one report of a snowmobiler being killed by a deer. He had been harassing the buck, chasing it in the snow, and the deer had turned on him with its horns.

There was a picture in the local newspapers. It had been taken in Fargo, North Dakota, immediately after a blizzard. The picture was of a car mostly buried in a snow drift. The

Fargo Air Traffic Control Tower could be seen a short distance away, beyond a chain link fence. Five people had sat in the car and frozen to death. The wind and the snow had blown so hard that they could not see where they were.

Blizzards were also common in North Dakota, where Louise had grown up. We were visiting her grandparents after one such storm. They lived in a little one-story ranch house three miles out of town. They showed us the only place where they had been able to see outside. One tiny area of the top right-hand side of their living room picture window had remained clear. Otherwise their entire house had been buried under snow. In this case the reason was fairly clear. They had planted a windbreak of trees too close to their house. When the wind slowed down it dumped snow on their house. I was somewhat surprised they had planted the tree line that close. They had lived on the Dakota prairies all their lives. They should have known better.

Interstate 94 at Alexandria had a unique feature. The on-ramp for westbound traffic was protected by a heavy metal gate. Most of the time the gate was wide open. But during blizzards the gate would be closed and traffic was not allowed to enter the interstate.

I clearly remember eyeing that gate one Christmas as we departed Alexandria, headed for Dickinson in far southwest North Dakota, about 400 miles away. I had worked a mid-watch from midnight to eight. Our little family had scheduled a Christmas gathering with grandparents and family. Louise had all the presents wrapped and ready to load into the car. The weather situation was extremely hazardous. The temperature at both the departure point and the destination was twenty-eight below. The wind was howling at forty MPH or more, dropping the chill factor to somewhere around seventy below. We were scheduled to depart as soon as I got off work. But with the weather the way it was and the fact that I had been working all night, I announced that we would have to cancel the trip and remain at home for Christmas.

That brought about tears and howls of disappointment from both our two children and Louise. Christmas was a special time to spend with family. I relented, but with the proviso that if we got as far as Fergus Falls, forty miles down the road, and it proved to be too hazardous we were turning around and coming back. We all agreed on this rule.

That said, I stuffed a sheet of cardboard in front of the car's radiator. It was a common practice in those days. It helped to keep the water mixture in the radiator from cooling down. We loaded presents and goose down sleeping bags and candles and emergency food into our little red, 1980 Buick Skylark and set out. (It was the last new car we ever bought. Late model used cars were a better deal.) I was somewhat surprised that the on-ramp gate was still open. It did not take long before every window in the car except the windshield was completely iced over, even with the heater cranked up to full power.

There was very little traffic on the interstate that day. The thought struck me that if our car froze up and stopped running it could be a while before someone came to our rescue. Remember that in those days the only way to communicate from a vehicle was via a CB radio, and we owned no such radio. It had been a foolish thing to do but somehow we made it without any major problems.

We were required to measure the amount of precipitation we received. Rain was not a problem. It fell into a collecting tube that measured the amount in tenths of inches. Snow was more of a challenge. We melted what had fallen into the collecting tube, then converted that from tenths of inches of water to inches of snow. The general rule was that one inch of water converted into about ten inches of snow. But, in fact, it was more subjective than that. There was wet snow and there was dry snow. I estimated that one inch of water measured out to about eight inches of wet snow and maybe ten or twelve inches of very dry snow.

I have to smile when I think about it. People probably think that when weather observers measure snow they go outside and stick a ruler into it. The problem is that snow tends to drift. It may be three inches deep in one place and ten in another. It would be difficult to find a truly representative depth.

My memory is somewhat fuzzy but I recall that there was another estimate that we had to forward to the National Weather Service in the spring, before the snow had melted. That was to estimate the snowpack, the total depth of the snow on the ground. It was a means of attempting to figure out how much of a problem spring flooding would be, especially farther south, when the snow did melt. I have to smile when I remember it. It could have been that some of the snow I was looking at in Minnesota would eventually end up flowing in the Mississippi River past my old home town in Illinois, near St. Louis.

There was a written report we had to fill out in order to record a weather observation. We had what we called a weather shelter outside. It held two thermometers. One was used to give us a "dry bulb" reading of the air temperature. The other had a wick on the end which was dipped into water. We turned on a fan to blow air over this second thermometer. That gave us a lower, "wet bulb," reading that we used to calculate the dew point, an indicator of relative humidity.

I remember that the thermometer shelter was a wooden structure about two feet square, with louvered sides for ventilation. It was painted white and stood on legs about five feet above the ground. In thirteen years I must have exited out the side door of Flight Service at least 10,000 times and walked twenty feet on the sidewalk to where the shelter was located. Oh my, there were a couple of winters when the snow was so deep that we had to get down on our hands and knees to see into the shelter.

The thermometer shelter served one more purpose. It had an electrical outlet. In the winter most vehicles would start on their own when the outside air temperature was around minus ten degrees or warmer. Colder than that and starting a car became problematic. Electrical engine block heaters that warmed the radiator fluid or oil pan heaters that warmed the engine oil solved the problem. I still had an oil pan heater in my Jeep Wagoneer. I'd had it installed when I was living in Alaska. I would extend a long electrical extension cord from the Jeep and plug it into the thermometer shelter.

The extension cord worked fine for one vehicle. It did no good when three or four of us were at work. We had to take our chances. I remember several times when I had popped the hood and was bent over the engine spraying ether into the carburetor. Another specialist would turn the ignition key. There would be a minor explosion when the ether caught fire. Most often it was enough to cause the engine to start. But I remember there were a couple of times when I sprayed too much either from the can. The result was a fire that probably came close to destroying the Jeep.

After we had finished our readings at the thermometer shelter, we needed to make note of the visibility, the clouds, precipitation, and any remarks. Then we needed to pencil in the barometric pressure and the wind speed and direction.

It took time, generally about ten minutes or so, to gather all the data. At night we needed to turn off the inside lights about ten minutes before we stepped outside, to give our eyes a chance to adapt to the dark. Then we had to type the report and have the tape ready when our teletype machine was polled at the top of the hour. Some reports were straightforward and simple. Others were more complex. Thunderstorms, especially, caused a lot of extra work. We had to keep up with them, to send out special reports as we tracked the storms through the area. There were many remarks we needed to append to the main report. For example - TB SW MVG NE FREQ LTGCCCGIC - meant that a thunderstorm was southwest of the station, moving northeast, with frequent lightning cloud to cloud, cloud to ground, and in the clouds.

The weather observations were sometimes stressful to the extent that it was difficult to get them out on time. They were an added duty. They had a lower priority, for example, than talking to a pilot on the radio. And we had to decide whether or not to answer a telephone call when it was close to the time for an observation. Wouldn't you know it, it would be time to step outside and begin an observation and a telephone would ring or a pilot would call in on the radio. There was no question as to how we were to handle the radio call. It had the highest priority. But the telephone, that was a judgement thing. We could either ignore it or answer it. I wanted to be helpful so I often would answer it, hoping that it would be a short and simple weather briefing or a pilot calling to cancel a flight plan. It was so damn frustrating when it would turn into something that took ten of fifteen minutes to complete, so that I would be late in transmitting the weather report.

Taking weather observations really was a serious business. Pilots depended on us to keep them safe. I paced the floor many a long hour, knowing that an airplane was scheduled to arrive, and watching the weather deteriorate. Would the pilot arrive in time or would he have to look for another destination? Would he do something foolish?

The general public also wanted to know whether schools should be closed that day, or if it was too windy to move mobile homes, or whether rain would ruin their cement work. Many assumed that the forecasts we received from the National Weather Service would be more reliable than what they could get by watching their local TV weatherman. Unfortunately that was often not the case. Louise learned that the weather forecasts I brought home from work were often inaccurate. She coined a humorous way to describe it. "You can never trust a weather man," she used to say, while she looked at me with a twinkle in her eye.

Louise and I had a silly game we would sometimes play. I would call home and say – "This is the weather man calling. I am waiting for your report. Is the coast clear?" It meant that if I were her lover and her husband was not home then the "coast was clear" and I could come over.

There were compensations for the hard work and the stress - stepping outside just before sunrise, breathing in the clear air, listening to the birds beginning to sing even before the sun was up, watching a fox hunt for mice. In a way it was like stepping into nature, of looking around to observe what was going on, of sniffing the air and feeling the wind on my face. It was the same milieu in which the pilots operated. It felt good to get a sense of it.

Other times I would step outside on a clear, cold winter night, bathed by the light of a full moon. It brought about a kind of spiritual feeling. It was as if my parent was Mother Nature herself and I was an unborn child floating in a protective womb of amniotic fluid.

Then there was that one special time. It was coming up on two o'clock in morning, the middle of winter, the airport covered with snow. I had turned off the lights to get my eyes dark adjusted. I opened the side door and stepped out. I needed to check the temperature and dew point, any clouds, and the visibility.

Soft snow flakes were floating lazily to the ground. There was not a sound. Suddenly a jackrabbit came hopping past me on the sidewalk. It was not six feet away. That seemed strange. What was it doing there? The question was soon answered. A very large white bird floated soundlessly out of the darkness, not more than fifteen feet above the sidewalk. It was a snowy owl and it was stunningly beautiful. It was checking out the jackrabbit as a possible meal. The owl landed atop a nearby hangar. It perched there the next couple of hours and hooted at me every time I stepped outside.

I remember one occasion when there was some humor involved. At the time, the 1970s, most people in the country had heard of International Falls, Minnesota, near the Canadian border. It often recorded the nation's coldest winter temperature. This notoriety was not achieved without some rivalry and some jealously from other competing towns.

I was working a mid-watch and I was feeling terrible. I was exhausted and I had a nasty cold. At six o'clock in the morning I took a weather observation. It was twelve degrees below zero. I finished the report and sent it out on teletype.

I completed the watch, went home, and crawled into bed. Later in the day I was watching the evening weather report on the local TV station. I was surprised to learn that Alexandria had recorded the lowest temperature in the nation for that day. We had been twenty-two below while International Falls had been a mere nineteen below.

What had happened became immediately apparent. I had been so sleepy that I had mistyped the actual minus twelve temperature and had made it minus twenty-two. I could imagine what would happen if anyone found out the truth. The headlines in the newspaper would have blared – "Alexandria Humiliated By Lazy, Incompetent Government Worker." I kept my mouth shut and have not revealed until this day how I goofed up and gave, at least for a day, the record to Alexandria. If I had revealed my guilt I would likely have been drummed out of town. You can't take something away from people once they have accepted it as the truth. It could have sparked a civil war between the patriotic citizens of Alexandria and International Falls.

People tend to forget about it but in the late 1940s to the early 1960s there had been a real concern in our country about a possible invasion of aliens from outer space. There were reported sightings of flying saucers. Other testimonials told of earthlings being kidnapped, flown away in a spacecraft, and returned safely back to earth. I had even at a young age been entirely skeptical of these reports. My thinking was that I would not believe in alien spacecraft until I had witnessed them with my own eyes.

When I was in the Air Force in the 1960s we had been required to forward reports of Unidentified Flying Objects (UFOs). I mentioned in an earlier book that I had forwarded one such report while I was stationed at Stewart Air Force Base in New York State. The sighting had corresponded with a meteor shower.

The Air Force's Project Blue Book had collected data from 1952 to 1969. Their goal had been to determine whether UFOs posed a threat to national security, and to scientifically analyze the data. After years of study they had concluded there was no threat, that supposed UFO sightings were mostly a misidentification of natural phenomena, that in many cases the sightings were a mild form of mass hysteria, and in some instances a hoax to seek publicity.

I mention all of this because I faintly remember that in the 1970s there were still voluntary organizations collecting information on UFOs. It is still being done even today, in 2020. I received a telephone call just after sunset one evening. A lady was reporting a possible UFO on the southwest horizon. I looked out the window. There sat the planet Venus, shining brighter than normal, probably because we were looking at it through an atmospheric haze.

The human imagination is phenomenal. But it can often be influenced by something called *the power of suggestion*. Someone can put a thought into our minds, the possibility, for example, that aliens from outer space have visited our planet. Then when we witness something unusual in the sky we can jump to the conclusion that it is a UFO. Thus there is often a wide gap between what we *believe* and what exists in *reality*.

There was a close relationship that developed between the National Weather Service and our Flight Service Specialists. A NWS Quality Control Officer (QCO) would evaluate us on a regular basis. He would listen in on our pilot weather briefings and monitor our weather observations. Then he would sit down with us and try to help us get better. He would answer any questions we had. It was a learning situation and it was conducted in a casual and friendly tone rather than being anything confrontational. We appreciated his professionalism.

It was sometime in 1982 when we got our first live weather radar. It was relayed from a local TV station. It was quite a move up from the teletype reports we'd had to rely on. Now we could actually help to vector aircraft around severe weather.

Oh my, the way things were in those days, the 1970s and early '80s. Weather forecasting was a mixture of science and art. It involved some poor prognosticator shuffling through piles of paperwork and trying to figure out what the hell was going on. Quite often he was wrong. Today mountains of raw data are fed into huge computers where it can be refined and correlated to produce more accurate and timely forecasts.

Our job was of course to use the forecasts we were given and not to try to forecast on our own. We were in no way qualified to do so. There were many times when I felt inadequate to get a grasp of what was going on with the weather. I think the pilots sensed my hesitation but did not blame me for it. Nobody expected perfection. We all knew there was a lot of guesswork involved but we had to work with what was available.

Perhaps in a way it was like life in general. We try to learn as much as we can, then we go out and poke our noses into the world, into reality, to explore and to experience life itself.

1410 BRYANT STREET

I mentioned in the introduction that Louise had not been feeling all that well on our long drive down the Alcan Highway from Alaska. She'd had mild intestinal problems. When we'd arrived in Alexandria we'd checked into a small motel on the edge of the airport. We lived there for probably about a month before we found a house to buy. The FAA paid our housing and meal costs.

We'd probably been in town a couple of weeks. Louise's nausea had not gone away. She made an appointment to see a doctor. I didn't think too much about it. It did not seem like anything serious but in an important way it was. Louise returned from the doctor's office to announce that she was pregnant. We were going to be parents. Well, we had thought that we would wait a couple of years before we would start a family, that the two of us would spend some time together enjoying each other's company. We found out that using protection was not a guaranteed way to prevent pregnancy.

But of course it was okay. We both adored children and we both wanted a family. Louise went through the usual problems with pregnancy. She had morning sickness. Her lower back began to hurt. She had to watch what she ate and drank.

I remember that there was a downtown restaurant, the Traveler's Inn, where we liked to dine. One time while Louise was still pregnant she had their baked stuffed peppers, which were tasty, but she could not hold them down. She could not tolerate the sight or even the smell of baked stuffed peppers for a few years after that. I have fond memories of the Traveler's Inn. It was where I was introduced to a culinary delight by the name of sour cream raisin pie. I had never heard of it before but it became one of my favorite desserts. It also turned out that the people who owned the restaurant lived just across the street and down a couple of houses from us.

I was proud of Louise. She was quite progressive in her views of childbirth. She had recently read about something called the Lamaze technique of childbirth. It involved focusing on deep breathing for the management of contraction pains. It was a more natural form of childbirth that encouraged women to be confident in their ability to give birth rather than to live in fear.

Louise signed up for a prenatal class at the hospital. She wanted to learn more about pregnancy and childbirth. She asked the nurse about Lamaze. The nurse discouraged her from attempting it. She knew of one lady who had tried and it had not turned out well. But Louise, who is a stubborn Bohemian lady, persisted. The nurse referred her to a lady in town who was just beginning to teach Lamaze. Her name was Jean.

Louise's doctor, Dr. Hunt, encouraged her in this more natural way of childbirth. He had been born in China, had gone to medical school in Canada, and had married an American woman from Minot, North Dakota. Dr. Hunt said that in China women would be working in the field, would squat in the shade of a tree to give birth, and then return to work. It was not the big deal that western societies made it out to be.

Nevertheless, we knew there were risks involved in childbirth. Both the mother and the baby could have serious medical problems. For my part, I was appalled at how ignorant I was of the whole process. Perhaps it is a subject that men are not normally attracted to. I suspected, though, that there were a lot of women who were just as uninformed as I was.

I remember that Dr. Hunt was a Catholic. One of his patients was also a Catholic. She was young, I think around thirty, and already had given birth to six or seven children. She and her husband wanted many more, as many as possible. Dr. Hunt warned her to slow down, that having so many children so quickly could do long-term damage to her health.

I attended the Lamaze classes with Louise. I learned to coach her on her breathing technique. But underneath I was scared. I told Louise that when the time came for her to give birth I would probably remain outside the room. It would be between her and the doctor and the nurses. She was not at all thrilled with my cowardice. I wasn't either.

Finally the day came. On July 18, 1972, we rushed to the hospital at a quarter to six in the morning. I remained in the labor room with her, coaching her breathing and timing her contractions. That was all I had intended to do. But when they wheeled her into the delivery room I had to go with her. I did not want to leave her alone.

There were a couple of other women giving birth in adjoining rooms. We could hear them screeching and moaning. But Louise lay there, concentrating on her breathing, as she had been taught to do. We had heard that giving birth was a lot of hard work. Now Louise found that it was true. At 11:15 a beautiful baby girl was delivered. Jenifer Rebeca weighed in at six pounds two and a half ounces. She was eighteen and a half inches long.

I called our mothers right away. It was old hat to my mom; she already had several grandchildren. But it was a first, or at least nearly a first, for Louise's mother. "Oh, no," she exclaimed, "that's my second call today." Louise's brother, Ron, had called from Denver a few hours earlier to announce the birth of their first child, Shea. Louise's grandmother Ficek (Fit-sick) is shown holding the two babies who were born on the same day.

Mothers were kept in the hospital longer in those days. Louise remained in the hospital for three days as a summer storm roared through the area. There were power outages and the hospital had to go on its emergency generator backup system. Much of those three days is fuzzy in my memory. The clearest picture I have is of holding this little bundle in my arms. I remember feeling a flush of tenderness. I was flooded with emotion. It felt as if I was looking at life for the first time. A baby's first cry, its later joyous laughter, those are sounds which surely must echo through the universe. Jenifer was swaddled in a blanket and she sneezed. It surprised me that a baby only a day or two old was even capable of sneezing.

Louise and I had lived in the motel for about a month while we had looked for a house to buy. There was not that much available in the little town of 7,200. We toured one newly constructed house. It was nice but there were a couple of problems associated with it. For one thing, it did not have a garage, which we thought was odd in an area where winter snows were common. The other problem was that the builder would not tell us how much he was asking for the property. It was as if he expected us to first make an offer and then we would negotiate from there. I had sold real estate for a short time while I was living in Anchorage. There was nothing normal about this deal so we decided to back out.

We looked at another new house across the street from the Middle School. It was smaller but the workmanship was outstanding. Some problems emerged. It had a sump pump in the basement. Neither Louise nor I had ever been around a sump pump. We were concerned about a possible flooded basement. We were to learn years later that sump pumps work well when houses are built in lower lying areas where drainage is a problem. The second concern was about the noise level when children were let out of class. The final concern was affordability. I think the builder was asking something like $32,000 for it. Could we handle the payments?

I don't know. We had both grown up poor and now we did not set our sights very high. All we really expected was a starter home, something we could fix up, something we could build some sweat equity in and then sell for a better place. We would work our way up.

The third house we looked at was more to our liking. It was an old, two-story farm house that had been moved onto a lot at 1410 Bryant Street in Alexandria. It measured 24 X 24. The downstairs had a living room, a dining room, and a kitchen. Upstairs were a bathroom and two bedrooms. All the rooms were small. There was a full basement and a tiny attached garage.

The owner was a sixty-five-year-old lady who had recently retired from teaching. In a move that had surprised all her neighbors she had married an older gentleman and moved to his home in the Minneapolis area. It was her first marriage. She was asking $16,500 for her house on Bryant Street and she was willing to carry the mortgage herself. Louise and I agreed to pay 6% interest on the loan and make monthly payments of $200. On December 14th, 1971, we signed a contract for deed.

When we moved in we did not possess even one piece of furniture. Now we had to buy what we needed for our bedroom, living room, and dining room. We would furnish the second bedroom later. We did not have the cash we needed to pay for all of it. We made monthly payments.

The house was heated by a hot water, radiator system. The boiler was in the basement, as was the fuel oil tank. It was not long before we decided to update the heating system. Alexandria had its own power plant. Electricity was incredibly cheap. We installed electric baseboard heating.

I remember when the contractor came to remove the radiators. Holy cow, were they ever heavy! They must have weighed 300 pounds each. One of the younger workers was heavily muscled. It looked as though he was a weightlifter. I can still visualize him carrying one of the radiators down the stairs. He was groaning with the effort and sweat was pouring off him. I did not understand why he was not using a dolly. I thought he was probably trying to show off his strength.

We had not lived in the house more than a few weeks when Nugget ran away. It was cold and snowy outside. I drove around the neighborhood until nearly midnight but could not find him. I tossed and turned all night worrying. First thing in the morning we got a telephone call. It was from the downtown drycleaners, about a mile away. I had dropped off a few shirts and some trousers with them. They wanted to know if I had lost a dog. A cold and shivering yellow Labrador had shown up at their door. They had checked the dog tag on the collar and remembered my name. Dumb mutt! He wandered off a few more times over the years. He would spend the whole night rummaging in garbage cans and searching for female company. It was party time for him.

Over the next few years I did some basic electrical and plumbing work. One of our family stories was the time I was installing new paneling in the upstairs bathroom. I was just hammering in the final finish nail when Louise called that supper was ready. For some reason the nail did not want to go in. I pounded harder. Then I heard a hissing sound. Oh no, I had driven the nail through a water line! I had to quickly run down to the basement and turn off the main water supply. Later, I cut a small hole in the paneling and soldered the copper pipe.

I finished part of the basement and installed a commode and a shower. I built a wood fence around the back yard. In 1977 we sold the house for $27,000 and began building a new home.

There were things to learn about living in the North Country. People told us that during the summer months we needed to use a dehumidifier in the basement. The cooler air could not hold as much moisture. Nuts, I thought, I'll just open the basement windows and let the flow of fresh air move the moisture out. There's no need to pay good money for a dehumidifier. Well, after I found my best pair of Eddie Bauer leather boots covered with mold and had to throw them out I changed my mind. And there was the time when a gray squirrel entered the basement through an open window and I had a hell of a time trying to catch it. I finally laid a wooden plank from the basement floor to the open window and the varmint made its escape.

There was another problem. Field mice apparently had a long-established route from the nearby grassy area of the airport to 1410 Bryant Street. They invaded every fall and early winter. There were a few times when Louise and I felt them running across us when we were in bed at night. Naturally, that bothered Louise a lot, even if she had been a farm girl. She said they belonged outside, not in the house.

I thought they were cute little varmints, and they were clean. I had taken care of lab rats when I was in college so I was used to wiggly creatures. Still, I had to agree that our bed was no place for them to be hanging out. After weeks of searching, Louise discovered that they were entering through the garage, climbing up the wall to the second floor, and passing through holes in a closet to our bedroom. I plugged the holes and that was the end of the problem.

Cold winter temperatures could present other problems that I had never heard of while growing up in southern Illinois. Frost was a problem, or more particularly, something called the frost line. I had first encountered it in Anchorage, where it was said to be five or six feet deep. That meant that water and sewer lines had to be buried deeper so that they would not freeze up in the winter. I think in Alexandria it was more like three or four feet. It was something that had to be taken into consideration when constructing a new building or laying new water and sewer lines.

Frozen water pipes were another hazard. If they were not properly installed so that they were well insulated from the cold they could burst in the winter and flood the house with water. Those who traveled during the winter would turn the thermostat down to forty degrees while they were gone. There was no sense keeping the house fully heated while they were away and forty degrees would keep the pipes from freezing.

In that regard, it was common for Minnesota retirees to spend part of their winters in the South. Texas and Arizona were popular destinations. Some dreamed of moving permanently but few did. The North Country had a hold on them.

I had complained that winters in Alaska were nine months long. Minnesota was an improvement. Now the winters were only six months long! In southern Illinois, where I had grown up, I had never had to be overly concerned with shoveling snow. Now I had to spend hours and hours shoveling snow in Minnesota. I got lots of fresh air and exercise. Those who were better off owned a snow blower.

I put my time in shoveling snow out of driveways, digging cars out of drifts, and raking snow off roofs. I and my back are achingly familiar with all the various tools used to move snow. But all in all there was nothing that could compare to a good, old fashioned aluminum grain shovel for the efficient removal of snow. I got the idea when we lived on Bryant Street. I watched our 75-year-old neighbor, a retired farmer with thick hands and large calluses, as he finished his driveway before I was half done with mine.

At first I figured the shovel was just a leftover from his farm days, something he had been reluctant to discard when he and his wife had moved to town. Why buy a new shovel when you have a perfectly functional old one, scratched and dented though it may be? But when I drove around town after the next blizzard I noticed a number of men using grain shovels. Either we had an abundance of retired agrarians or somebody knew something I didn't. It called for a quick trip to the Fleet Farm store and a hasty purchase. I tried the new shovel and, by golly, it worked just fine. I liked it. It brought back memories of shoveling wheat and corn as a farm boy in Illinois.

I remember that old retired farmer and his wife. They always had a large patch of strawberries in their summer garden and they were happy to share them with our little family. There was a problem, though. His wife had read somewhere that mothballs were a good way to keep bugs out of a strawberry patch. The berries she so generously gave us smelled and tasted like mothballs. We had to accept them with a smile and a thank you and then dump them into the garbage when she was not looking.

Louise and I were in our own home with a new baby. It must have been in August of 1972 that my parents flew up from Illinois for a two-week stay. They would spend time with their new granddaughter and help out around the house. One afternoon I rented a pontoon boat at a nearby lake. Dad and I fished while the women visited. Our little daughter was wrapped in a blanket. She can brag that she was probably about a month old when she first went fishing.

It was an exhausting time for Louise. She was nursing Jenifer and she could not bear to hear her cry. Jenifer was not a good sleeper then nor has she been for the past forty-plus years. Louise would get up several times in the middle of the night to feed Jenifer. She did not want to wake me because she knew I was worn out from work.

Now Louise and I had to seriously consider what we wanted in the way of family. Louise expressed a desire to have children quickly rather than dragging it out. She wanted to return to her teaching career. We agreed that maybe two or three children should be the limit. We had to laugh when we thought about it. When Louise was younger she had dreamed of having twins. Now that she'd had a baby she had given up on that fantasy. Babies were a lot of work!

It must have been around May of 1973 when Louise found out that she was pregnant again. She continued nursing Jenifer until Dr. Hunt told her she had to stop. The fetus was smaller than normal. There could be a chance of a miscarriage. Medical opinion has changed since then. Today pregnant women can continue to nurse.

We went through the Lamaze training again. One would think that after experiencing the first childbirth parents would begin to relax. But that was not the case, at least not with me. Something could still go wrong.

The due date was mid-December. We have a picture of Louise on Christmas Eve, opening presents with Jenifer. Oh my, was her tummy ever extended. It was a quarter to six in the morning, just as it had been with Jenifer, when we again rushed to the hospital. It was Christmas day. Our neighbor, Fern, came over to stay with Jenifer. Christopher was born at six forty-four. He weighed seven pounds six ounces and was twenty and a half inches long. I was back home by seven thirty. Fern was asleep on the couch and Jenifer had not yet awakened.

Louise and I talked it over in her hospital room. We had speculated that if we had two daughters we would want to try one more time and then call it quits. But now that we had a daughter and a son, we thought that was enough. Dr. Hunt performed the procedure. He tied Louise's fallopian tubes so that she could not get pregnant.

We tend to visualize newborns as they will appear in the future – a princess girl in a prom dress – a shy boy tossing baseballs in the back yard. Then they grow up and we remember them as they were in diapers. It is difficult to look at them when they are in their teen years and visualize them as parents. In fact, it makes us shudder to do so. We do not want them to produce babies too darned early.

I had constructed a cradle out of plywood before Jenifer had been born. Louise and I had kept it in our bedroom for a few months before buying a used crib and moving Jenifer into the second bedroom. We had found the crib at Ron's Railroad Salvage. I had cleaned and repainted it. We were living paycheck to paycheck and every dollar counted. Ron's Railroad Salvage had a lot of bargains.

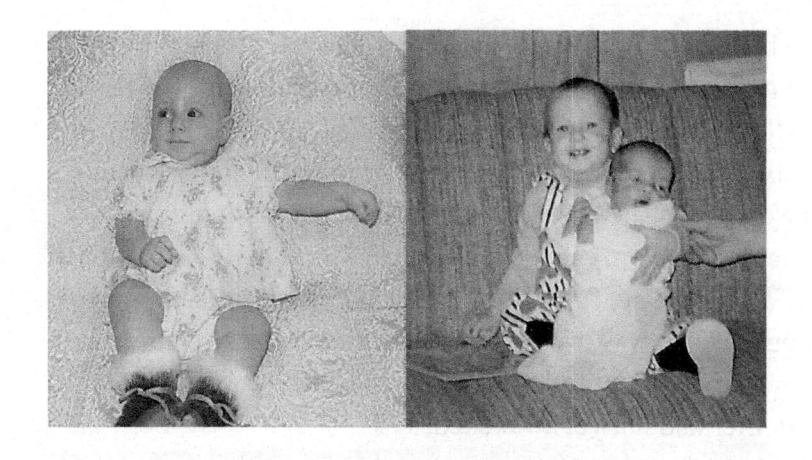

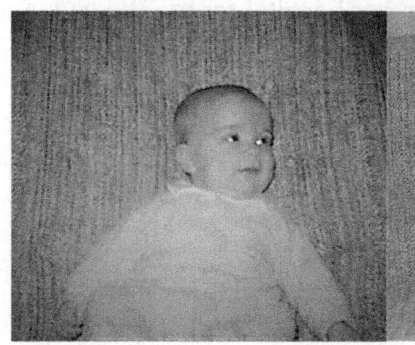

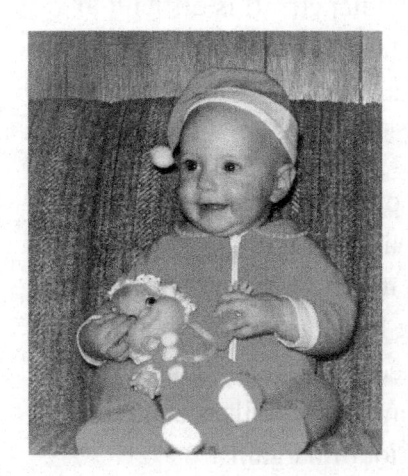

Left to right, from top: Jenifer with sealskin mukluks, Jenifer and newborn Chris, Chris, Chris, Jenifer at 1st Christmas.

Our son and daughter-in-law later inherited the cradle for use with their children. It is stored in their basement.

I remember how tiny that second bedroom was. A slanted dormer wall took up much of the space. The children played hopscotch so far as sleeping was concerned. For a few months Chris slept in the cradle in our room. Then he went into the crib and we returned to Ron's Railroad Salvage to buy a small bed for Jenifer. Eventually both children slept in their own beds.

Now the real joy began. I had ached for a family. I had worried that it was never going to happen. Louise had taken care of that for me. I sat the children in my lap and read to them. We read the same stories over and over. At first the children were more interested in chewing the pages than in paying attention. Then they became fascinated by the pictures. Finally they began to memorize the words and the story so that if I skipped over a word they would correct me. Soon we made a game of it. I would substitute something silly for the real word. Instead of a rabbit chewing on a carrot I would say it was an elephant. Jenifer and Chris would burst into giggles. They had memorized the story and knew I was being silly. The rule was that they would have to point out the correct word and sound it out phonetically. Learning to read thus became a fun thing that they picked up before they were in kindergarten.

The Disney children's books were some of our favorites. They featured animal characters such as Donald Duck, Mickey Mouse, Bambi, Dumbo, and Thumper. One of my favorite stories starred Goofy, a canine friend of Mickey Mouse. There was a drawing of a combination restaurant and gas station that Goofy owned. A large sign on the roof encouraged patrons to "Eat At Goofy's and Get Gas." It was humor obviously intended for the adult reading the story rather than for the child.

Another favorite was a book of world animals. It was a larger format volume with pictures of hundreds of animals, from beavers to kangaroos to gnus. We spent many pleasant hours with both children on my lap, the open book in front of us. I would point to an animal and ask the children to name it. It was something they enjoyed. It was amazing to find out how bright they were. They were like two little sponges when it came to learning something new.

I fantasized about writing a children's book myself. I had already thought of a title. I would call it *YAH BUT*. It would be based on my experiences with my own two children, little rug rats that they were. "Pick up your toys," I would tell them. Or - "Find your coat and let's get ready to go." Often the response was "<u>Yah</u>, <u>but</u> Dad I don't want to."

Louise and I took the children along when we went bird watching. We would drive slowly along the country roads, binoculars and bird books in hand. When we identified a new bird we would check it off in the book.

Memory of those country drives reminds me of the times when I had days off during the week and Louise was working. I remember how frustrating the teaching situation was in Alexandria. Louise had applied for jobs in elementary education. She had been turned down. The rumor was that if the husband had a good-paying job there was no reason for the wife to be working. It apparently was associated with religious beliefs; a woman's place was in the home. As a result, Louise had accepted a lower paying job to teach Head Start, a federal program that provided early childhood education, plus health and nutrition training, to low-income families.

At any rate I would take the children for a drive in the country. I had taught them a couple of farm expressions that I had learned as a young boy. It was said that when our bladders were full and we needed to pee that "our eyeballs were floating," and that when we boys had a strong stream it "sounded like a cow peeing on a flat rock." One day we were driving by a farm south of Alexandria. Half a dozen cows chewed their cuds while standing in a muddy barn yard. One of them began peeing. Chris and Jenifer jumped in excitement (seat belts were not much used in those days) and began howling with laughter. "Look, Daddy, look, there's a cow peeing on a flat rock." I looked and sure enough there stood a cow standing on a big flat rock and peeing up a storm. It was hilarious.

If Louise would have been with us on some of those drives she would have pitched a fit. The children were interested in doing everything. I would let them sit on my lap, one at a time, and steer the car. Of course I would have my hands on the steering wheel as well. Sometimes we would be going fifty or sixty miles an hour. Those were the days too when seatbelts and child restraints were not much used. Jenifer and Chris would <u>stand</u> in the front seat as we raced down the road. I remember one time when I had just gotten my good Eddie Bauer down jacket back from the dry cleaners. Chris stood beside me as I drove, his hand on my shoulder, his fingers covered with peanut butter and honey.

Those were halcyon days with our two young children. We hardly ever hired a babysitter. Jenifer and Chris went everywhere with us. There were many, many days by the clear lakes which surrounded Alexandria. Chris would spend hours skipping rocks across the water. Jenifer would explore among the autumn leaves that littered the shores. Louise and I would watch.

We had not lived in Alexandria for more than a few years when we traded in the Jeep Wagoneer on a new Ford station wagon. The Wagoneer's tires were noisy on the highway and the vehicle was rough riding. The station wagon was more suited to our family. The children and the dog could sleep in the back on long trips. But that damned Ford, it was not reliable! It would not run in cold weather. It was obviously a carburetor problem. I had it in the shop several times but nobody knew how to fix it. In 1980 we traded it in for a little Buick Skylark. The Skylark was the last new car we were ever to buy.

In Alexandria we were assailed by Ole and Lena jokes. The area was heavily populated by the descendants of Swedish and Norwegian settlers. I called them "Scandihuvians" and I developed a theory that immigrants tended to resettle in places that were similar to the land they had left. The farms around Alexandria were small and the soil was laced with rocks. I imagined that must have been the way it had been in the old country. I had not heard of "rock picking" when I had grown up in southern Illinois. The soil there had been deep and rich and loamy. But in central Minnesota it was still common to see piles of rocks farmers had "picked" out of the fields and there were many, many rock fences that had been constructed decades earlier.

I surmised, too, that sometimes there could be a relationship between the land and the personalities of the people who settled it. West-central Minnesota was a land of often grim and flinty farms, it was somber during the long and dreary winters, and there was a lot of water in the many lakes. Life was often a struggle to eke out a living from the poor soil. Surely it must have reminded early settlers of their native Scandinavian homes.

The Scandinavian personality seemed reserved, perhaps reflecting life's struggles, and they seemed closed and suspicious of others outside their social group. Life and religion were a serious matter to them. They were not topics to be toyed with by asking frivolous questions or having unfounded doubts. A more extremist brand of the Lutheran religion was popular. Bible-thumping Baptists held sway in many churches. They were even more suspicious of outsiders. There was a single Catholic church in Alexandria.

We learned that there was a darker, almost hidden side to some of the life in Alexandria. Louise and I talked to her priest about it. The priest said we would not believe some of the things that went on, things that he heard about in the confessional box. He mentioned sexual abuse and wife beating among other things. Surely this dark side of humanity exists everywhere.

One of our local pilots was an attorney in town. I think he flew a Piper Comanche, a twin-engine airplane. He said he had moved his family out of Minneapolis to get them away from crime. One Sunday his son and his son's girlfriend were driving to church in a little community north of Alexandria. They were ambushed and shot to death by her former boyfriend, a young farmer who lived alone. The farmer returned to his house, set it on fire, and burned himself to death. What a life of quiet desperation he must have been living.

A man was due for a hearing. He came armed to the court house. He shot a deputy to death and then fled in his car. Police followed him to his farm home where he hid behind a tree. When he stepped out another deputy armed with a 12-guage shotgun killed him. It was crazy behavior. There were too many things that spoke of frustration, of suppressed anger, of mental illness.

There was a kind of self-abasing humor when it came to the Ole and Lena jokes. Some of them were too off-color to relate here. I will give a few examples of the cleaner ones.

It was said that Lena had a difficult time distinguishing between the front and the back of Ole's underwear. "It's simple," Ole explained to Lena, "All you have to remember is that the yellow goes in the front and the brown belongs in the back."

Ole and Sven were in a tavern one evening when a good friend fell off one of the bar stools and died. "Someone will have to tell his wife," the bartender said. "Ole and Sven, you do it. You knew him as well as anyone." The two approached the house and knocked on the door. "Why don't you tell her?" Sven said. "You have a better way with words than I do." The woman opened the door. "Are you the widow Olson?" Ole asked her. "No, I don't think so," she responded. "The hell you're not!" Ole said. Yes, he certainly had a way with words.

Ole went to Minneapolis, looking for work. Nothing panned out. He decided to try Duluth. Approaching the bus driver, he asked: "Does dis bus go to Dalute?" "No," the driver responded. "it yust goes beep beep like all dem udder buses."

In Nome we had learned that "Eeeee" with a long "e" meant that the Native person understood what we were saying. In Minnesota we learned that "uff da" was a Scandinavian exclamation or interjection that expressed a wide range of sentiments – from bafflement to surprise to dismay, from disgust to concern to being overworked. It could be "Uff da, I don't know the answer to this test question," or it could be "Uff da, I sure am tired of shoveling all this snow."

There was a jingle we learned to memorize. "My name is Jon Johnson (or Yon Yonson, as you prefer). I come from Visconsin. I work for a dollar a day. I go to see Nellie. She lay on my belly and take my dollar away."

The Scandinavian influence was everywhere. The "Big Ole" statue located in downtown Alexandria was said to be the biggest Viking statue in America. The Runestone Museum was famous for the 200-pound slab of sandstone that was covered with runic characters - letters from ancient Germanic alphabets. The rock had been "discovered" in 1898 by a couple of farmers who lived near Kensington, Minnesota, twenty miles west and a little south of Alexandria. Thus it came to be known as the Kensington Runestone. The letters were interpreted to say that Nordic explorers had visited the area in 1362.

Runologists and other scholars roundly condemned the artifact as a hoax, which it likely is. Still, questions remain. Could a group of Vikings have wandered down from the Hudson Bay area? There is no historical or anthropological evidence. Today, in 2020, locals continue to prop up the legend. Big Ole, the statue, holds a sign that declares "Alexandria – The Birthplace Of America." Surprisingly, no other state in America has ever heard anything about the Kensington Runestone.

In my reading I stumbled across something called the Icelandic Eddas. They are a pair of manuscripts that had been copied down and compiled in the 13th century. They are regarded as one of the main sources of Norse mythology and skaldic poetry that relates to religion, cosmology, and Scandinavian history. I read them in an attempt to better understand the history behind the Viking personality.

Every culture seems to have its specialty foods. For the Scandinavians around Alexandria it was lutefisk and lefse. Lutefisk was dried white fish that had been soaked in a lye solution to soften it. It was one of those dishes, like ham hocks and sauerkraut, or pickled herring, which are best described as an "acquired taste." In other words, the food stinks. Most people closed their nose and stifled their gag reflex the first time they tried lutefisk. Lefse, on the other hand, was quite tasty. It was a flatbread made from potatoes and topped with butter, sugar, and cinnamon. I had a sneaking suspicion that the idea was to challenge one's palate with something gross, then reward it with something tasty.

Thirty miles southeast of Alexandria, alongside Interstate 94, was the little town of Sauk Centre, population around 3,500. Novelist Sinclair Lewis had lived there from 1889-1902. In 1930 he had been the first U.S. writer to be awarded the Nobel Prize in Literature. His satirical writings were critical of middle-class American life in the 1920s, of the social pressure toward conformity. I particularly enjoyed reading *Babbitt,* among Lewis' other books. I had to visit Sauk Centre, to get a feel for what Lewis was writing about.

The picture Sinclair Lewis painted was of very provincial, self-serving, self-centered, and mindless people who considered themselves to be the salt of the earth, and their little town darned near the center of the universe. They were smug and self-satisfied and not much impinged on by the outside world. George F. Babbitt was a prime example. He sold real estate and he was a community "booster." Babbitt rebelled for a while. He explored liberal politics and had an extramarital affair before he returned to the fold.

I had occasion to talk to a few of the residents of Sauk Centre. To them Lewis was "Red," in deference to his red hair. They were offended at the way Lewis had written about them. My sense was that the writing had been an act of courage and brutal honesty, something a true artist would engage in. Would I have that kind of courage if I were ever to become a writer?

I was somewhat amused to find this brand of "boosterism" prevalent in Alexandria. We had our own Babbitt. Oh my, I no longer remember his real name, only that I called him Harvey Hamburger. He headed up the local Chamber of Commerce or some such organization. His job was to promote Alexandria and he went about it with childish zeal. I was amazed at some of the exaggerated claims he made, how Alexandria was the most ideal place on the planet to live, to raise a family, or to start a business.

Louise and I met an idealistic couple who had moved themselves and their family from the big city of Minneapolis to the little farm community of Parkers Prairie, population around 1,000. Parkers Prairie is twenty-five miles north of Alexandria. She was a teacher; he was an artist-type. They hoped to get involved with the community, to contribute, to help make a change for the better. I don't remember how long they stayed – it may have been eight or ten years. Finally they gave up in disgust and discouragement and moved to Arizona. They found that no one was much interested in change.

Alexandria turned out to be a good place to raise children. We did not worry about our kids roaming the neighborhood. Our house was located one block away from airport property, which in those days was not fenced in. There was a gravel pit on the airport for Jenifer and Chris to explore. There were wonderful and relaxing picnics on remote areas of the airfield. We let the children and the dog run while Louise and I spread a blanket on the grass. Our menu usually consisted of fast food we had picked up at Kentucky Fried Chicken.

There was also a park in town where we sometimes went on a picnic. The problem there was that it was filled with Canadian geese. We had to be careful. The adult geese were extremely protective of their goslings. They would attack if we got too close. The geese caused another, stickier problem. Their poop was everywhere. It was difficult to avoid stepping in it.

Fillmore Park was located even closer. It had a few pieces of playground equipment – a seesaw, a merry-go-round that spun in circles, a slide, and a large swing set. We began a family tradition on the swing set. I would stand behind the children, then run forward and underneath them as I pushed the swing as high into the air as I could, all the while yelling "Yabba Dabba, Doo," the catchphrase of a TV cartoon character by the name of Fred Flintstone. It was probably a hazardous thing to do but the higher I pushed the children the better they liked it. Many years later I did the same thing with my grandchildren.

There was an A&W Root Beer stand on the northern edge of town. One of its specialties was fried chicken. But they did not make use of the whole chicken; they did not cook the livers. They sold the raw livers for fifty cents a pound. Well, that was quite a stack of livers. There must have been thirty or forty or more. Louise made a tasty casserole with them. She combined them with rice and cream of mushroom soup and onions. It made for an inexpensive but delicious meal.

I read in the newspaper that the Root Bear was scheduled to make an appearance. He was a big brown bear with orange clothing and he was the official A&W mascot. Of course we knew there was a person inside the costume. This must have been in the mid-seventies when Jenifer was about four years old and Chris was two and a half.

Louise and I thought the children would love the bear but that was not the way it turned out. They took one look and fled in terror. They took refuge in our car. The Root Bear was handing out candy, tiny root beer barrels wrapped in cellophane. The only way Jenifer and Chris would accept the candy was if we rolled down the passenger window just an inch or so and let the bear poke candy through the opening. It is one of my favorite memories. A couple of years later the children had gotten over their fear. They were more than happy to pose for a picture with the Root Bear and to accept more of the free candy he handed out.

A tiny Taco John's food stand was located about half a mile away. It must have been among the original franchises. We bicycled though idle city streets. There was indoor seating for about a dozen people or less. Oh my, we loved our Taco John's. Something went wrong on one visit. Apple desserts are among my favorites. I had an Apple Grande and within an hour was vomiting. I could not stand the smell, the taste, or even the mention of an Apple Grande for a couple of years after that.

Mention of vomiting brings about another family story. It took place while we were still living on Bryant Street and the children were small. Our entire family came down with a stomach flu. We had just gone to bed. First we heard Jenifer get up, pad into the bathroom, and urp up her supper. Shortly thereafter Chris followed suit. Pretty soon Louise vomited. All three barely made a sound. It was as if they were being polite about it.

Then it was my turn. When I regurgitate it is not something pleasant to witness. The sound comes all the way from my toes to the top of my head. You can hear it a block away. It sounds like two grizzly bears locked in mortal combat. It is a gut-wrenching experience for me. Louise and the children listened in stunned amazement. They had never heard anything like it. They hesitated for a minute then they burst into uncontrolled laughter. Holy cow, Dad, what the heck was that?

A few of the evening watches at Flight Service, from four P.M. to midnight, became family time, especially when there was not a lot of traffic. Louise would bring the children out to the airport. While they practiced typing on the teletype machine or spinning in the swivel chairs Louise and I would visit over a cup of coffee. One of the enjoyable things for the children to do was to watch while I filled a weather balloon with hydrogen and launched it to measure the height of the clouds. Of course, being the doting father that I was I would fill two extra balloons for Jenifer and Chris to take home with them. They tell me now, forty years and more later, that going out to the station to spend time with Father is one of their favorite childhood memories.

Speaking of a doting father, one of our daughter Jenifer's most vivid recollections is of the time when her younger brother, Chris, wanted to ask for something. He was ready to talk it over with Louise. "No, you dummy," Jenifer advised, "if you want something you have to ask Dad. Mom will just say no." Obviously I was the softy in the family.

We had not lived at 1410 Bryant Street too long before we reestablished a relationship with some Nome, Alaska, friends. Paul and Patti Norman and their adopted Native daughter had moved from Alaska to Holdingford, Minnesota, a little farm town of 600 or so people sixty miles southeast of Alexandria. Paul had accepted a job as a shop teacher in the Holdingford public school system.

What could one say about His Honor Paul Norman, founder and Past President of the DPUN – the Dump Pickers Union of Nome? I have written about him in Volume III of my autobiography. I had dump picked with Paul one time. I had returned home with a rotted ice skate and a busted ski. Now we were practically neighbors again. Our two families spent some time together.

In southern Illinois where I had grown up, the weather at Easter time had always been warm. In Minnesota, though, it was a different story. Easter weather was iffy. There could be three feet of snow, some of which still remained from the previous November. The egg hunt then took place inside the house – behind the couch, beneath the kitchen sink, or high on a shelf.

I remember one Easter when we hid the baskets behind furniture. Paul and Patti's little girl and our two youngsters still had fun searching for them. It may have been a year or two later when we were able to hide the baskets outside in the backyard lawn. There were only a few patches of snow remaining and much of the grass was showing. I still have a visual memory of Jenifer and Chris racing around in their bathrobes, pajamas, and fuzzy bathroom slippers.

An obvious disadvantage of the rotating schedule was the many, many evenings, nights, weekends, and holidays that I had to work while my family sat at home. And there were the many days they had to remain quiet while I tried to sleep after getting off work at eight in the morning.

I remember there was one holiday weekend when a C-130 cargo plane from an Air National Guard unit in Minneapolis landed and taxied in. It came to a stop directly in front of Flight Service while a passenger deplaned. Its turboprop engines were roaring. Oh my, my heart started thumping. Oh to be a part of a flight crew again, as I had been for five years in the Air Force! Hand me a flight suit and my captain's bars and I would be ready to go. Then I remembered that the crew and I had something in common. They were not spending the holiday with their family and neither was I. I would be no better off flying than I was working in Flight Service.

I had to remember that there were many occupations which kept workers away from home on evenings and weekends and holidays – police and firemen and medical personnel, salesmen and long-haul truck drivers. I was thankful that Louise was always there to parent our children on the many odd hours I was working.

The 1970s were another time, another era in American history. Milk in glass bottles was delivered to our front door. The deliveryman was a little on the eccentric side. He was a smaller man who bowed and scraped and hopped nervously about. He engaged in nervous chatter. His name was Fred, though we never referred to him with that simple moniker. To us he was always "Fred the Milkman." There came a time, though, when we heard that Fred had had a horrible accident. He had been backing his delivery truck out of a driveway and had accidently run over and killed a child. Fred seemed a simple, kindly, and friendly man. The accident must have devastated him.

Then there was Barney the mailman. He walked door to door delivering the mail from a leather pouch slung to his side. He took his time, poking along, and stopping to visit. To him work meant doing things at an easy, relaxed pace. I watched him one day as an inspector walked with him, checking, I supposed, to make sure that Barney's route was a full day's work. Otherwise, he would assign more customers for Barney to take care of. Now, with the inspector in tow, Barney had to hustle from house to house. He had to demonstrate that he was working hard. I had to chuckle. What a hangdog look Barney had on his face. If he had routinely hustled as much as he did now he could probably have covered his route in half the time it normally took and he would have been exposed. Sweat poured from him. He stretched his steps as much as possible. Instead of ambling across lawns as he normally did he walked back out to the street after every delivery and then on to the next house. What a character!

I had purchased a decent Voitlander 35mm camera in Germany while I was on leave from the Air Force. I had dragged it along while I flew combat missions in Southeast Asia and during the three years I had lived in Alaska. Now, in Alexandria, I took it out of its case again. There was a creative side of me that called for exploration. I enrolled in a photography correspondence course, hoping that some professional guidance would help me. I mailed in the assignments and waited for the feedback. I do not remember now whether I ever finished that course or not. I may have grown disillusioned with it after a bit. I was more interested in outdoor photography than anything else. I had no desire to shoot weddings or portraits.

I do remember taking a photo of a country church. I thought it turned out rather well but the instructor's comments were not at all positive. I also remember a time when I was walking in a natural area that had been set aside by the State. I was wading through about a foot of snow. Ahead of me were the remains of a rotted out wood fishing boat. I thought I saw movement but instead of stopping to investigate I kept walking. Suddenly a beautiful snowy owl erupted into flight. It had taken refuge inside the boat. If only I had been more patient, quieter, it is likely I could have gotten a picture of it peeking over the boat. An all-white bird against a background of all-white snow could have made a stunning picture. It should have been a lesson learned, that outdoor photography demands concentration and patience.

Years later I got deeper into outdoor photography. Searching for pleasing compositions was an enjoyable pastime. But I also learned that people have widely different artistic tastes. More often than not, when I thought I had taken a special picture others were not all that impressed. And sometimes when I judged a photo to be mediocre others loved it. It was a crapshoot, plus the market was quite competitive.

Our family stories grew. A few of our kids' favorites were the following. When we went out to eat I had the habit of taking the easy way out. Instead of poring over the menu and agonizing over a decision I would order whatever was the "special." Besides, being the cheapskate that I was, the special was often marked down in price. I allowed this cheap side of me to dominate when I went shopping. I could buzz through a shopping mall in fifteen minutes while Louise spent an hour browsing. The only thing I was interested in was sifting through the bargain bins. There was a pink shirt I purchased that was a bit on the garish side. Louise and the children laughed at me. But who cared? It had been in the bargain bin.

Our little family often went for drives on local farm roads. We wandered around. I never really paid much attention to the turns we made. It would come time to head back home and I had no real idea how to get there. We would wander around some more before we found our way back. I refused to accept, though, that we were lost. We ex-Air Force navigators never admitted to being lost. We were merely taking the "scenic route." Again, Louise and the children laughed at me. There were times when we had to stop and ask for directions.

A young married couple lived in a tiny house across the street from us. They did not have much in the way of income. The husband added an addition. He ignored the requirement to obtain a city building permit. He found used lumber somewhere. He was basically a gravel truck driver with a hammer and a saw and a level. He had no experience with basic electrical work or with plumbing. (A plumber once told me that plumbing is not all that difficult, that all we have to remember is that shit flows downhill.)

The finished product looked a bit lop-sided. It tilted towards the north. The city building inspector condemned the whole thing as unsafe to live in. It had to be torn down. This likely created a life-long anti-government agitator. I could understand and emphasize with the husband's desire to make thing better for his family. But, my god, there are some common sense rules that need to be followed. How would the husband have felt if the house had burned down as a result of his shoddy electrical wiring and his little family had perished?

We had not been in the little house on Bryant Street for too many weeks when Nugget got us into a bit of trouble. I had been outside shoveling snow in the driveway and had not kept a close eye on him. I had allowed him to wander a bit. It was after dark and Louise and I were inside when we heard a noise at the front door. I opened it to find a pile of dog poop on our front step. A neighbor, shovel in hand, was just crossing the street back to his house. It apparently was his way of saying keep your damned dog out of my yard.

Holy crap, that was no way to act. Of course I did not want Nugget to be pooping in other people's yards. I was a more responsible owner than that. I wanted to be a good neighbor. All he'd needed to do was tell me and I would have cleaned up the mess in his yard myself. I would have apologized. Now I was angry and offended at the way he had handled it. I do not recall that neighbor ever speaking to me in the six years we lived on Bryant Street, and I'm pretty sure I never attempted to strike up a conversation with him. The rumor was that his wife ruled the roost, that she used to beat the crap out of him. Maybe he deserved it.

Cyril the barber lived in another house across the street. His shop was downtown. He was my regular barber though I did not get to know him on a personal basis. I remember he gave Chris his first haircut. It was not uncommon for little boys to become terrified the first time they felt electric clippers buzzing around their ears. But Cyril handled the situation well and I was there to reassure Chris.

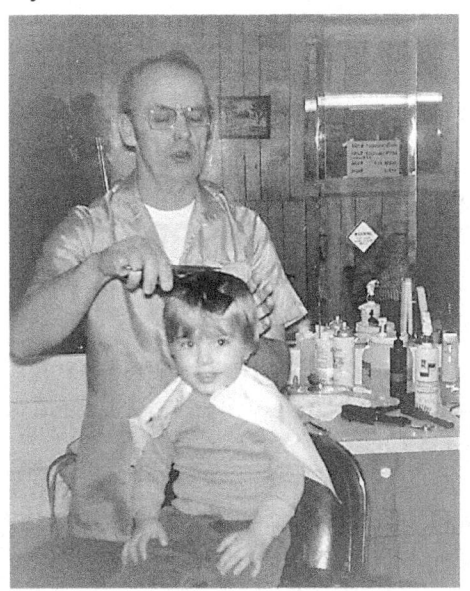

There was a men's state prison in St. Cloud, seventy miles southeast of Alexandria. Louise paid close attention to every newspaper or TV account of an escaped prisoner. Surely he was headed directly for 1410 Bryant Street! We should lock the doors, check the windows, and sleep lightly.

For the first couple of years we were restricted to an old and inexpensive black and white television set. It was all we could afford. Its interior was filled with vacuum tubes. I had been given a modicum of electrical training while I was in Air Force navigator school. It was mostly bookwork. I had never seen the inside of a TV set. Now, with our restricted budget, it was up to me as a husband and a provider to take on the role of TV repairman.

As it turned out, it was not all that difficult. When a tube burned out it would stop emitting a light or it would be cold. I would unplug it, take it to the hardware store downtown, and buy a replacement tube. The numbers were clearly marked on the bottom edge of the tube. I had to be careful, though, when I was fiddling around inside the TV set. I remembered from my Air Force training that many pieces of electronic equipment had something called a capacitor. The capacitor stored electricity so that a person could get a hell of a shock even if the TV was not plugged in.

Oh my, the TV programs from those days, the 1970s and early '80s. James Garner played the lead role as a handsome ex-con and private investigator in the *Rockford Files*. His best friend was a scummy character by the name of Angel Martin. Angel was no angel; he was always getting Rockford entangled in some mess. It was a rare episode when Rockford was not shot at or beaten up or wrecked his car. He was mostly rooked out of the pay he was due. Jenifer was so young at the time that she had difficulty pronouncing the title of the program. To her it was the "Rockport Piles."

We howled with laughter at every episode of *The Honeymooners*. Ralph Kramden, portrayed by comedian Jackie Gleason, was a New York City bus driver. He bellowed and roared and made hollow threats against his wife, Alice. But underneath he was softhearted. Ed Norton was his best friend. Ed worked for the sewer department. Ralph was forever involved in some get-rich-quick scheme. None of them ever worked out. He and Ed would then retreat to a meeting of the Loyal Order of Raccoons.

Why is it that stories involving losers are so popular? And why is it that they are often portrayed as comical? Perhaps it prepares us for the failures in our own lives. Perhaps we learn that it is sometimes better to laugh things off than to take them too seriously.

We became Minnesota Vikings football fans. Bud Grant was the coach in those years, the 1970s and early '80s. I was particularly interested in one of their running backs. His name was Bill Brown and he had graduated a year ahead of me at the University of Illinois. I was happy to see him doing so well at the professional level. The Vikings had good players and a winning record. But they were never able to win the Super Bowl.

Thus settled in on Bryant Street, I spent the time immediately after supper letting my food digest while I grabbed the daily issue of the *St. Paul Pioneer Press* and headed for the lazy boy lounge chair. It was a good newspaper with interesting articles and competent writers. Louise and I also enjoyed watching the news and weather on the Minneapolis TV stations, particularly WCCO. A couple of their reporters were exceptionally good. They ended up moving on to national TV networks.

Minnesota's slogan was that it was the "Land of 10,000 Lakes." But if there were 10,000 lakes then surely there must have been 10,000 resorts and another 100,000 summer homes and cabins. People living in Minneapolis and Chicago and Omaha dreamed of moving to the North Country. They could quit their stressful city careers and buy a resort, where they could be their own boss, where life would be more relaxed and the fishing was always good.

It seemed that hundreds attempted it every year. A rare few actually succeeded. They discovered that the resort business involved a lot of hard work and years of stress. First of all, most of them paid too much. They owned a $50,000 home in Minneapolis, so that a small house with half a dozen cabins for $70,000 - $80,000 did not sound too bad. They did not think to look at the books, to get some idea of what kind of profits they could expect, whether they would earn enough to make the monthly mortgage payment and cover household expenses. Nor did they often examine the structures too closely. They did not notice the rotting boards in the dock, the windows that needed repair, or the boats that needed replacing. All that amounted to thousands of extra dollars.

Still, they dived in. Optimism was the name of the game. If it took hard work for a short time they would accomplish that. Then reality would set in. They had not realized that owning a resort meant being on call twenty-four hours a day, seven days a week, all damned summer long. They had to take care of the customers. They were continually exhausted and there was no time to enjoy life.

Nor could they have foreseen, apparently, how incredibly difficult it was to squeeze a living from eight or ten small cabins that provided income only in the summer. They would need to find outside work in the winter, when few jobs were available. Thus a mechanic who had earned a good wage in the city would find himself pumping gas part-time for minimum wage. More resort owners existed closer to starvation than lived the high life. Many said to hell with it, sold the resort for a loss to the next dreamer, or turned it back to the bank, moved back to the city, and started over from scratch, their dreams and their bank accounts bankrupt. It was another case where reality proved to be a harsh taskmaster.

One of the Flight Service Specialists I worked with, let's call him Ralph, backed his way into the resort business. He had a married son who was struggling with health issues – with severe diabetes. Ralph and his wife were desperate to help. They sold their newer home and bought a resort. It would be ideal. Ralph could help out in his spare time while his wife and son and daughter-in-law ran the resort. I paid a visit one July weekend. It had rained for days. Glum-faced vacationers sat around with nothing to do. If I recall correctly, the son quickly lost interest and wanted out.

Louise needed to earn six college credits every five years to keep her Minnesota teacher's license current. She attended classes during the summer. She took one class at the University of Minnesota, Morris. It was about forty-five driving miles west and south of Alexandria. It was a small campus of about 1,500 undergraduate students. I remember playing hide and go seek outside with our children while Louise was in class.

She attended a couple of classes at Minnesota State University Moorhead. The campus body there was comprised of about 5,000 students. The city of Moorhead was located just across the Red River from Fargo, North Dakota. The whole family went along. It gave us an opportunity, after Louise's class was over, to hop across the river to Fargo, there to shop at the large mall and to dine at what was to us the fancy Red Lobster seafood restaurant.

As a side note, I found it curious that the Red River flowed north into Canada, whereas where I had grown up in the central U.S. the rivers always flowed south. I learned there was a simple explanation. Rivers always run downhill. The land around Fargo sloped to the north, towards Hudson's Bay. The land in the central parts of the country sloped south and east, towards the Gulf of Mexico.

1501 RIDGEWAY DRIVE

(SWEAT EQUITY)

When I was living in Anchorage, Alaska, I had worked for a short time as a real estate agent. I had learned about something called "sweat equity." It was the increase in the value of a property as a result of the added labor, or "sweat," an owner put into it. Louise and I had made improvements to our home on Bryant Street, then we had sold it for a profit. Now we were about to dive into the real meaning of sweat equity. We would build a house from scratch. It would be labor intensive.

By 1977 we felt we had outgrown our first little house and were ready for something larger. Jenifer remembers that she was five years old. A new home turned out to be quite an adventure. We had first looked around a bit in town but had not found anything that appealed to both of us. Oh my, I almost got myself into trouble. We were looking through an older home. It had recently been rewired and had new plumbing. I was not at all enthusiastic. The house still looked as though it needed lots of work. When everything was completed it would still be an old house.

Louise, though, was more than interested. She thought the house had some real possibilities. I had to think of something fast if I was going to talk her out of it. We were standing in the living room. It had been decorated with deep red, flocked wallpaper. I thought it was garish; Louise kind of liked it. A sudden inspiration came to me. I had no idea of its origin. "It reminds me," I murmured piously, "of the wallpaper I once saw in a French whorehouse." Well, that did it. Louise was not going to have any part of a house that reminded me of a bordello. We walked away and never returned. Of course, I actually had never been in a French whorehouse but I had a hell of a time convincing Louise otherwise. Nonetheless, the story fulfilled the purpose of getting us away from that house.

Louise had a big part in getting the next step started. If we could not find an existing house we liked then perhaps we should build our own. She bought several large paperback books of house plans and a packet of graph paper. She would pick out a house that she liked the looks of and redraw the floor plan on the graph paper, modifying it to make the foot traffic flow better, or to enlarge the dining room, and so forth. It became a hobby that she enjoyed. Over the next few years she spent many pleasurable hours modifying house plans.

In Alexandria, Louise came up with kind of a modified tri-level design that we both liked. There was the main entrance. On the left were a study, a family room, a laundry, and a bathroom. On the right, raised about three feet higher, were a large living room, a dining room, and a kitchen. A flight of stairs led from that second level to the upstairs, where there were three bedrooms and two baths. There was a crawl space under the first level and a full basement under the rest. I remember the total area as being somewhere around 2,200 square feet. It was quite a move up from our cramped 1,000-square-foot house on Bryant Street.

After we had built the house and moved in it was a pleasant experience to walk into the new house and view that raised living room to the right. I installed a railing which accentuated the view even more. Large windows let in lots of natural light.

Housing contractors in Alexandria were non-union so that building costs were lower than in larger cities. Still, by the time we had finalized our house plans we were too late for the building season. All the contractors were booked up. We decided to act as our own contractors. We would find someone to frame the house, to hang the sheetrock, to do the wiring and the plumbing. We would do the rest of the work ourselves. It was the way both of us had been raised. Both our families had been too poor to hire workers. If they wanted something done they had no choice but to do it themselves, and to do it as cheaply as possible.

We found a half-acre lot at 1501 Ridgeway Drive, on the west edge of town. Its official description was Lot Three, Block Two, in the Westview Acres subdivision. It was a prime location for us. Our children could walk the few blocks to Lincoln Elementary School. Lake Winona was just down the hill. In the evening we could hear loons calling from the lake. Canadian geese nested there in the summer. Their flight path seemed to be right over our house. They would come gabbling over, not fifty feet above our chimney. They were within easy shotgun range. I would pretend I had my .12 gauge in my arms, raise it to my shoulder, aim, and murmur "Pow, Pow," as if bagging a couple of the fat geese for our Sunday dinner table.

The back side of our lot butted up against airport property. There was no fence at the time. When there was no snow I could walk across the airport to my work at Flight Service. Better yet, when I was working I could look out the window at Flight Service and see my house. Things could not have been much more convenient than that.

We found a company in Minneapolis, Martin Homes, Inc., that sold pre-built homes. They took Louise's house plans and prepared a full set of blueprints. They packaged most of what we needed – lumber and sheetrock and insulation, shingles and nails and cedar siding, carpeting and parquet tiles for the floors, windows and doors.

We went to the bank and on May 17th, 1977, signed a loan for $27, 749, with monthly payments of $265.23, and an interest rate of 8%. Building a house was one hell of a project to take on. Would our marriage survive it? I was forever exhausted from the rotating shift work. Plus I had a family to take care of. Thankfully, I had Louise. She had been a farm girl and she did not shy away from work. As the years went by we were to build a total of three houses together. We made a good team. I did much of the grunt work while Louise oversaw the interior decoration and the landscaping. She had a much better eye for those projects than I did. I remember that we did lots of wallpapering together. Louise spent many days looking at wallpaper and paint samples. It was not an easy job.

We had to get the foundation and the basement ready. We found a local contractor to do the work. His crew dug the basement with a bulldozer, poured the concrete foundation, and constructed the basement block walls. That contractor - I will not forget him. He supervised the work, all the while quoting bible verses. He wanted to impress us with his religious piety. It must have been a year or so later when we received a letter from the Internal Revenue Service. They wanted to know how much we had paid the contractor and whether or not it had been in cash. We read later in our local newspaper that the contractor had been accused of hiding some of his income from the IRS, thus avoiding taxes.

All the lumber was precut at the factory. One afternoon a large flatbed truck pulled up at the lot. It was piled high with lumber – roof trusses, floor joists, two by fours, and two by sixes. They would send along a three-man crew to frame the house. Then the problems started. That uncovered lumber had not laid on the ground for more than a few hours when the sky opened up and the rain poured. Everything was soaking wet. Our family had sold the house on Bryant Street and was temporarily living in an apartment house on the edge of the airport. We listened as it rained all night. There was nothing we could do about it.

The rain may have been the same deluge that spawned another favorite Powers family story. Chris was nearly four years old when we were living in the apartment while building the house. He and Jenifer soon found some little friends to play with. The rain had left a huge mud puddle and Chris, no doubt egged on by the others, had decided to roll around in it. When Louise and I found him he was covered with mud from head to toe. I had to take a picture. I carried him dripping wet to the bathroom and tossed him into the shower, clothes and all. We call it the "Mud Man" story.

The framing was completed in a few weeks, with all the windows and exterior doors installed, and the crew departed. Now it was our turn. The first item on the agenda was to nail down the shingles. We needed to keep the interior dry. Jim from Flight Service volunteered to get us started. He'd had some experience with roofing. We did not use nail guns in those days. Everything was done with a hammer and special roofing nails. The shingles were cut with either a utility knife or tin snips. I will not forget the day we started. We had worked for maybe an hour when the skies opened up again and the rain poured. We watched helplessly as water dripped everywhere inside the house. I remember that later that winter, after it had turned cold, there was so much moisture left in the wood that the attic was covered with frost.

A bundle of asphalt shingles weighs sixty pounds. I learned how to climb a ladder with a bundle on each shoulder. There was a lot of roof area to cover, taking into account both the house and the attached two-car garage.

One day Louise and I were nailing down shingles. My, my, that Bohemian lady from North Dakota could swing a mean hammer. (Nobody uses a hammer anymore for driving in nails. Carpentry and roofing work are done with an air compressor and nail guns.) We were interrupted by our children. "Mom and Dad," Jenifer called out, "can Chris and I come up?" "No," we responded in unison, "it's too dangerous." I think Jenifer was about five years old and Chris was four. "What if we're already on the roof?" Jenifer wanted to know. And they were. The ladder was out of sight from where we were working. The two little stinkers had climbed it and were sitting on the roof. We allowed them to remain by us, well away from the edge, where we could keep an eye on them. They thought they were pretty special. We could see for miles and miles when we were on top of that roof.

Bill, one of the electronic technicians from Flight Service, undertook the supervision of wiring the house. I paid him a fair wage and undertook much of the grunt work myself. I must have drilled a thousand holes through wood as we strung wire from outlet to outlet to a 200-amp circuit breaker in the basement. A city electrical inspector made sure all the wiring was safe and up to code. Alexandria had its own power plant so that electricity was the least expensive energy source. We found an electric furnace and Bill figured out how to hook it up. It called for extra-heavy wire.

The next step was insulation. We had ordered 2 X 6 studs for the outer walls rather than the usual 2 X 4s. This was a time, the 1970s, when there was an energy crisis. The Organization of Petroleum Exporting Countries had begun an oil embargo in 1973. It was in retaliation for the U.S. support of the Israeli military during the 1973 Arab-Israeli War. Gas prices had more than tripled, from $.36 a gallon in 1970 to $1.19 a gallon in 1980. There were long lines at gas stations. Many stations periodically ran out of gas.

Most homes were heated with petroleum products - heating oil or natural gas. The thicker insulation in our walls meant we could conserve energy and save on our heating costs. We did not have to worry about air conditioning. We were far enough north so that in the summer the air cooled at night.

The batts of fiberglass insulation came in large bundles. They were individually precut to fit snugly between the wall studs. But oh my, were they ever itchy. The tiny fibers were everywhere. I had to wear gloves and long-sleeved shirts. Even then, it took two or three showers to wash everything off. It was a large house to insulate. I no longer remember how long it took me. Later, I insulated the entire attic with more batts of fiberglass insulation.

When the insulation was finished I hired a contractor to hang and plaster the sheetrock on the walls and the ceilings. It was sweaty, grunt work best done by a crew of professional installers, not by an amateur working alone. It would have taken me months to complete the job.

Plumbing was another area where I needed help. I had done a bit of it at our little house on Bryant Street when I had installed a shower and a biffy in the basement. Now I hired a professional. I had to laugh when he provided a pithy formula for his vocation. "All a plumber has to know," he informed me, "is that shit flows downhill."

Soon we moved out of the apartment building and into our unfinished house. I remember driving home from work the first time. The little house on Bryant Street had never really felt like home. It had felt like a temporary dwelling. This was different. This was *our* home, something Louise had designed and we had built together. It was the first feeling of home I had felt since I had left Illinois for the Air Force fifteen years earlier, in 1962. It was a warm feeling, a feeling of comfort and acceptance, like snuggling under a heavy quilt on a snowy winter night.

We had settled on cedar siding. I learned that what the company had sent us was not of the highest grade quality but I worked with it anyway. Much of it splintered easily and had to be thrown out. I split those pieces and used them for kindling in the fireplace. They could be lighted with a match. I had no tutor to guide me. I had to learn how to cut and fasten the siding as I went along. It would have been better if I had been a craftsman. I had difficulty figuring out some of the angles that had to be cut. God, it must have been a couple of months before I was finished and I must have dug a thousand splinters out of my hands.

I installed parquet tiles on the floor of the first level, and in the living and dining rooms. There must have been a thousand of them. I spent so much time on my knees that I have had problems with them ever since. I cannot kneel on a solid surface today without it being painful. I have to wear knee pads.

I like old things; I always have. I form a relationship with them, an emotional connection. I have my favorite winter coat, my old pair of scuffed hunting boots, a battered desk. They all have something in common – they all have character and they all have memories.

With this in mind, I have a story to tell. As I sit here typing on April the 6th, 2020, I am wearing a Harris Tweed jacket instead of a sweater to keep me warm. I own two of the wool coats. I ordered them fifty-five years ago in Bermuda. We were flying Air Force radar missions off the east coast of the U.S. and when we were fogged out we would divert to Bermuda. A men's clothing store would send our measurements to London, where the jackets would be tailor made. We would pick them up the next time we landed in Bermuda. I was young and slim at the time. But it was not too many years before my chest migrated down to my waist and the jackets no longer fit. They have hung in my closet for nearly fifty years now. I was determined not to give up on them.

I have aged the past couple of years. Soon I will be eighty years old. My muscle mass has eroded, my skin has gotten flabby, and I have lost weight. I have gone from 192 pounds down to 172 pounds and now I can button the jackets again. To me they are more than just an item of clothing, they are a story and a host of memories. They are like old friends. They help me recapture my youth.

I remember another story about the living room in our new home on Ridgeway Drive. We had not lived in the house more than a couple of years when Louise decided we needed a change. She was the interior decorator and she had a good eye for it. We had moved a side table from our old house on Bryant Street to the new one on Ridgeway Drive. I protested when she determined that the side table had to go, that it no longer fit in with the rest of the house.

For me, it took a minimum of two or three years to even welcome a new piece of furniture into my life, let alone to feel comfortable with it. It had to prove itself first. It had to develop a history, a collection of memories. It was what I asked of any new friend.

But for Louise the table was a piece of furniture and little more. I had sweet memories of my cup of coffee sitting on that table as I pored through a newspaper or cuddled two children in my lap. I knew every stain and scratch and chip on it. I was concerned that if we threw out the table we would throw out the memories that went along with it. I had to accede, though reluctantly, to Louise's practicality.

Hanging the interior doors and installing the oak moulding proved to be a lengthy and labor-intensive endeavor. Everything had to be stained and varnished first – one coat of stain and two coats of varnish. I laid the pieces out on the basement floor. The work called for the skills of a craftsman and I did not have them. Some of the joints were not as tight fitting as I would have liked them. I will have to say, though, that nobody complained. It was one of those cases where we look at every mistake we make while nobody else pays any attention.

One last project was to hang the large garage door. I read the directions carefully. It involved winding a heavy spring with a long screwdriver or a bar. It could be dangerous. If the screwdriver or the bar slipped the spring could unwind with tremendous force and break my arm. I was nervous but I succeeded.

There was one final matter. We paid to have a 110-foot well drilled. The water in Alexandria was foul. It stank and it left a scum in the pan when it was boiled. Some of the local residents preferred it that way. They had drunk it and cooked with it all their lives. Most of us, though, resorted to using water softeners. Salt removed most of the minerals. There was an argument as to whether the soft water was better for us. It certainly was an improvement so far as laundry was concerned. White clothes remained white instead of turning gray. It was said that hard water was healthier for drinking but we did not like the taste of it. I don't know how many bags of salt pellets I dragged to the water softener in the basement. It was a chore.

I had made an attempt to improve the water situation. Our well had been drilled down to more than a hundred feet. The water was still terrible. A neighbor down the hill had sunk a sand point well in his basement. The water was pure and clear. I hoped I could tap into the same source of groundwater. Before the concrete basement floor had been poured I had driven the steel pipe with its perforated point down about sixteen feet. The maximum depth I could go in order for the pump to still work was thirty feet. But at sixteen feet I had hit a rock or a layer of clay. The pipe bent. I could go no deeper. I gave up.

I don't know, it was probably four or five years, and maybe more, before most everything was completed. We loved that house. As I said before, it was pleasant to walk in the front door and see the raised living room to the right. The large windows let in lots of natural light.

We had many pleasant family meals in the dining room. Our young son, Chris, was such a messy eater. He would drop crumbs of food everywhere under his chair. Our dog, Nugget, would lay waiting under the table. He would eat every crumb that Chris dropped. We kept Nugget's water and food bowls in the laundry room. One evening we were watching television in the family room. We heard a crunching sound. What the heck was that? We could see Nugget lying in plain sight on the family room floor. We found Chris in the laundry room, eating the dry dog food out of Nugget's bowl. Chris must have felt that turnabout was fair play. If Nugget could eat his food then he could eat Nugget's food. Mom and Dad put a quick stop to that.

I remember many happy days when I walked home from work. It may even have been that the airport maintenance crew had cut a path through the weeds, from Flight Service to Ridgeway Drive. The children and the dog greeted me at the door. Nugget sometimes almost knocked Jenifer and Chris over in his hurry to get to me first, his tail wagging furiously. Louise would be relieved to see me. She had been keeping up with two active children all day and she needed a break.

Our children also walked home from Lincoln Elementary School, a few blocks away. Jenifer was usually the first to arrive. She did not linger along the way. Chris, on the other hand, had to explore every puddle and visit with every friend. But when he reached the end of our driveway he would suddenly erupt into a frenzy. It was not until then that he paid attention to his overextended bladder. He would pound on the front door while his feet drummed a little dance of desperation. On more than one occasion he wet himself before we could get to him. What is it about boys, and males in general, that causes them to not pay attention, to be so easily distracted?

Chris arrived home from elementary school one day. He was in tears. "Daddy," he said to me, "our teacher told us that if you do not stop smoking you are going to die!" Well, I had been a cigarette smoker since I was eighteen. I usually smoked about a pack a day. Now I was thirty-eight. I had made a couple of abortive attempts to quit in recent years. It was time for me to try harder.

I was working by myself on an evening shift. It must have been around 8 P.M. when I ran out of cigarettes. I had no money on me so that I could buy more cigarettes in the vending machine next door. I began to panic. It was then that I finally began to realize how addicted I was, and how absurd it was that I could not get through even a few hours without lighting up a cigarette. I decided to take it one hour at a time, to see if I could make it through the night. Well, that did it. I quit cold turkey, as they say. I was grouchy as all get out for about a month, and it must have been a couple of years before the addiction was totally eradicated. Every time I was tempted to light up I had a vision of that little boy with tears running down his cheeks.

It did not take long before I had put in a small garden. We had grown much of our food when my family had been dirt poor and living in a little farm town in Illinois. Now I planted sweet corn, beets, onions, tomatoes, potatoes, green beans, kohlrabi, cucumbers, and lima beans. The onions grew large and sweet. Louise canned many quarts of stewed tomatoes that she used when she was cooking chili. She pickled and canned beets. I gave much of the corn over to Jenifer's care. She picked it and sold it to the neighbors. It was a way for her to earn pocket money and to accumulate pleasant memories.

Then there was Chris, that little rascal. Watermelons and cantaloupes were difficult to grow in Minnesota. We were too far north. The growing season was too short and the summer temperatures did not get hot enough. One summer I had nursed along three or four cantaloupes. They were small but I licked my lips in anticipation of how they would taste when they had ripened. I checked them almost every day and bragged at how well they were doing.

One day I checked the cantaloupes only to find that the largest and best of them was gone. What the heck? Had an animal gotten to it? I scouted around and discovered the remains. They had been tossed into deep weeds in the airport. Chris confessed to the crime. He was about seven years old. He and his pal, Benjy, a neighbor boy, had listened to me brag about that cantaloupe. Finally, they could not stand it any longer. They had filched a knife from the kitchen and sliced the melon open. It had not been quite ripe enough for eating so they had thrown the evidence away. I was disappointed but I could not get too upset. I could still remember what it was like to be a boy and to roam the neighborhood looking for adventures.

There is one special memory that nobody in our little family has ever forgotten, even though the children were young at the time. We had spent one pleasant autumn evening visiting Louise's former Lamaze instructor and her family. They lived on the east side of the airport; we lived on the west side. It was a about a three-quarter-mile hike across the open, unfenced, and grassy field. On the way home, well after dark, our way was lighted by a huge harvest moon. The air was cool, the evening enchanting. We carried a couple of small bags of fresh-picked and crisp apples the family had given us. It was one of those magic moments when life could not have been more perfect.

There were those clear nights on Ridgeway Drive when the family and I would step outside. I wanted to teach them what little I knew about the stars, what I could remember from being an Air force navigator. Two of my favorite constellations were Orion the Hunter and Ursa Major, the Great Bear or the Big Dipper. I showed Louise and the children how two of the lip stars in the Big Dipper pointed directly to my favorite star – Polaris, the North Star or the pole star. I explained that it was always within plus or minus two degrees of true north and that its degrees above the horizon were always the same as the observer's latitude.

I have often thought to myself, would it be reasonable for an old Air Force navigator to request, when they bury me, that they point the head of my casket directly at Polaris, so that I will be properly oriented? Perhaps it would seem an oddly primitive thing to do.

When I was growing up in Chesterfield, Illinois, a farm village with a population of 250, there had been no competitive sports in which I could participate. As a result, when we moved to a larger town and I entered high school I had no confidence in my ability. I attempted sports as a freshman and then dropped out. The other boys had much more experience.

I wanted my children to have more confidence in themselves than what I had had when I was their age. Louise took the children for swimming lessons. Jenifer took to water like a fish. She spent half the summers swimming in the nearby lakes. It was a great confidence booster for her. Chris, on the other hand, could swim but it was not his favorite thing to do. He was skinnier, was chilled by the cooler water, and sank like a rock. He took more naturally to hockey and to baseball.

Jenifer's self-confidence eventually centered more around academics than athletic activities. Both she and Chris participated in the Talented and Gifted program that Lincoln Elementary School offered. The school hosted a science fair when Jenifer was in the sixth grade. I helped Jenifer design an experiment by making use of a concept I had learned as an undergraduate student in psychology. It was called Operant Conditioning and it had been developed by a famous psychologist whose name was B. F. Skinner. It involved rewarding good behavior and punishing bad.

I remembered that the experiment I had conducted in college was to first weigh a healthy rat, then reduce its weight 15 % by feeding it less food. The idea was for the animal to be good and hungry. I no longer remember what task I wanted to train the rat to perform but basically I rewarded it with food when it made a correct move and withheld food when it did not. The same technique can be used to train a dog to sit or to roll over. Praise can be used in the place of food.

Jenifer and I plotted out a maze on graph paper and I constructed it out of plywood. She had two pet hamsters – George and Henry. Jenifer remembers that George was a bully. He would eat all of Henry's food. We had to separate them or Henry would have starved to death. We put them into the maze one at a time. If they made a correct turn they would find a pellet of food to reward them. If not, there was no reward. They learned one turn at a time until finally the only food they found was when they had completed their way through the entire maze. They were amazingly quick learners. Jenifer received an

nts compete in science fair

award for her experiment though it was not the top prize. She is standing on the viewer's right in the above picture.

Jenifer attended a summer Russian language camp in Detroit Lakes, Minnesota. The students bathed in the lake and slept in rustic cabins. Jenifer reported that there were several times she felt mice running over her as she lay in her bunk. She would have had a fit if that would have happened at home. The camp must have been a good experience for her, though. Years later she graduated from Georgetown University's School of Foreign Service. Louise and I were extremely proud of her.

Oh my, hockey in Minnesota was quite the thing. Boys began skating at an early age. Chris was five when he began his first lessons. I remember him clinging to the back of a folding card table chair as he pushed it around the hockey arena. He soon progressed to being a member of a team. It was fun to watch those little ones tumbling around on the ice as they used their hockey sticks to shoot the puck. Minnesota high schools paid for uniforms and equipment. Their hockey teams played for an annual state championship. We were disappointed when we moved to Green Bay in 1984 to discover that Wisconsin high schools did not offer hockey as a team sport.

Hockey became even more popular nationwide during the 1980 Winter Olympics, held in Lake Placid, New York. The U.S. team had the youngest players in the hockey tournament. They were mostly amateurs and they were pitted against a very professional Soviet Union team that had won the last four Gold Medals. Nobody expected the U.S. to win. But we did, by a score of 4-3. It was called the "Miracle on Ice" and it became one of the most iconic moments in all of Olympic and U.S. sports. The Cold War between the U.S. and the Soviet Union was still in full effect. The win gave the U.S. renewed optimism in the ideological struggle against the Soviets.

Two days later our team beat Finland 4-2 to take the Gold Medal. Chris must have been about six at the time. I remember how pumped up he and his fellow hockey players became. I remember, also, observing the difference between the way the U.S. played hockey and the way it was practiced in the Soviet Union. Our players were much more physical, slamming into opposing players and knocking them out of action if they could. There were lots of penalties. The Soviets, on the other hand, were skill players. Their passes were sharp and crisp. They concentrated more on moving the puck than on hitting opposing players. I liked their style of play better.

As I said earlier, hockey was huge in Minnesota. I went to a couple of professional games at the Met Center in Bloomington, a suburb of Minneapolis. It was the home of the Minnesota North Stars. I remember sitting in the "nosebleed" section, high up near the rafters, and looking down on the players far below. It was hard to believe when in 1993 the franchise was sold and relocated to Dallas. Who the heck played ice hockey in Texas? There was no ice.

When Chris was about eight years old, he and I were practicing hockey in the basement. We were going at it pretty hot and heavy and the little stinker had scored several goals on me. I was getting frustrated. My competitive spirit began to kick in and I started shoving my weight around (against an eight-year-old). I was near to scoring a goal on him.

Chris started yelling out "Tweet Tweet, Tweet Tweet." I didn't pay any attention. I kept muscling my way towards the goal. "Tweet Tweet," he yelled out even louder, "Tweet Tweet,"

Finally I overpowered him and slid the puck into the net. He threw down his hockey stick in disgust. Panting and sweating, I raised both arms in the traditional victory salute when a player scores a goal. What the heck, a goal is a goal even if the opponent only weighs sixty pounds. "Dad, that doesn't count," Chris informed me. "The heck it doesn't," I responded. "You've scored a lot of goals on me and just because I score one on you, you get upset."

"It doesn't count," he insisted. "I went Tweet Tweet."

"What do you mean?" I wanted to know.

"I went Tweet Tweet," he insisted a little stronger.

"I don't understand. What do you mean by Tweet Tweet?"

"That's the way my friends and I play," Chris told me. "When we say Tweet Tweet that means the official is blowing his whistle and you have to stop play."

It finally sunk in. My ignorance of the rules meant that the goal I had scored had not counted after all. My brief moment of glory had been snatched away.

Joe and I were working in Flight Service the next day when I told him about my hockey misadventure with my son. I may have embellished the tale just a bit to add to the effect. The story struck Joe's funny bone. He was in such agony from laughing so hard that he had to lie on the floor. I am certain that today, many years later, if I were to meet Joe on the street and go Tweet Tweet he would break into laughter again.

We had a big back yard. Jenifer and Chris and the neighborhood kids would play baseball. I remember one corner of the garden being designated as first base and a cherry tree as third base. At other times I would throw fly balls for the kids to catch. This probably led to later shoulder problems and rotator cuff surgery.

There were hardly any organized sports for girls in those days, the 1970s. It's too bad. I think Jenifer would have enjoyed softball.

Chris played baseball from about first grade on. He loved it. I remember one game in Little League. Chris was probably about ten years old. Our pitcher was struggling. His pitches were wild and he was walking too many batters. Our coach asked me if we had somebody who could do better. Chris was playing center field. I told the coach that Chris was pretty accurate with his throws. Chris had never pitched before.

Chris finished that inning for us. I think he struck out a couple of batters. Then, when it was his time to return to the mound he gave a sigh. "Do I have to?" he asked. Well, he finished that game and was a pitcher forever thereafter. He threw left-handed –

"southpaw" was the baseball term for it. The more he pitched the more he grew in self-confidence.

It must have been some time in 1982 when we lost Nugget. I say "we," but in fact it was me. Nugget had always been my dog. Louise and the children had mostly tolerated him. He'd had a history of bladder stones. I'd taken him in for surgery twice. Nugget was suffering and the veterinarian said he could not do a third surgery. We had no choice but to put Nugget to sleep. I could not stay to watch it. I was sobbing like a baby. It was like having a child die. It brings tears to my eyes to think of it even today, in March of 2020. That mutt and I had gone through a lot together.

My father had retired in 1974. He was sixty-five and he had been a janitor at the high school I attended. I do not remember for certain but it must have been around 1980 when he had a stroke. He was sitting in his favorite tavern when he fell off the bar stool. That was the end of his drinking. He had been an alcoholic as long as I could remember. He stopped drinking but he continued to smoke cigarettes. The stroke had left him partially paralyzed on his left side but he had still been able to function at almost a normal level.

It was said at the time, though, that a person never fully recovered from a stroke, that they gradually went downhill. That is what happened to Pops. His daily routine was to hang out at a nearby gas station, where three or four old geezers like him drank coffee and gossiped. Otherwise, he would sit on the edge of the cot in the little bedroom where I had slept and watch television. He seemed lonely. I talked to him one last time. He had been sick with the flu and it seemed like he was having a difficult time recuperating from it. I told him that we were worried about him. He did not respond. It seemed like he no longer cared, that he had given up. It scared me.

It was four o'clock in the morning on April 4th, 1984, when the telephone rang. Louise and I were fast asleep. I sensed right away what it was. My sister, Mary, was calling. She was living with Mom and Dad in the little house at 223 Madison Avenue in Wood River, Illinois. Dad's aorta had burst and they had not been able to save him. He was gone.

I went through the rest of the day in shock. We started packing. At 9 A.M. I rushed downtown to a men's clothing store. I did not own a suit that fit anymore. They hurried me into something somber and suitable. We loaded the luggage and the children into the Ford station wagon and hit the road. Louise did all the driving. I sat in the front passenger seat and cried. I could not stop. God, I had loved that old man! He had not known how to be the greatest father but I felt he had done the best he could. I remember Chris and Jenifer looking at me with some concern. I don't know if they had ever seen their father cry before. Our family picture is on the back cover.

Dad had taken care of everything. He and Mother had purchased their burial plots. Dad had made arrangements with the funeral home – Gray Memorial Chapel. Friends and family gathered for the wake.

It bothered me a lot when so few people showed up. Everybody had liked Wimpy, as my father had been nicknamed for as long as I could remember. There were old friends from the early days in Chesterfield, including my mentor, Myron Nixon. There were hardly any from the thirty years Dad had lived and worked in Wood River. I was disappointed that were only a couple from the high school Dad had retired from a few years earlier. A younger man who worked at the gas station where Dad had hung out and gossiped paid his respects. He said that Wimpy had been a good old guy and he would miss him. That meant a lot to me.

I was put off by a few church people who showed up. They seemed arrogant, as if they were special people, as if they were better than the rest of us, as if they were some of the elite, the chosen few. None of them had even known Dad. What the hell were they doing there, anyway?

Then I had to ask myself – how many people would attend my funeral? The answer was - probably not a lot. Aside from the fact that funerals are painful and we want to avoid them, men in our society generally do not form all that many close friendships. We end our lives in near obscurity.

Dad was buried on April 7th in Rose Lawn Memory Gardens, alongside Highway 140 in Bethalto, Illinois. I took note that the Civic Memorial Airport, now renamed the St. Louis Regional airport, was just across the highway. Departing aircraft buzzed low over the cemetery. The closeness of the airport appealed to me. It was likely related to my own involvement in general aviation. There seemed a connection between Dad and the airplanes.

It may have been a day or two later when my younger brother and I sorted through Dad's things. I still had tears. There was not much for us to divide up. I took Dad's papers from his days as a Mason. There was a small card which announced that Virgil A. Powers had been given an "Army-Navy Production Award" from WWII. The Western Cartridge Company in East Alton had produced three billion rounds of ammunition for the war effort. I can still envision the time when I must have been about four years old, in 1944, when Dad had shown me the brass casing from a round of 20mm ammunition. He must have snuck it home from his work.

Dad had kept a copy of the "Non-Resident Individual Angling License" he had paid $6.50 for when he and mother had visited us in Alexandria in June of 1975. Louise and I and the children had still been living in the little house on Bryant Street. The license shows that Dad had been born on August 23rd, 1909, that he had brown eyes, was five feet five inches tall, and weighed 170 pounds.

I also took a small pocketknife Louise and I had given him a couple of Christmases earlier. He had not used the knife. It was still in the original box. I have it somewhere in my belongings. My brother must have taken a few items. I no longer remember what. As I said, there was not much for us to divide.

A year later one of my sisters and I visited Dad's grave. It was so peaceful. The sun was warm, there was a refreshing breeze, and as we sat there without speaking we heard a cardinal calling in a nearby birch tree. Cardinals were a special bird in Illinois. We had listened to them all our lives. Now the moment seemed almost spiritual. It sparked a creative urge. I should write a short story about it. I would recreate the moment and call it "I Heard a Cardinal Calling." That was thirty-five years ago and the story has yet to be written. Maybe someday….

We were back home in Minnesota a week or so after Dad's funeral. I awakened in the middle of the night. Everything was bathed in inky darkness. I felt lost. I could not remember who I was or where I was. It was terrifying. It took a few minutes for my memory to return. I was an Air Traffic Control Specialist and I lived in Alexandria with my family. Surely the feeling of being lost was a psychological event that had something to do with my father's death. He had always been a part of my life and now he was gone. It had left a hole in my psyche.

Dad had never been able to show much affection. There had been no hugs or kisses or words of praise. At the same time, though, he had not been critical or demeaning. I supposed that is the way he had been raised. As far as our father-son relationship had been concerned, he had seemed to view me more as a pal than an offspring. Perhaps it explained why my siblings and I were different. We found it emotionally rewarding to cuddle and to kiss our children. I especially enjoyed sitting Jenifer and Chris on my lap, reading books to them, and telling them how wonderful they were. I was the soft one in the family. Louise was the disciplinarian.

1984 turned out to be quite a hectic year. When Louise and I had gotten married in Nome, Alaska in 1971, she had been excommunicated from the Catholic Church. We had been surprised to learn that it was not because I was a non-believer, an agnostic, but because I had not been baptized, even in the Protestant religion. Both our children had been baptized in the Church. In the spring of 1983 we had begun the process of getting my earlier marriage annulled so that Louise could get back into the good graces of the Church. The Diocesan Tribunal in St. Cloud, Minnesota, would render the final judgement. We were told that the process would take about fourteen months.

Thus it was that a hearing had been held in St. Cloud on December 13th, 1983. Both Louise and I were interviewed.

I was raked over the coals a bit by a priest who was acting as "Defender of the Bond," to make certain that our marriage would in fact be morally correct. It made me smile when after our separate interviews were over Louise was more concerned about me than about the Church. She was quite protective of me.

We were notified on June 12, 1984, that the annulment had been granted. It was two months after my father had passed. Louise and I were remarried in Alexandria's Catholic Church. Her parents drove in from North Dakota. They gave us a Catholic bible which we still have and which I have read.

Then, by the autumn of 1984 we had put our house on the market and had moved to Green Bay, Wisconsin. I had been transferred. As I said, 1984 had been a very busy year.

FAMILY ADVENTURES

Both Louise and I had had our horizons severely restricted when we were youngsters. Her family had never once gone on a vacation; mine had not even owned a car. Education and books had been our only exposure to an outer world, to diverse cultures and landscapes. We wanted our children to have more.

My family lived in Illinois, about twenty miles northeast of St. Louis, Missouri. It was an area of oil refineries and heavy industry and farming. Smoke stacks spewed grit and grime and carbon dioxide into the air. Both air and water were polluted. We called our little town of Wood River "Stinkyville" as a result of the odors from the oil refineries.

Louise's family, on the other hand, lived in the big, wide open country of far western North Dakota, in Dickinson, a hundred miles west of Bismarck, the state capitol. The air was clean, there were few trees, and I was introduced to something called "buttes," isolated steep hills with near vertical sides and almost flat tops. Hers was a land of big farms, of wheat, and of beef cattle. For decades Dickinson had been nicknamed the "Queen City of the Prairies."

Illinois was the land of Lincoln, so named after Abraham Lincoln, our most famous historical figure and one of my favorite people. Dickinson was Teddy Roosevelt country. Teddy, "Old Four Eyes" he had been called due to the glasses he wore, had first come to North Dakota in 1883. He had been twenty-four years old and stinging from the death of both his wife and his mother. He had fallen in love with the badlands along the Little Missouri River Valley, north of Medora. Over the years I have pored through many histories and biographies written about both Lincoln and Roosevelt.

A notable difference between our two families, though it did not seem to bother anyone, was that I had been raised in a mostly Protestant environment while Louise had gone through twelve years of Catholic education. I did not identify with either religious leaning; I was agnostic.

Thus there were three states where our family spent most of our time – Minnesota, North Dakota, and Illinois. Everything was encompassed within a 500-mile radius of Alexandria, a long day's drive by automobile.

I mentioned earlier (page 144-145) that shortly after Louise and I had arrived in Minnesota in the autumn of 1971 we had reconnected with Paul and Patti Norman, friends we had met in Nome, Alaska. Paul had become a teacher in the Holdingford, Minnesota public school system. I remember Paul complaining about the low pay. The teachers had asked for a raise, the school board, which was composed mostly of a bunch of old farmers, laughed and offered fifty dollars a year. Paul had left in disgust.

It was about that time that Paul's brother, who was operating the fishing resort that their grandfather had started and their father had built up, died in an accident. Paul and Patti took over the resort.

I also talked earlier (page 154-155) about how difficult it was to make a living in the resort business. During the summer the owners were tied down twenty-four hours a day, seven days a week. Then during the winter they needed to find a job to supplement their income. By then all the tourists had returned to their homes. The only work available was pumping gas or some such minimum wage job.

I telephoned Paul a few days ago, in mid-March of 2020. He and Patti are long retired and still living in Minnesota. Paul confirmed that there had been good years and bad years in the resort business. He said most often they had needed to borrow money from the bank to make it through the winter. They would repay the loan in the summer when money started flowing in. It was a scenario that was just about universal to resort owners.

That did not prevent Paul and Patti from being generous. Oh my, our little family spent a week just about every summer at their resort, and there were times when they refused payment. I remember one summer when we sent them a large container of Amway laundry soap as partial payment for our week's stay. Patti had lots of extra bed sheets and linens to keep clean.

Those summer days at Lake View Camp were idyllic. Paul and Patti had a daughter they had adopted from Alaska.

Then they had adopted three Korean children, two boys and a girl. The children swam and played together while the adults visited. I remember Chris spending hours standing on a dock while he fished for panfish. Jenifer spent hours swimming out to a lake raft and back.

The resort was located on two lakes – Blackwater and Mule. I remember that there was a loon nest on Blackwater. We would sometimes see baby loons riding on their parent's backs. I also remember one evening when Paul had enough time off to take me fishing on Blackwater. It was near dark. We cast our floating lures near the edge of a weed bed. Paul showed me how to let the lure lay idle for about a minute then twitch it slightly. The twitch was enough to trigger the feeding urge of largemouth bass. It was thrilling to watch a bass smash into a lure floating in the water. It caused quite a commotion.

There are so many wonderful memories associated with the Lake View Camp, of our two rumpled-hair children waking up from a good night's sleep, of coffee in the morning with

Paul and Patti, of Patti's wonderful cooking when we shared evening meals, of roasting marshmallows over a fire, of clean air and clean water, of relaxation, of friendship.

Louise and I made several shopping trips to St. Cloud and to Fargo. St. Cloud was seventy-five miles southeast; Fargo was a hundred mile northwest. Both were on Interstate 94 and both had many more shops and restaurants than small-town Alexandria could offer. It was a good excuse to get out of town for a day.

Of course Minneapolis had a lot to offer. There was a huge university and theaters and art galleries. The airport connected to international travels. The city was 140 miles away and it usually entailed an overnight stay in one of the Bloomington motels, ten miles south of downtown Minneapolis. I do not recall that we spent much time downtown. I remember wanting to introduce our children to the theater but the productions in Minneapolis were too expensive. We could not afford the tickets on our budget.

Talk of Minneapolis brings about another Powers family story, another misadventure. It must have been the early 1980s when Louise and I took the children to the Valleyfair Amusement Park in Shakopee, a southwestern suburb of Minneapolis. It was kind of a short notice trip. I did not make a reservation in the nearby Bloomington motel where I usually stayed when I was in Minneapolis for Flight Service training. Louise was concerned. I assured her there were plenty of other motels where there would be vacancies if the place in Bloomington did not work out.

Well, the children had a wonderful day on the roller coaster and the other thrill rides at Valleyfair. Late afternoon rolled around and we took a break for something to eat. I found a telephone and dialed the number for the Bloomington motel. I was somewhat surprised to find they were booked up. That had never happened before. I found a phone book and began dialing other motels within a reasonable driving distance. Everyone was full.

I began to panic as I noticed Louise giving me the evil eye. Our whole family was worn out from the day's activities. We did not have the energy to engage in a protracted struggle. Finally, in desperation, I found one room still available. It was in the nearby Savage Motel. Looking back, I should have smelled something rotten. Why did that motel have a vacancy when everything else was full? But I was desperate. I booked the room.

Oh my, we had to compromise. But what could we do when all of us were exhausted? We had to make do as best as we could. The motel was shabby, loud and scruffy long-haul truck drivers roamed the halls, keys jangling from their belts while they belched beer. They made us nervous.

The door did not have a lock. I pulled a dresser against it, just in case one of the drunken drivers tried to force his way into the wrong room. Then of course I did not sleep all night. Loud voices and roars of laughter filled the hallway. Who could sleep through all that racket? Louise and the children find great hilarity in retelling the story. We will never forget the infamous Savage Motel.

We found that the Minnesota Zoo was wonderful. It is located twenty miles south of Minneapolis, in Apple Valley. We watched tigers roaming in a natural habitat and beluga whales swimming behind large sheets of glass.

There are a couple of other Minnesota adventures that stick in my memory. Camp Ripley was a huge Minnesota National Guard training facility located fifty-five miles east of Alexandria. Each year we must have dealt with hundreds of helicopter flights that originated out of Ripley. They landed at Alexandria quite often. If I remember correctly, we had a direct telephone line from Flight Service to Ripley Operations.

One bright summer day Louise and I loaded our two children into our little Buick Skylark and headed for Camp Ripley. It would be an adventure for them and a way for me to become better acquainted with what was going on. I do not remember a lot, except for one visual memory that has remained in my mind all these years. We were walking along when we encountered a National Guard troop exiting from a mess hall. He stood about five feet four, had a big belly, looked flabby, and was bedecked in camouflaged clothing. He appeared to be between thirty-five and forty years old, had a baby face, and all the ferocity of a marshmallow. But attached to his belt was a huge knife whose tip dangled damned close to his knees. He looked at us with questioning eyes. "Here I am, a fierce warrior," he seemed to be saying. "Do you believe me?" None of us did. We hid our grins behind our hands.

We followed backroads on the return drive to Alexandria. The sky looked wicked. Heavy, black clouds and lightning were a few miles south. We kept a close eye on them, looking for funnel clouds or a tornado. We hoped we could make it home before the severe weather moved a few miles farther north and engulfed us. We did.

We set out to explore a bit more of Minnesota. Pipestone is located in the southwestern corner of the state. It is 155 miles south and a little west of Alexandria, and fifty miles north of Sioux Falls, South Dakota. I have no memory at all of how I heard about it but it remains one of my favorite places. It is filled with stories about American Indians. There was a family legend that said I had Cherokee ancestors. It had sparked an interest in the history and culture of Native Americans and it was something I wanted to pass along to my children. Louise has done a lot of genealogical research into my family tree and has not been able to uncover any solid evidence of a link to the Cherokees.

Pipestone is a soft red stone that Natives have quarried for about 3,000 years. Today the quarry pits have been incorporated into the 300-acre Pipestone National Monument. Our little family hiked the ¾-mile Circle Trail. It was one of those times when it felt as though I could feel the spirit of the place. Legend had it that generations upon generations of Natives had worked there in peace, that no fighting or warfare had been allowed in this sacred place. Modern Indians still use hand tools – sledges, hammers, pry bars, and shovels – to quarry the mineral. It is a difficult undertaking. Non-Natives are not allowed to mine the quarry.

The soft stone is carved into sacred pipes, which are used for prayer, important rites, and to conduct civil and religious ceremonies. Tradition has it that smoke from the pipe carries prayers to the Great Spirit. I remember that we used to call them "peace pipes" because in American history they were often used during the signing of treaties. But that designation does not fully describe their purpose. The pipestone material was traded extensively throughout much of North America.

The official name for the rock is "catlinite," after the early American painter, author, and traveler, George Catlin. Catlin was the first to have the mineral analyzed. He specialized in painting portraits of Native Americans in the 1830s. He had long heard of the sacred pipe mining grounds and had traveled to Minnesota in 1836 to have a look.

It must have been a year or two after our trip that I read one of Catlin's books. It may have been *Letters and Notes on the Manners, Customs, and Conditions of the North American Indians*. Catlin described how he had been threatened by members of the Santee Sioux tribe, who had an economic interest in the quarry. They did not want any white man to go near it. But Catlin persisted. He was the first white man to paint the quarry.

We made several trips to visit my family in Illinois. I remember one Christmas trip in particular. Louise and I had learned through experience that long-distance travel with the children was difficult. They sat in the back seat, not buckled up in those days, and were easily bored. They would fight in order to break the boredom. "You have your hand on my half of the seat. Mom and Dad, make Chris get back on his side." It was distracting and of course dangerous to try to turn around and swat at them while I was steering the car down the highway at sixty-five miles an hour. Threats seemed to have no effect on them.

Louise and I devised what we thought would be a foolproof plan. We would drive at night while the children were sleeping. We placed a pad and a couple of blankets and pillows in the back of the Ford station wagon. We started out around seven in the evening and by eight thirty both children were yawning. I soon joined them for an hour or two of sleep while Louise sped on in the darkness.

Our plan would have been a great success except for one thing – the weather. A major snowstorm was moving across our route. The highways were drifted over with blowing slow. Large semi-trucks littered the ditches. Our station wagon slipped on patches of ice. We arrived in Wood River shortly after dawn. Both Louise and I were exhausted. We went to bed. Grandma and Grandpa could watch the kids.

It was likely on that Christmas vacation that we paid a visit to my Uncle Albert and Aunt Marjorie in the little town of Manchester, seventeen miles south of Jacksonville. Aunt Marjorie knew something about Illinois history. She told Jenifer and Chris how one memorable Illinois winter storm had dumped snow up to the level of window sills, indicating with her hand snow about two and a half or three feet deep. The children hid their amusement behind their hands. They were products of Minnesota winters. They had seen drifts six and eight feet deep, and had listened to the stories Louise and I told them about winters in North Dakota and Alaska. They had heard of houses being completely buried in snow. Two or three feet of the white stuff was nothing to brag about.

We had a wonderful trip to Illinois in June of 1982. We decided to make a leisurely journey of it, to drive backroads instead of following major highways. We discovered that it was a delightful way to travel. If we were passing through a small town and we were hungry for a milkshake all we had to do was pull over to the curb and order, instead of exiting off a road buzzing with traffic and big semi-trucks.

1982 was about the year I read an autobiographical travel book written by William Least Heat-Moon. The title was *Blue Highways: A Journey into America*. The author described his journey and the people he met while driving the secondary roads, colored in blue on a road atlas, that connected much of rural America. He felt they offered a more scenic and relaxed way to travel, that they were better suited to introspection. Based on our drive to Illinois, I had to agree.

Eventually, we came to a river crossing. There was an Illinois state ferry that transported passengers and cars across the Mississippi River, from Iowa to Nauvoo, Illinois. I had been born and raised in Illinois but I had never heard of Nauvoo. Apparently our high school class book on Illinois history had been wiped free of any reference to Mormons in Illinois, just as our American history book had not said one word about American soldiers massacring Indian women and children at Wounded Knee, South

Dakota, in 1890. Those of us who were concerned with historical accuracy had had to learn the whole story sometime after high school. But in the 1950s it had been considered "unpatriotic" to mention anything bad about any part of our national history. Conservatives thought it was better to keep our children ignorant.

The Mormons, or Church of Jesus Christ of Latter Day Saints, had emigrated from western New York State to Nauvoo in 1839. Their leader was Joseph Smith. They'd had a troubled time in Nauvoo. Anti-Mormon sentiment had run high. Joseph and his brother had been murdered by a mob in 1844. In1846 the Mormons had moved farther west to the Salt Lake City, Utah, area.

Little were we to know that the initial exposure to Nauvoo in 1982 would continue to the present day, 2020. It was some years after 1982 when Louise was doing some genealogical research into the Powers family. She ran across a story that concerned my great grandfather, Aaron Powers, and the Mormon Church. I outlined the tale on page 10 of Volume I of *We Are Born*. I will briefly recount it below.

The story goes that Aaron had been a farmer in northern Illinois when he had joined the Mormon Church. One day Joseph Smith told Aaron that God had talked to him, Joseph, and had advised him that Aaron needed to donate his farm to the church. Aaron had thought it over and then had asked Smith when this conversation had taken place. Smith answered that it had been the night before. "Well," Aaron was said to have replied, "he talked to me this morning and told me not to do it."

Last year, 2019, Louise and I decided to follow up on the story. We drove from Wisconsin to Nauvoo. We were surprised at what we found. Sure enough, on the Nauvoo tax records of 1842 Aaron had owned two city lots, his sons had owned others. John Milton Powers had owned one, Solon Powers had owned two, and James Colby Powers had owned one. If I remember correctly, Aaron had purchased his property from Hyrum Smith, the brother of Joseph. Also, if I remember correctly, Aaron had dropped out of the Mormons and joined the Missionary Baptist Church. So far as we know, none of the Powers moved west when the Mormons fled to Utah.

That vacation trip in 1982 led to more family adventures. I wanted to show Jenifer and Chris where I had grown up. We drove by the Lewis and Clark Junior High School where I had attended the eighth grade. I took them to the mouth of Wood River Creek, where it emptied into the Mississippi, and where Lewis and Clark and the Corps of Discovery had encamped in the winter of 1804-1805, prior to heading up the Missouri River. We toured my old high school, East Alton-Wood River Community High School. It was where my father had worked as a janitor.

Of course I had to show the children Chesterfield, the farm village where I had spent the first thirteen years of my life. I introduced them to Dave and Nita Rigsby. I had for years kidded Jenifer and Chris about eating gooseberry pie. They had assumed I was joking, that I was teasing them, that I was telling a story. Now Nita had a fresh-baked gooseberry pie waiting for them. It was delicious.

I had to tell the children about finding Indian artifacts in Chesterfield gardens. And the tour would not be complete until I took them to Coop's Creek, five miles south of town, where Myron "Nick" Nixon and I had found arrowheads and pieces of pottery. The wonderful spring of sweet, clear water, that Nick had shown me, was still there.

I parked the station wagon at the bridge where Route 111 crossed over Macoupin Creek. We needed to walk about a quarter of a mile through brush and weeds to get to Coop's Creek. The children were wearing shorts. I advised them against brushing against the "itch weed" (stinging nettle) as I had done thirty years earlier when I had first visited the site. I remembered that the skin on my bare arm had burned like fire for about fifteen minutes. Nick had told me that the itch would go away if I did not scratch it.

We stumbled across an old cabin. I no longer remember for sure but I suspect the owner had posted his name and telephone number on the door. He was Cliff Davidson and he lived in Godfrey, a few miles north of Wood River. I called Cliff and we arranged to meet at his cabin the following day. We found that Cliff was an older retired man, probably in his mid-60s. He proved to be a wonderful host for our little family. Unfortunately we found no artifacts.

But there was more to learn about the Native Americans who had long ago inhabited the area. I remembered that when I was in high school my buddies and I had driven by Indian mounds a few miles south of Wood River. They were at a place called Cahokia. Now we discovered that in the past quarter of a century the State of Illinois had conducted extensive archeological research into the mounds. I was surprised to find a small museum and interpretive center. Today, in 2020, there is a much larger and more expansive interpretive center. It is a fascinating place to visit and to learn the history behind the mounds. The United Nations has listed Cahokia as a World Heritage Site.

The tour of Indian heritage would not be complete without a drive up the river road that ran alongside the Mississippi River from Alton to Grafton. I had hiked the road with a Boy Scout troop when it had been nothing more than an old rail bed. Now it was fully paved. We of course had to stop and take a close look at the Piasa Bird (pie-eh-saw). It is a dragon-like monster that Natives had originally painted on the bluff centuries earlier. Pere Marquette had made note of it in his journals when he had explored the area in 1673. We had to continue on to Pere Marquette State Park where we feasted on a Sunday dinner of fried chicken and mashed potatoes at the lodge, which had been constructed by the Civilian Conservation Corps during the Great Depression. It was a wonderful family time with my parents and the rest of us.

We attended St. Louis Cardinals baseball games a couple of times over the years. Busch Stadium was located in downtown St. Louis, a short drive from Wood River. We could sit in the bleachers and watch the ball game, and at the same time have a wonderful view of the Gateway Arch, which was situated nearby.

I remember a game in 1981 when the Cards played the Cincinnati Reds. Johnny Bench was catching for the Reds.

He had a legendary baseball career. I remember that Dad and I, plus Jenifer and Chris, had good seats in the right field stands. Chris was playing baseball and Johnny Bench became his favorite player. I remember that Grandpa Wimpy spoiled Chris. Every time the hot dog vendor came by Dad would ask if anybody wanted another hot dog. Chris must have eaten three or four.

Another time we went to an Old Timer's game at Busch Stadium. We sat right behind the third base dugout. Bob Gibson pitched for the Cards. He is another legendary baseball figure. Chris remembers him to this day.

Every vacation in Wood River involved at least one trip to Alton's Seventh Street hill. The hill became famous in Powers family lore. I would come to a full stop at the top of the brick street. The hill was so steep that we could not see the bottom. There must have been about a sixty-degree slope. A stop sign was located at the bottom. We had to make damn sure the car's brakes were working properly as we pitched over the crest and came careening downhill, riding the brakes all the way. It was almost like being on a roller coaster. The children loved it. Louise fussed. Forty years later our son Chris had to take his wife and three children for a ride down that hill. It had become a family legend.

There were family houses on both sides of the street. People sat on their porches and watched us speed down the hill. I had this crazy vision that those who lived on that hill all their lives must have had one leg shorter than the other. Otherwise, how could they have stood upright on such a slanted surface?

We traveled to North Dakota two or three times a year. Louise's family treated me and the children royally. Lou's mother, Martha, was especially understanding. She knew I was not much interested in the Church. "That's okay," she said, "not everybody needs to be a Catholic." She was a quality lady. We spent a fair amount of time with Louise's two sisters, Kathy and Rose, and their husbands, Gene and Tom. I used to say that I had the world's two best brothers-in-law. The young children of our three families played together.

North Dakota – to me the very name has a romantic ring to it. It speaks of vast stretches of prairie, of wind and wildness, of buffalos and badlands, of a proud Native American heritage.

The landscape was so different than what I had known in southern Illinois. The eastern part, as we passed by Fargo and headed west on Interstate 94, was as flat as a pool table. Sugar beets and sunflowers were the major crops. The central and western portions eventually gave way to buttes. Wheat was the main farm crop and there were lots of beef cattle. The far western area, along the border with Montana, was known as the "Badlands," so named because of the deeply eroded terrain. Theodore Roosevelt National Park is located in the Badlands. The future president had had a cattle ranch there in the 1880's. "Old Four Eyes," as he was called because he wore glasses, wrote fondly of his North Dakota days. We saw many buffalos in the park. My god, those huge buffalo bulls were magnificent! I could understand why Native Americans had had a spiritual connection with them.

I remember one time when I had planned to take my Voitlander 35mm camera and shoot pictures of the sunrise in the park. My nephew, Brent, and niece, Christina, wanted to come along. They must have been about ten or twelve years old. I told them I would pick them up at 4:30 in the morning, and that if they were not ready to go I would leave without them. I fully expected them to remain in bed.

But sure, enough, when the beam of my headlights shined on their porch the next morning there they sat, ready to go. They watched the sun come up while I shot pictures. By six thirty we were enjoying breakfast at the Cowboy Café in Medora. Then we drove through the park. It was a memorable day for all three of us.

I grew to love North Dakota. Oh my, you could see forever. There were blazing sunsets and the air was fresh. There was not enough industry to cause significant pollution. It was so different than Illinois. A few cottonwood trees grew naturally along the river bottoms, otherwise there were very few trees. Farmers could earn a decent living from 200 acres in Illinois. They flourished if they had 600 or 800 acres. But in North Dakota nobody talked in terms of acres, it was how many *sections* they owned, each section being 640 acres. "I have a couple of sections over here and another couple over there."

Louise's Bohemian ancestors had immigrated from the Russian Crimea to North Dakota in the late 1800s. Her Grandmother and Grandfather Kubischta had lived in a sod hut in the early 1900s. They had burned sheep manure for fuel. What it must have been like for those early Dakota settlers, with the summer storms and the bitter winters! I read stories about women who went insane in the numbing isolation, and families who gave up in despair and returned to their native countries. I suspect, though, that Louise's grandparents had had an active social life with their Bohemian- and German-speaking neighbors. These are stories not much talked about in American history classes.

Now, in the 1970s and '80s, Grandma and Grandpa Kubischta were long retired and living in a newer ranch-style home on the outskirts of Dickinson. I will never forget that Grandpa called me "Big Boy," though I was only six feet tall and weighed about 185 pounds. The old couple maintained a big garden every summer and did lots of canning. Potatoes and other garden vegetables were harvested in the autumn and stored in a basement root cellar. Grandma Kubischta still made lye soap.

Louise's other grandmother, Grandma Ficek, lived in the tiny village of New Hradec, ten miles north of Dickinson. Her little pale green house was tiny and there was still an outdoor toilet. I can still see Grandma Ficek in my mind. Her gray hair was always tied in a neat bun. Louise had very fond memories of her. She had lived with Grandma Ficek for three years during elementary school. Every time we visited, even if it was mid-morning or mid-afternoon, she would put on an apron, fire up the wood cook stove, and begin peeling potatoes. She had to cook something for us to eat. She was a kind and lovely lady.

In Illinois I had grown up with stories of Lewis and Clark. I had attended Lewis and Clark Junior High School in Wood River. I had hunted and fished in the same place where they had had their first winter encampment, before heading up the Missouri River in 1804 on their exploration of the Northwest. They seemed a part of my personal history.

Now I ran into Lewis and Clark once again. The first year they had made it as far north as the Mandan and Hidatsa tribal villages a few miles north of present day Bismarck. They had built a fort and wintered. They had hired a Native girl by the name of Sacajawea to travel with them and to act as an interpreter. She was a Shoshone who had been captured by the Hidatsa warriors and later sold to a French-Canadian trapper by the name of Toussaint Charbonneau. Her name was to become famous in American history. North Dakotans mention her with pride.

In 1978 an author by the name of Anna Lee Waldo published an historical fiction novel about Sacajawea. The paperback book was more than 1,300 pages long. My family bought me a copy as a birthday present in May of 1979. The children knew I loved to read. I always had my head buried in a book. Their goal was to go to the bookstore and look for the thickest book they could find. It did not matter what the subject was, the book just had to be thick. *Sacajawea* became one of my all-time favorite novels. I was fascinated by the description of Lewis and Clark and their travels, and by the portrayal of Indian life in the very early 1800s. I pored through the book three or four times. I still have the battered copy of the paperback somewhere in my collection of books. Its front and back covers are held together with tape.

The land, Louise's family, the Lewis and Clark connection, all conspired to make me fond of North Dakota. There was an additional pull. In Illinois I had grown up surrounded by Native American legends. I had picked arrowheads and pottery shards from the soil. Now, twenty years later, I was fascinated by what Native life must have been like in North Dakota. There were the remains of long-abandoned Hidatsa and Mandan villages along the eastern banks of the Missouri River, just north of Bismarck. Circular rings from their dome-shaped earthen lodges were still clearly visible in the soil. I wrote a poem about one of the villages. It was called *Double-Ditch*, and it is in a book of poetry titled *A Moment Passed By*.

DOUBLE-DITCH

In North Dakota, north of Bismarck
On a scenic bluff overlooking the
Meandering Missouri River
Lie the circular remains of earthen
Mandan Indian lodges
In a long-abandoned village
We moderns call Double-Ditch.

There the natives lived
Behind their palisaded wall
Behind their two protective ditches
Safe from enemy raiding parties.

There smoke from their many fires
Cast a thin blue haze
Across limitless skies and prairies
Across limitless grazing herds

Of the sacred buffalo
There the tribe lived in harmony
With original nature.

There as I stood alone
On a shimmering summer day
My thoughts and my imagination
My only companions
I felt the spirit of the place
As it flowed into my soul.

And in my imagination, as if in a vision
I saw ghostly shapes rise from the sacred soil
Saw the ancient residents
Wandering among their homes
Among their hopes and dreams.

I saw ghosts of mothers in deerskin dresses
I saw proud painted warriors and swirling dancers
Ghosts that seemed to ride the wind
That rode the river in bobbing bull boats.

And was that sound the keening of Indian women
Singing in their grief
Or was it how the wind speaks
When it has gathered memories
From a thousand generations
From a thousand miles of open prairie?

I wondered at the culture
Of these olden people
Were they gripped by the mystery of things
By the possibility of gods
By life passing into eternity?

> Silent, somber, questioning were their faces
> As if trying to comprehend me
> A mysterious modern man
> Tracing the footsteps of Lewis and Clark
> Bearer of changes, of destructive diseases.
>
> Turning, I retraced my thoughts back to the present
> Planning to return another day
> To restore my hearing
> With the silence of the place.

Lewis and Clark had explored the region in 1804-1806. In 1839 Prussian Prince Maximilian of Wied-Neuwied had followed up the Missouri River in their footsteps. He had brought along a Swiss painter by the name of Karl Bodmer. Bodmer's paintings of the Natives and their surroundings are some of my favorites.

I was fascinated by the Mandan and Hidatsa religion. It was a form of Animism, where the universe and all natural objects – animals, plants, trees, rivers, mountains, rocks – have souls or spirits. I had been briefly exposed to these beliefs as an Air Force navigator flying across Greenland and the Canadian Arctic - Native Inuit country. To my mind Animism was kind of a brotherhood, a kinship, between Man and Nature, between Man and the Universe. It was about humans finding their place in the order of the world. It seemed like such a genuine way to live – at one with Nature. There was no talk of sin and salvation, of feeling like crap about oneself, of guilt, of burning in hell. It was not a religion that was shoved down people's throats.

On our many drives along Interstate 94 between Alexandria and Dickinson we could not pass by Jamestown, North Dakota without looking for the world's largest buffalo monument. It stood atop a hill on the north side of the highway. We stopped by several times to tour the National Buffalo Museum. In the 1990s a white buffalo calf was added to the small herd that roamed the museum grounds. To many of the Plains tribes, the birth of a sacred white buffalo is a sign of hope and an indication of good times to come, that one day all races will unite and live in harmony.

In July of 1982 our family had just returned from a vacation in Dickinson. We had stopped for a bite to eat at one of Alexandria's fast food restaurants. The following night, a Saturday, Jenifer had invited some of her friends to a sleepover at our house. Her birthday was on Sunday, the 18th. Jenifer was not feeling all that well and by Sunday she had gotten worse with intestinal problems. On Monday Louise took her to see Dr. Hunt, who immediately put her in the hospital. She had salmonella. She was in the hospital for eleven days.

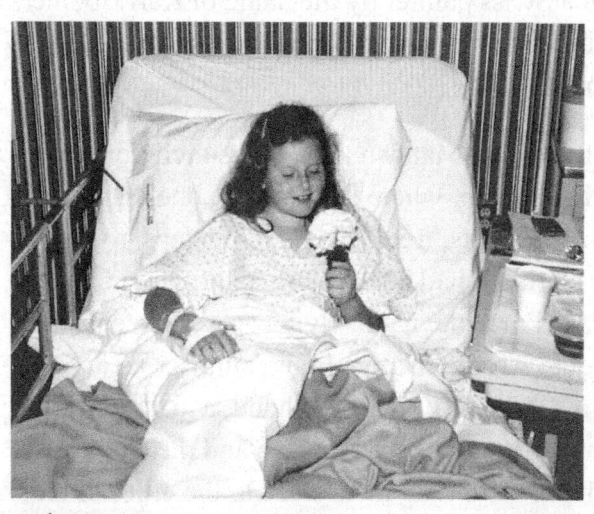

It was 1983 when our family set out on one final family trip to the Dakotas, before we moved from Alexandria to Green Bay in 1984. It was probably our most enjoyable adventure of all. We departed Alexandria on a late June morning and headed first for Fort Sisseton, South Dakota, 140 miles west. The fort was historic. It had been erected in 1864 as a response to Indian troubles. It had been an active Army post and frontier waystation for twenty-five years. It had been abandoned by the Federal Government in 1889, after the Native population had been largely subdued. A few of the original buildings remained.

The highlight of our short visit at Fort Sisseton was a one-hour ride in a heavy wagon pulled by a team of horses. The driver was dressed in a period uniform. We were the only visitors at the time. We had the driver and the horses and the wagon all to ourselves. Jenifer and Chris thought it was quite the adventure.

We pressed on. Rapid City and the Black Hills area was our intended destination for the day. We drove 220 miles southwest towards Pierre, the state capitol on the Missouri River. I was surprised along the way to see pelicans soaring high in the sky. I had thought they were strictly a sea bird. I had not expected to see them hovering over a north-central inland reservoir.

South Dakota is big, wide open land with lots of Native American history. I faintly remember a road sign that pointed to a rock cairn that had been erected by Natives centuries earlier. The cairns were piles of rocks that had been heaped up by the Plains tribes for a variety of purposes, for landmarks and burial sites and so forth.

The thing that impressed me about those lonely cairns in the vast expanse of South Dakota prairie was that long ago some Native American had piled them there for a reason. It had been such a simple thing yet filled with so much meaning. The cairns spoke of nature in their isolation, of earth and air and sky. And yet they whispered of humanity, too, of man's limited importance in the universe. A Native person had been here; he had left a symbol to remember him by. His physical presence was long since gone yet something of him remained.

We stumbled upon the Prayer Rock near Ipswich, South Dakota. It was a five-ton boulder that had originally overlooked the Missouri River near Mobridge, South Dakota. There were two distinct sets of handprints etched into it. It was said that in its original location there was a deep footpath worn into the earth where Indians had knelt before the rock to pray.

We stopped by Pierre for a late lunch, then pushed on for Rapid City, 175 miles farther west. The only thing I remember about Pierre was that it was on a high site overlooking the Missouri River. The thought went through my mind that the river had been a transportation route for humans for untold centuries.

Wall, South Dakota, calls itself the "Gateway to the Badlands." We'd already had a long day, and we were familiar with the badlands of North Dakota, so we did not take the time to tour South Dakota's badlands. The main reason for our quick detour to Wall was to say we had been to Wall Drug. It was a tourist trap and we knew it. It had thousands of souvenirs on display – coffee cups and flags and so much more. The only thing we were interested in was one of their bumper stickers. We had seen dozens of them proudly displayed on other cars. We were traveling so near to Wall that there was no excuse for us not to stop and get one. There were such cute sayings as "A Blast From The Past Wall Drug," and "Have You Dug Wall Drug." Our favorite, and the one we had seen most often, was "Where The Heck Is Wall Drug."

For the next two days there was much to see and do within a fifty-mile-radius of Rapid City. Custer, South Dakota, was the home of Flintstone Park, named after the popular Flintstones television series. Fred and Barney and Wilma were animated Stone Age characters. Dino the dinosaur as their pet. Our son, Chris, had had a stuffed Dino as a companion when he was a baby. There was a twenty-foot tall Dino statue that the children were able to climb on. The park was closed in 2015 and everything was bulldozed in 2019. The TV series had run from 1960-1966. I guess nobody was much interested in the Flintstones fifty years later.

We swam in the wonderful indoor pool fed by hot springs, in Hot Springs, South Dakota. The children, especially, enjoyed it. Nearby was an indoor mammoth dig. We could see bones of the ancient animals sticking out of the sand. The story went that more than 20,000 years ago the site had been a swampy sinkhole that the mammoths had fallen into. It was a natural history lesson for all of us.

Wind Cave National Park was another learning experience. We had not even heard of it. Now we descended and crawled through an hour and a half tour of the underground wonder. I remember that Louise and I were a little reluctant to enter the cave. We both had difficulty with claustrophobia. But we could not disappoint our children. Once we were in the cave we were fine. The tour guide informed us that the small opening to the cave had been discovered by a rancher in 1881. The Natives had known of its existence but had wanted to keep it a secret.

We could not of course leave the area without visiting Mt. Rushmore. It is a nationally known memorial featuring the faces of four famous U.S. presidents carved into the granite side of Mt. Rushmore. The presidents are George Washington, Thomas Jefferson, Theodore Roosevelt, and Abraham Lincoln. I was mildly disappointed. The massive faces were sixty feet high but seemed somehow small when we viewed them through the museum windows.

We hurried seventeen miles down the road to the Chief Crazy Horse Memorial, which was a work in progress. There was a wonderful museum with many Native artifacts. Rumor had it that the Natives were not at all happy with the carvings at Mt. Rushmore. It was the white men who had stolen the sacred Black Hills from the Indians. It was their Native ancestors who should be honored and not the white intruders. Crazy Horse had been a famous war leader in the 1870s. He had fought against white encroachment on Native lands and to preserve the traditional way of Lakota life.

I later read more about the history of the Black Hills. They had indeed been considered sacred by the Lakota Sioux, who considered the mountains to be the center of the universe, and where their culture had begun. The Indian name for the Black Hills was Paha Sapa. The Treaty of Fort Laramie in 1868 had guaranteed ownership to the Sioux. Six years later, in 1874, Lieutenant Colonel George Armstrong Custer had led an expedition out of Fort Abraham Lincoln, near present day Bismarck, North Dakota. The stated purpose was to find a suitable location for a new military fort. A secondary purpose was to explore for the possibility of gold.

Members of Custer's party did discover gold near Custer. By 1875 the Black Hills gold rush was on. In 1877 the federal government took back ownership of the Black Hills. The U.S. has broken many of the treaties it made with Native American tribes. A landmark 1979 Federal Court decision called the government's seizure of the Black Hills one of the most dishonorable acts in American history. The government has offered to pay hundreds of millions of dollars in retribution but the impoverished Sioux say the land is still not for sale.

The forty-mile drive along the Needles Highway to Custer State Park gave us an insight into why the Sioux so much adored the Black Hills. It felt like being at one with Nature. We made frequent stops to admire the many scenic views. The air was incredibly fresh and scented with the aroma of pine trees.

We drove the eighteen-mile Wildlife Loop through Custer State Park. Buffalo and deer and pronghorn antelopes roamed freely. We could understand why the park had been named a World Class Wildlife Refuge. We had come across many bison on prior visits to Theodore Roosevelt National Park in North Dakota. Oh my, how I admired them, especially the big bulls. I could understand why Indians had so loved them. A couple of years ago, around 2018, two friends of ours were driving through Custer State Park. A big buffalo bull attacked their car and caused several thousand dollars in damage.

We had slept three nights in a Rapid City motel. On the fourth day we headed north. Our destination was Dickinson, North Dakota, where Louise's family lived. We passed through Sturgis and saw a road sign that pointed to a place called Bear Butte State Park. We had never heard of it. We found that it was another sacred Indian place. The monolith rose a thousand feet above the surrounding prairie. Native Americans, especially Cheyenne and Sioux, believed it was a place where the creator had chosen to communicate with them through visions and prayer. We hiked the 1.85-mile rail to the summit. Current Native worship was evident. We saw colorful prayer bundles and tobacco ties hanging from shrubs. There were several tiny sweat lodges.

The land had been under private ownership until 1961, when it had been developed into a state park. It struck me that in all fairness the butte and surrounding area should rightfully belong to the Natives, that the ownership should be turned over to them. But today, in 2020, Bear Butte is still owned by the State of South Dakota.

We arrived in Dickinson around the first of July. We stayed with Louise's parents. Tom and I went a bit overboard. We bought over $200 worth of fireworks. On the Fourth of July the whole family gathered at Gene and Kathy's house in the tiny farm village of New Hradec, ten miles north-northwest of Dickinson. The village had been established by Bohemian ancestors in 1887. Louise had stayed in New Hradec with her Grandma Ficek for three years while she was in elementary school.

We doled out bottle rockets and firecrackers to the children. It was not long before an alarm was sounded. There had not been much rain. Everything was bone dry. One of the bottle rockets had landed in a ditch and set the grass on fire. A moderate wind was blowing, causing the fire to spread rapidly. Who knew how many hundreds of acres of farmland could burn if we did not take quick action? We grabbed buckets of water to form a fire brigade. Gene hooked up a garden hose and we soon had the fire out. It was a heart-thumping way to celebrate the holiday.

We headed back for Alexandria the following day. It had been a vacation packed with fun and adventure and learning. None of us has ever forgotten it.

FIREWOOD 101

(Beginning college courses are usually numbered in the one hundred-level series, such as Psychology 101 or History 105. It is an indication of an introduction to the subject. Higher level courses are indicated with two- and three-hundred-level numbers. Logging 101 is about my introduction to the subject of logging, or cutting down trees for firewood.)

Due to the oil shortage imposed by Mideast countries in the 1970s many people experimented with solar energy. I had thought about installing solar heating panels on the south side of our new house, where they could capture the maximum amount of winter sun. I never did. Those first solar panels were not very efficient. I remember that one of the Flight Service Specialists bought a couple of cheap four feet by eight feet panels that he could assemble himself. He pumped the heat into his house and waited for the savings. He was disappointed. I asked him about it after the winter was over. "Al," he said, "a person would expect that when the temperature is twenty below the skies would be clear and the sun would be shining. It would seem a perfect time for solar panels. But you would not believe how many days the temperature was well below zero and the sky was overcast. The solar panels did not work out at all. I'm going to get rid of them."

I remember driving by the International Business Machines (IBM) company in Minneapolis in the late 1970s. They were experimenting with solar energy. They had a large array of several hundred solar panels. It was later determined that the panels were not cost efficient. They were removed.

The next heating source of choice was wood. Efficient wood heating stoves soon found their way into the market. Modern fireplace units were redesigned to burn more efficiently. They made use of outside air for burning rather than drawing cold air through the house. We found an award-winning local manufacturer and had a fireplace installed in our family room.

Hot dog, it was my time to shine. I had lived in a tiny southern Illinois farm village when I was young. We had been so poor that we had mostly heated with wood. I had thoroughly enjoyed using a buck saw and an axe to cut and split the oak firewood.

But that had been in the 1940s. Now it was the 1970s and things had changed. People no longer used a hand saw for cutting firewood, though a metal-framed crosscut saw in the shape of a bow, called a bow or Swede saw, was sometimes used for lopping smaller branches. The most-used implement for cutting firewood was a chain saw. It cut with a set of teeth attached to a rotating chain that ran along a guide bar.

It seemed as though I could not help myself. I always had to shop around, to look for the least expensive solution, to find a bargain. It likely was associated with my post-depression era upbringing. Jim, my fellow Flight Service Specialist, had an old chain saw that had been used in Michigan for many years to cut cedar fence posts. It was big and clunky. It must have weighed twenty pounds or more. The muffler was shot, so that the user needed to have ear protection if he did not want to go deaf. The chainsaw later earned the nickname of "The Beast." I bought it at a bargain price and over the next fifteen years I must have cut a hundred and fifty full cords of wood with it, a cord being a stack of firewood four feet high and four feet wide and eight feet long, or 128 cubic feet.

I will never forget the first time I fired up "The Beast." It seemed extraordinarily dangerous. Those sharp teeth whined only a few inches from my hands. If I were to slip and lose my grip on the chainsaw it could chew through a leg or an arm as if they were nothing.

Writing about The Beast and being thrifty brings to mind an aside. I remember that the circular saw I bought to make the thousands of cuts for the cedar siding I installed on our house on Ridgeway Drive had been the least expensive one on the market. It was big and clunky and underpowered. I struggled with it. Ten years later I was working in Green Bay. One of the younger specialists and his wife were building their first house. I passed along my hard-earned wisdom. "Don't be cheap like I was," I advised him. "Go for the good stuff. Tell your wife you will need all new tools if you are going to take on such a large project. Tell you will need that table saw and that nail gun and that air compressor. Make a list of all the tools you ever dreamed of. Catch your wife in a moment of weakness. How can she deny you what you will need to build her a new house?"

It was said that logging was one of the most dangerous occupations. There were injuries and fatalities. I was to discover that it was not just a matter of the chainsaws. Sometimes trees did not want to cooperate. They would fall where you least expected them. Over the years I read several newspaper accounts of woodsmen being crushed by falling trees.

Louise and I searched for some wooded acreage. I had some mutual funds I had purchased while I was in the Air Force. We cashed those in and signed a contract for deed to buy forty acres of land northeast of Parkers Prairie. The purchase price was $10,000. We agreed to a down payment of $2,000 and monthly payments of $100. The interest rate was 8% per annum. The drive from Alexandria to the property took us north on Highway 29, past Lake Carlos and Lake Miltona. The distance was twenty-five miles.

The owners were Leo and Deloris Blashack. They were an older couple, probably in their sixties. On May 5th, 1978, the Parkers Prairie real estate agent drove to Alexandria with the papers for Louise and me to sign. He had some tragic news. Leo and Deloris had signed the day before.

Then Leo had been killed. He had been driving his farm tractor and it had tipped over on him.

I want to add here, before I forget it, that I felt comfortable in our real estate dealings, in the two houses and the wooded land, and I continued to feel comfortable in future deals. My time as a real estate agent in Anchorage had given me enough experience to know about contracts for deeds and the like. I never hired an agent to sell property for us. I took care of it myself, saving us many thousands of dollars in commissions.

Now I had a chain saw and I had some trees I could cut. I needed something to haul the wood in. Bob, one of our neighbors, ran a landscaping business. He had recently bought a newer truck. The old three-quarter-ton white Ford pickup truck was still sitting in his yard. He was about to haul it away to the junkyard. It was old, it was beat up, the tires were bald, and the brakes were suspect. But it was heavy duty with stout springs. I could load most of a full cord of firewood into it. The wood probably weighed a ton and a half or more.

"Does it run?" I asked Bob. "Sure," he said, "but it's in pretty tough shape and it looks bad." "I'll give you seventy-five bucks for it," was my offer. "Oh, that's way too much," he countered. "All I can get for it at the junkyard is twenty-five." We reached a compromise. I paid him fifty dollars.

The truck needed an alternator. There was a junkyard halfway between Alexandria and Parkers Prairie. I drove right by it on the way to the property. I had a used alternator installed for $15. I talked to the owner. "I'm not sure how much longer that old heap will keep running." I told him. "If it craps out on me will you come pick it up? I'll never be more than fifteen miles away. You can have it for nothing." He had to smile. "Sure," he said, "just give me a call. I'll bring the wrecker out and tow it away."

I hauled wood with that truck, and drove it to work, for the next two years. I marveled at how much wood it could carry without getting bogged down. But at the same time I was being stupid. The truck became less and less safe to drive. Finally, it was down to one operational brake, the steering was loose, the back window was busted out (I had accidently thrown a piece of firewood through it), I could see the highway rushing by through the rusted-out floorboard, the top of the cab was crushed (Oops, the tree I had cut down was supposed to fall the *other* direction), and it needed tires and a muffler. Louise became concerned. She paid $500 for another used truck that was in much better shape.

One Saturday I drove the old truck slowly north on the highway. Louise followed closely behind in our family car, the emergency flashers on. We were on our way to the junkyard. We had notified the owner and he was waiting for us. He handed me thirty-five dollars as he kindly and gently took possession of the old Ford. So long, old pal!

Our woods were riddled with standing dead elm trees. Dutch elm disease had moved through in the 1970s and not one elm tree had survived. I cut them down for firewood. Most of them were quite large, three feet in diameter or more. I cut the wood into two foot chunks that would fit into the fireplace. Oh my, some of those pieces were quite heavy, maybe seventy-five pounds or more. It was hard and sweaty work to load them into the truck.

I had learned about elm firewood when I was young. It had a reputation for being difficult to split. The grain was twisted so that sometimes a person damned near had to rip the pieces apart. Now I hauled loads home in the spring and dumped them beside the garage. Then all summer long I would go outside after supper and spend an hour or so splitting wood. It was good exercise. I used an eight-pound splitting maul and splitting wedges. God, that wood was tough! There were times when I had two or three wedges embedded in the wood and could not get them out. I had no choice but to put the chunk of wood into the fireplace and burn it so I could get my wedges back.

Of course I could have purchased a gas-fired hydraulic log splitter and saved myself a lot of work. There were many models on the market. But the truth was that I actually enjoyed splitting firewood by hand, and as I said the exercise was good for me. It built up my muscles and it gave me a good cardio workout.

I don't know how many wood handles I broke using that splitting maul. I would have to go to Fleet Farm, buy a new one, and fit it into the steel head. It brought back visions of older men in Chesterfield in the 1940s. Chesterfield was the small farm town in southern Illinois where I had spent the first thirteen years of my life. These men had used a piece of sharp glass to patiently shave down a new axe handle so that it would fit smoothly into the head. My attempts to copy them were less than perfect. I used a rasp and sandpaper to reshape the wood where it fit into the handle. But I was never patient enough. There were gaps in the wood.

By the end of the summer I would have one side of the two-car, 22 X 22-foot garage completely stuffed full of split and dried firewood. I reckoned it amounted to nearly ten full cords. We would burn all of it by the time the snow had melted the following spring. I recall that the wood seemed to attract field mice. I set several traps. Then, suddenly, the mice seemed to be gone. It was difficult for me to believe the traps had been that effective. Something seemed amiss. An explanation soon made its appearance. I saw a weasel running out of the garage. It had a mouse in its jaws. That took care of the mouse problem.

I can still visualize that double-car garage so full of firewood we could barely fit our Ford station wagon inside. I had split and stacked every piece of it, in between working rotating shifts, completing the house, and spending time with our young family. It was a busy, busy time for both me and Louise. I would not have traded it for anything.

There is a memory about another piece of wood that was nearly impossible to split. It was a large chunk of swamp ash that I had cut in the early autumn. It was too heavy to lift into the truck. I'd had no luck trying to split it with the maul and wedges. For some reason neither the maul nor the wedges would penetrate even an inch into the wood. Local "experts" told me how to handle it. "Wait until it freezes," they advised, "then it will split easily." The following winter I waded through the snow to have another crack at it. The temperature must have been ten below. "Alright you sucker," I thought to myself as I raised the maul high above my head and prepared to swing with a mighty blow, "prepare to meet your match."

I had never swung with so much force. I expected to see the wood neatly cleaved into two pieces. But it was not to be. The cutting edge of the maul did not penetrate even a quarter of an inch. Instead, it bounced straight back up into the air. I felt the vibration from the tips of my fingers all the way through my shoulders and down my torso. I darn near swooned. I no longer recall what I finally did with that chunk of ash wood. It is likely that I took my chainsaw to it.

I remember harboring a deep suspicion that perhaps those so-called experts had set me up. Maybe they knew damned well what was going to happen.

Elm comprised the majority of the wood I cut. There were a fair number of aspen and basswood trees. The nickname for aspen was "popple." A few ash and paper birch and hornbeam trees were mixed in. I don't remember any oak trees on our property but I do remember cutting oak firewood in other places. The pure white paper birch made a nice piece of firewood to look at. Sometimes I would lay a few chunks of birch beside the fireplace instead of burning them. It looked homey.

I learned that different woods held different amounts of BTUs, British Thermal Units. A piece of oak, for example, is denser and heavier than a piece of popple. Therefore the oak has more energy stored in it. Popple burned faster and hotter; oak burned slower and lasted longer. I would use popple to get a fire going and to quickly heat the house, then I would stoke the fireplace with oak or elm. Elm wood held fewer BTUs than oak but more than popple.

There is something gratifying about grabbing a solid chunk of well-seasoned oak or hard maple, of using it to stoke a good stove or fireplace. The wood has some weight to it, by god, some heft. It is rich in BTUs. No sissies, these hardwoods. They do not flash and die quickly, like willow or cottonwood. No, they heat for hours. Stoke the stove or the fireplace before you go to bed at night, close down the damper, and there, snug under the ashes, will still be the embers to start a new fire in the morning.

There were items in the local newspaper advertising firewood for sale. I no longer remember for certain but I think at that time, the mid-1970s to the mid-1980s, the price for a cord of wood was around $75-$80. Today, in 2020, it is closer to $200-$300 per cord. Too, a person has to be aware that wood is sold either as a full cord or as a face cord. A full cord is 4 feet wide by 4 feet high by 8 feet long, or 128 cubic feet. A face cord is one-third that amount. It is a pile 4 feet high and 8 feet long, but only 16 inches wide. It is common to cut firewood into 16-inch lengths.

There is something about wood heat. It "feels" more penetrating – warmer. And there is something calming about watching a wood fire burn while listening to the snap and crackle of embers. The flames seem almost hypnotic at times.

Burning wood can be messy and it can be dangerous. There are always bits of bark and dirt which litter the floor. Ashes need to be carried out. Soot accumulates in the chimney and can catch on fire. We must have read about a dozen or more house fires that had been caused by chimneys catching on fire. The old timers said that the best way to prevent the house fires was to deliberately set the chimney on fire, to start a fire that was so hot it would ignite the soot. Well, that may have been one solution. I never got up enough nerve up to try it. Instead I made an effort to burn only dry wood. Wet and unseasoned wood caused soot to accumulate faster. During the summer I would climb up on the roof and clean the chimney with a special brush.

There were many adventures with the elm trees. As I said, logging is dangerous work and the majority of the time I was working alone. The technique for "dropping" a tree is to cut a notch on the side towards which you want the tree to fall. Then make a single cut from the other side and towards the notch. If everything goes well the tree will topple towards the notch. Wait until you know for certain which way the tree is falling and then run like hell in the opposite direction.

But holy cow, trying to figure which way those elm trees would naturally want to fall was sometimes difficult. If they were leaning it was not a problem. There was only one direction they were going to go. But some of them had grown straight up. I would circle them, trying to discern if there was even the least bit of leaning. I would even consider which way the wind was blowing. Maybe the wind would push the tree in a particular direction as it was falling.

It happened more than once. I would notch a huge elm, cut through from the other side, and nothing would happen. The tree was in perfect balance. It would not topple. Which way should I run when it did start falling? There was no way to know. Finally I would grow so apprehensive that I would walk away, keeping a wary eye on the tree. I did not want to die that day. I would leave the problem for Mother Nature to resolve. Hopefully she would brew up a strong wind that would push the tree over. It worked every time. I would return a week later and the tree would be down.

Another dangerous situation occurred when the tree would fall only part way. It would hang up in other trees. Then it was a matter of trying to cut off a section of the trunk at a time, hoping the tree would eventually disentangle itself and not fall on me.

The forty-acre wood lot was in low and swampy ground. I stayed completely away from it in the summer. I surmised the mosquitos would carry me away. I don't know how many times I got stuck when I was cutting firewood. Of course it was always after I had the truck fully loaded with wood. I would unload some of the wood, trying to decrease the weight to the point that the truck could move. Then I would unload more and try again, until eventually I would have the whole damned load back on the ground. Finally, it was a matter of knocking on a nearby farmer's door and asking him to bring his tractor to pull me out.

I read a humorous fiction story about a man who was going to save money by burning wood. He convinced his wife that he needed an expensive chainsaw and a brand new pickup truck to get started. Then, since he was such an amateur, he dropped a tree on the truck and demolished it. He spent thousands of dollars and got nothing but grief in return.

The story later struck a respondent note with me. I was cutting down an elm. I knew exactly which way I wanted it to fall. I parked my truck in the opposite direction and what I judged was far enough away so that even if the tree accidently fell that way it could not reach the truck. Holy cow, wouldn't you know it, that damned tree would not cooperate. It toppled 180 degrees from where I wanted it to go. I watched in disbelief as it fell directly towards the truck. Upper branches about four inches in diameter crashed on top of the cab, denting it. Oh well, it was an old truck and the damage had not been too bad. The truck was still drivable. Sometimes things do not work out the way we had planned.

I was cutting wood another spring day when I heard a couple of gunshots at what I judged were about a half mile east of me. It seemed a little odd but hunting rifles were so common in Minnesota that I soon forgot about it. Probably somebody was target practicing.

I finished loading the truck and headed back south towards Alexandria. I was probably two or three miles south of Parkers Prairie when I noticed flashing red lights behind me. I pulled over to the shoulder and parked. I suspected that the police had finally caught up with me. They were going to inspect my beat up truck and declare it unsafe to be on the highway.

I was surprised when a Minnesota game warden flashed his badge. He wanted to know if I had been deer hunting, which was illegal in the spring. Deer season was always in the fall. I asked him if he was talking about the gunshots I had heard northeast of Parkers Prairie. That did not completely reassure him. He asked if he and his fellow game warden could unload the wood. They wanted to search for a deer carcass. Of course I gave them permission. I waited while they unloaded the wood, found nothing, and loaded the wood back again.

I surmised that there probably had been some illegal deer hunting going on. The land by our woods was low and swampy. Farming would have been a difficult way to earn a decent living. The people were poor. Venison probably found its way to their tables year round.

One day I was walking by the southwest corner of the woods when my eyes suddenly focused on some animal tracks in the mud. They were large tracks. Could a wandering cow have made them? Something told me that was not the case. I had seen many moose tracks in Alaska.

These tracks looked suspiciously similar. I asked Deloris if anyone had reported seeing a moose. She'd heard nothing about it. But within the week several people reported seeing a moose. It was quite unusual. Moose were common in Alaska and in Canada, but not this far south. A few weeks later we read that moose had been spotted in Iowa.

The children and I camped on the property a few times. They slept in one tiny tent; I slept in another. I remember one particular trip when all three of us were up well before dawn. I prepared a quick breakfast of oatmeal and hot cocoa and we went for a walk. We had returned to the tents by the time the sun was up. We knocked on Deloris' door and had more cocoa. Deloris regaled us with stories about hard times during the depression. She told us they drank hot water instead of coffee because nobody could afford to buy the coffee. She was a nice lady and she enjoyed our company.

I have fond memories of those forty acres of woods. I enjoyed being an amateur logger. My one regret is that I avoided the property in the summer, fearing the mosquitos and the ticks. It is likely that there was an abundance of birds and wildflowers. We sold the property back to Deloris in the autumn of 1984, prior to my being transferred to Green Bay. We had paid $10,000 for it six years earlier, now it was worth $12,500. We had also paid down the mortgage quite a bit so that Deloris had to write us a check for $8,750 to settle the balance.

THE GREAT OUTDOORS

FISHING

I had hunted and fished all my life. I had purchased licenses in Illinois, in Missouri, in Massachusetts, in New York, in Alabama, in California, in Oklahoma, in Canada, and in Alaska. Now I continued the outdoor adventures in Minnesota.

Alexandria was lakes country. Summer tourists flocked to the many resorts. The ideal home for local residents was a house on one of the lakes, with a dock where they could tie up their boat. Building lots with frontage on the water were quite expensive.

Fishing season opened in the first part of May. I remember the first year well. I was looking forward to it. I was excited to be outdoors after a long Minnesota winter. The day dawned and it began to snow. I was cold and miserable. I quickly learned not to trust the weather on opening day of fishing season in Minnesota.

Bluegills and crappies and northern pike, plus bass and perch and walleyes, were abundant, though not as much we were told as in the good old days before the lakes had been "fished out" and their populations had declined. (Isn't that some kind of a law, though? Nothing is ever as good as it was in the good old days.) People fished year round, from boats in the summer and through the ice in the winter. Fish filets from the cold winter water were sweet tasting and firm. But in August, when the water was warm and scummy, the flesh was soft and muddy tasting.

Walleyes were at the top of almost any fishing list. They were the tastiest. Some people called them walleyed pike but in fact they are a member of the perch family. Northern pike had a reputation for being full of bones. Muskellunge were famed for their huge size, their ferocity, and the difficulty in catching them. They were known as the "fish of 10,000 casts." In all the thirteen years we lived in Minnesota I never heard of any of my fishing buddies landing a musky, nor did I.

If walleyes were at the top of the fishing list, then surely carp were at the bottom. They are an invasive species from Asia and Europe. They root in the bottom of lakes while searching for food. They degrade water quality and destroy habitat for fish and waterfowl. People in other parts of the world enjoy eating them but they are considered a trash fish by most people in our country.

In the 1970s the Minnesota Department of Natural Resources (DNR) made a concerted effort to rid lakes of carp. They were ruining the fishing for other species and they posed a threat to the tourist industry. The DNR set carp traps in many lakes. They killed and disposed of the fish.

There was a group of businessmen in Alexandria who hoped to make a profit from the carp. Instead of disposing of the carp they would turn the flesh into something useful. Oh my, the ideas they came up with. I remember there was one product that was supposed to taste like peanut butter. I no longer remember the other flavors they came up with. They also sold gallon jars of liquid fish plant fertilizer. I remembered hearing stories of Native Americans fertilizing their gardens with fish.

The corporation lasted a few years. Local people were encouraged to invest money in it. The products appeared on the shelves of local grocery stores. But, alas, the concept did not take hold. American consumers had no taste for carp no matter how its use was disguised. The corporation went bust and the investors lost their money. For my part, I still think the idea had merit.

People in southern Illinois where I had grown up, and the entire South for that matter, consider fried catfish to rank high on the culinary scale. Cripes, even McDonalds hamburger joints sometimes have catfish on their menu. But in the North Country people turn up their noses at even the thought of eating catfish. If they catch them they immediately toss them back into the water.

The first fishing boat I bought was a little 12-foot aluminum thing with a tiny engine. It came with a homemade trailer I could tow behind our Ford station wagon. I purchased it from an old man who lived across the alley from our little house on Bryant Street. I think I paid $150 for it. I don't remember using the boat much nor do I remember when I got rid of it. I mostly fished with friends who had larger and better equipped boats.

I remember a time when a pretty good hailstorm came roaring through. My $150 boat was safe in the single-car garage while our $4,000 station wagon was parked outside in the driveway. I watched in dismay through the front screen door. It was too late for me to do anything about it. Fortunately the hail did not damage the vehicle.

Some years later another neighbor sold me a larger boat, a fourteen-foot model, but the engine was too small. I took the kids fishing on Lake Le Homme Dieu one time. It was a larger lake of 1,800 acres and the wind came up. The little engine could not handle the wind and the waves. We all had life vests on but I was alarmed. We finally made it back to shore. A short time later I sold that boat.

There was a definite learning curve in fishing for walleyes. We had to learn about <u>structure</u>, how walleyes would hang around underwater points and drop-offs, which we could pinpoint with our sonar-like electronic fish finders. We would place buoys to mark the spot. I recall one particular underwater ridge in Lake Le Homme Dieu ("Man of God" – a French family name), on the northeast edge of Alexandria. In the spring and early summer walleyes would congregate along that ridge in about twenty feet of water.

Lake Le Homme Dieu had a great swimming beach which the children and I occasionally went to. Once we fished Le Homme Dieu until after dark. There were no mosquitoes in the daylight hours as we sat casting for walleyes in the middle of the lake, but as soon as we touched shore that evening and took the time to winch the boat back onto its trailer we were attacked by hordes of the pesky varmints.

We also were told that walleyes do not like bright light, that they will look for deeper water to avoid it, that they migrate to shallow water in order to feed only when the light is dim or dark. I remember one fall evening, after a couple of frosts had decimated the mosquito population, when a couple of us were fishing near shore in our hip boots. We waded out into shallow water and cast our bait. It was difficult to see the line or the hook in the darkness. We had no luck but, oh my, the northern lights put on a little show for us. They were not nearly as spectacular as what Louise and I had experienced in Alaska but they were still worthwhile. It was an experience to remember. I can still see and feel it in my mind forty years later.

Al and Ron Lindner were famous Minnesota fishermen in the 1970s and beyond. They were based out of Brainerd, Minnesota. They invented what became to be known as the Lindy Rig. It was mostly used to fish for walleyes. It consisted of a slip sinker and a plain hook. The sinker dragged along the bottom, where the walleyes normally fed. The sinker would "swim" over most rocks and other bottom obstructions without getting snagged.

We used a variety of baits when fishing with a Lindy Rig. Minnows and nightcrawler worms were common. The most effective of all, however, seemed to be leeches. These little, black, squirmy creatures were apparently abundant in the lakes and were a favorite food of the walleyes. Bait sellers captured the minnows and the leeches in special traps and sold them to the public. I remember that a lot of the worms were imported from Canada. My son, Chris, and I would occasionally go outside at night after a rain and shine a flashlight on the ground. We would capture nightcrawlers emerging from their holes.

Bait shops were open from before dawn until early evening, seven days a week. It was not a problem for the larger sporting goods stores who could afford to hire plenty of help. But one poor sucker, I watched him as he struggled all one summer. He had opened a tiny shop on one of the main streets in Alexandria. He had only himself and his wife to man it. What was he thinking? He opened the store by four o'clock in the morning and kept it open until six P.M. He put in probably eighty or a hundred hours every week. I noted that as the summer progressed his eyes grew more bloodshot and it was obvious he was losing weight. He had to have been utterly exhausted. I was concerned about mental exhaustion. I no longer remember what happened to him, only that the next summer the bait shop stood empty and vacant.

Those walleyes were sensitive fish. There was a trick to hooking them. If they felt the least pull on the line they would drop the bait. We held the loose line with our index finger, and if we felt the least little pull or tap we would drop the line and let it run freely from the open-faced spinning reel. We mostly used six- or eight-pound test monofilament line and a fishing rod with a "sensitive" tip that would alert us to any activity. We would give the fish time to get the bait into its mouth before we set the hook.

Trolling was quite popular when fishing for walleyes. Fishermen could cover a lot more territory than when anchoring in one spot and casting. We mostly trolled lures, but if we could go slowly enough, especially into a wind, we would troll Lindy Rigs. Rapala fishing lures were also popular.

One day three of us were fishing on Lake Latoka. We'd found a place where the electronic fish locator indicated there were fish hanging near the bottom. We'd made several passes over the spot without any luck. We were about to leave. I felt a little pull on my line and let it drop. Probably the sinker had momentarily hung up on a rock. But when I set the hook, holy cow, something big was on the line. We netted an 8-pound walleye. It was big enough to get my picture in the local newspaper. A little curly-headed girl is shown standing beside me. It is Jenifer, our daughter.

Though walleyes were a favorite prey, we often fished for other species. A good stringer of bluegills, especially when they were taken from cold water in the spring or fall, were quite tasty. Their flesh was sweet and firm. I remember one early summer day when another Flight Service specialist came by our house on Bryant Street. We both had the day off. He'd gone fishing; I was working in the back yard. He had a stringer full of crappies. He'd caught his limit and he offered to give them to me. He wanted to go back for more.

What the heck? Crappies tasted good. All I had to do was clean them and our family would have a nice meal. I set to work. I placed the fillets in a clean pan. I wrapped the entrails and the skin in newspaper. Nugget watched me as I worked. When I had finished I took the newspaper-wrapped waste to our garbage can in the alley. I made the mistake of leaving the fillets unguarded. When I returned I saw Nugget licking his lips. Half the fillets were missing. That scurvy mutt had eaten them. There was no use scolding him; it was my fault. It was another of life's lessons in humility.

In southern Illinois I had learned how to use live frogs to fish for largemouth bass. Now I tried it again. The bass loved them. The trick was to put on hip boots and wade out in shallow water near the shore. I would cast the frog and a weedless hook on the edge of weed lines. The bass were fun to catch - they put up a good fight.

As a side note, frogs were abundant in those days. My son, Chris, and his neighborhood pal, Todd, who were about eight years old, would catch them and sell them to bait shops. But even in the 1970s we had begun to notice a decline in amphibian populations. The worry was that the decline was an indicator of significant environmental changes, of an ecosystem out of balance. The decline continues unabated even today, in 2020. Scientists have been mostly puzzled by it. They believe there is no one simple answer. The latest thinking is that a combination of factors, including a disease called chytridiomycosis, global climate change, pesticides, and invasive species are the cause of the decline. At any rate, it has been decades since I last used frogs to fish for bass.

Our neighbor, Loren, and I were making one last fishing trip before winter set in. A chilly wind was blowing. The water on Lake Carlos was frigid and choppy. Loren's heavy wood boat handled it well. We had probably fished for a couple of hours when we'd had enough. We were shivering and the walleyes were not biting. The leeches on our Lindy Rigs went untouched. We headed for the launch ramp.

We were near shore when we anchored the boat and cast our rigs one last time. It is hard for a fisherman to give up. The fish locator indicated we were over a pile of rocks in about ten feet of water. Still, there were no bites. Loren put his fishing rig away and prepared to raise the anchor. I, being the stubborn man that I was, kept my bait in the water for that last few minutes. Then I felt a pull. I set the hook and could feel something heavy on the line. We netted it then tried to figure out what the heck it was. We later determined that it was a smallmouth bass. It was so big that we'd had problems recognizing it.

It was a trophy fish that weighed in at five pounds and four ounces. I did not want to spend the money to have it mounted. It would have cost $75 or more. There was a hardware store in downtown Alexandria that had an array of trophy fish mounted on its walls.

I checked to see if they would be interested in my smallmouth. Indeed they were. They had just about every local fish except a smallmouth. It was a win-win situation. They paid to have the fish mounted. I got to see it and my name in prominent letters every time I walked into the store.

There is something that always comes to mind with I think of Loren. He and his wife, Fern, and their children lived across the alley from our home on Bryant Street. They were a nice family. Loren seemed down to earth, a relatively uncomplicated man. He worked as a salesman. But he had what I thought was an unusual hobby. He loved to listen to opera. What the heck! Opera was something I could not make heads or tails of. How had Loren gotten into it? I admired him for it.

Open water fishing was widely popular during the warmer months. Ice fishing was as popular or even more so in the winter. There was a race to see who could get out on the ice first. Every year some of the early birds would break through the ice in their pickup trucks and need to be winched out. Old timers whose light trucks were equipped with wide tires thought that a couple of inches of ice were enough. Most people wanted at least eight or ten inches.

I had never driven on an ice-covered lake until I had moved to Alaska. I had been apprehensive the first time I had done it, that is, until we had discovered that the ice was five feet thick. In Alexandria I had no fear of driving on ice. But I remember when some Illinois relatives visited one Christmas. I drove them out to an ice fishing shanty. There was probably a couple of feet of ice. They were as nervous as all get-out.

Oh my, some of those ice fishing shanties were almost palatial. They were constructed or refurbished in the summer and then in the winter hauled to the lake on a trailer. Most of them had wood runners on the bottom so that they could be towed from one place on the lake to another. There were always those few who waited too long in the spring to get their shanties off the ice before it melted. They would either float away or sink to the bottom.

Inside, there could be paneled walls, a small library of books, a small wood or propane heating stove, and a cooler filled with beer and sandwiches. Perhaps there would be a battery-powered radio so they could listen to the Vikings football game. There could be a card table with a deck of cards and a scrabble board.

Two or three holes, about a foot in diameter, would have been cut in the floor. Holes would be drilled through the ice. Short fishing rods about two feet long were equipped with "tip ups" that would indicate when a fish was biting. Minnows were the most common bait but tiny wax worms were frequently used when going after panfish, such as bluegills and crappies. Oh my, fish from the frigid water sure tasted good.

I will close this section on ice fishing with a short story I wrote years later when we were living in Wisconsin. It was in memory of an ice fishing adventure that had taken place while Nugget and I had been living in Alexandria. The story was, in fact, mostly true with perhaps a bit of exaggeration sprinkled throughout. I had submitted the story to the *Woodsman* magazine, a little rag of an outdoor publication based in Spooner, Wisconsin. I was thrilled beyond reason when the editor accepted it for publication. It appeared in the December, 1993, issue.

I can remember to this day opening the mailbox and reading the letter of acceptance. It is likely I stood there for a few minutes and let my mind wander, dreaming of worldwide fame. Maybe this would lead to a Pulitzer Prize or, wonder of wonders, to a Nobel Prize in Literature. (My imagination knew no limits.) I think my payment was ten or fifteen free copies of the magazine. I remember that I rushed three or four more short stories to the editor. All were rejected. The editor said they had too much dialogue.

My fantasy of immediately becoming a famous writer was dashed.

****

ICE FISHING IS FOR THE DOGS

An outdoorsman's day rarely is perfect, often is frustrating, and at times is downright humiliating. There are those occasions when, no matter how hard we try, things just don't turn out right.

Jim and I were at work one winter afternoon. For the past month we had been mostly stuck indoors as one snowstorm after another rolled through. We were getting edgy, victims of cabin fever, and desperate for something to do.

"How about some ice fishing?" Jim suggested. "My shanty's still out on Godfrey Lake, if the wind hasn't blown it away, and the walleyes should be plenty hungry by now."

"Sounds good to me," I said. "But can I bring my yellow Lab along? He's getting a little nutty being inside all the time."

"Hey, no problem," Jim said. "All the really wimpy fishermen are staying home. We'll have the whole lake to ourselves. That mutt of yours can run around all he wants."

I called home. "Woman," I said, "you can put that hamburger back in the freezer. Jim and I are going fishing. You and I are gonna have fresh walleye instead of meat loaf for supper tonight."

What sounded suspiciously like a snigger came back across the line. I chose to ignore it. Life is too short to worry about the non-believers. Besides, I could almost taste those fish fillets already.

After work, Jim and I met at his house and drove to Godfrey Lake. Good thing we had four-wheel drive. We had to bust through some mighty big drifts. But Jim was right – we had fooled everybody else and were alone on the lake.

We parked at the access and began wading through the quarter-mile of deep snow that lay between us and Jim's fish house. The sky was all gray overcast and a bitter northwest wind stung our faces. The two of us, bundled in our heavy parkas and long underwear, were soon gasping for air. But this is the manly way to stay in shape, not on some sissy indoor treadmill. The dog zigzagged around, poked his nose into every drift, and rolled happily in the dry snow.

Panting and perspiring, we were near collapse when we finally had plowed our way through to the shanty. Our legs felt like rubber and our lungs were raw.

"Oh, _ _ _ _!" Jim groaned, smacking himself upside the head.

I was alarmed, thinking perhaps he was undergoing the same heart attack I was just then experiencing.

"What's the matter?" I asked.

"I just remembered – there's a padlock on the door and I forgot to bring the key."

"Oh, _ _ _ _!" I said.

"Can't we break in?" I suggested.

"We won't even consider it," Jim said. "I've put too much work into this fish house to wreck it now."

There seemed nothing else to do. We started back. Lesser men would probably have called it quits right then and there. But we were woodsmen, and a few minor setbacks meant nothing to us. Besides, there was that matter of the snigger . . . .

We had already busted a trail through the drifts, so our return trip probably wasn't half as bad as it seemed. Our enthusiasm for this outdoor adventure was down a notch or two, and it was near dark by the time we returned to the shanty. The dog took everything in good-natured stride.

Fortunately, Jim was right. We no sooner had our minnows in the water before the walleyes were biting. Sure, they weren't the five-pound lunkers we had envisioned. They were probably more like a pound or so, but, hey, they were fish.

"Good eating size," Jim said, smacking his lips.

As we unhooked each fish, we opened the shanty door and tossed the walleye into the snow, where it would quickly freeze.

Soon, the fish abruptly stopped biting. We had just enough for supper. We turned off the stove, gathered our gear, and locked the door. But when we turned to shine our light on the fish, they were gone!

We scratched our heads in amazement, searching for some logical solution to this mystery.

"Maybe someone came along and stole our fish while we were yukking it up inside the shanty," I said.

"That must be it," Jim agreed. We know for sure those walleyes couldn't get up and walk away by themselves."

"But look," I showed him, calling upon my finely tuned woodsman's skills. "the only tracks in the snow are yours, mine, and . . . the dog's!"

Our heads swiveled in unison as we focused our attention on the Labrador. His brown eyes brimmed with affection, and his tail wagged violently as he licked his chops. There was a noticeable bulge in his belly. It was as if he were saying: "Thank you, thank you, thank you! The fish were delicious. May I have more?"

It was the final humiliation. Jim and I hunched our backs into the icy wind, our shoulders sagging in defeat as we struggled through the drifts and the darkness to the truck. The dog, paying no attention to our gloom, raced around us in happy circles.

There were no walleyes on our plates that night. I stopped by a fast food joint and brought home a meager meal of beans and burritos. Louise was all hand-over-the-mouth giggles as she fondly petted the dog. I wasn't in much of a mood for pleasant conversation.

The Lab, worn out by the fresh air and exercise, and with his belly full of fish, soon lay stretched out full length under the dining room table, fast asleep. Every so often, his tail would thump emphatically on the floor and his teeth would snap shut. Somewhere in the mists of his canine dream world, a door opened, the light shone, and another walleye came floating towards his waiting jaws.

****

Okay, so maybe the writing was not something John Steinbeck or Ernest Hemingway would have laid claim to, but, hey, it was a start.

THE GREAT OUTDOORS
TRAPPING

One autumn day in about 1973 I was exploring the farm roads west of Alexandria. I was passing by a tiny pond of water on my right when suddenly I braked the Ford station wagon to a sliding halt. I stepped out of the vehicle for a closer look. The pond could not have been more than a hundred feet in diameter and it looked shallow. It lapped up against the road's shoulder on the near side and was bordered by a corn field on the other.

But, holy cow, there must have been a dozen muskrats swimming in the muddy water, and I could see a fair number of muskrat houses. There was not a cattail to be seen. Cattails are a muskrat's favorite food. Their houses are often constructed of decaying cattail stems and mud. In this case, though, the muskrats had stumbled onto a food bonanza. That field of corn provided all the food they could possibly use and the stems help hold their houses together.

My heart started thumping. I had run a small trap line in 1952 when I was living in a tiny farm town in southern Illinois. I had been in the seventh grade. Trap lines were fairly common for farm boys in those days. It was a way to earn some pocket money. I remember using my earnings to buy some jeans and a pair of shoes. The following year we had moved to a more urban area and my trapping days were over.

I had been thrilled with that early trap line. It had brought me closer to nature. Now, twenty-three years later, I was in my mid-thirties. Could it be that I could rekindle part of my youth? I had to give it a try.

I had no idea who owned the land. I looked for a farmhouse and saw one about a quarter mile away. I don't know – the accepted philosophy in our little Illinois town had been that if we asked permission to hunt or fish on someone's land and they turned us down, we were screwed. If they later caught us trespassing there was no way we could lie our way out of it. But – if we snuck onto their land without first asking permission, and they did catch us, it was okay, it was appropriate behavior. We at least had a case we could plead. It was entirely customary to play humble and stupid, to cast our eyes to the ground as we muttered abject apologies. Heck, we had thought we were on somebody else's property.

It was a kind of game we played. In actuality, everybody knew everybody. If we trespassed on somebody's property it was likely they were aware of it. There could be a problem if the trespasser was an adult and the two men did not get along. But boys with a fishing pole over their shoulder or a .22 rifle cradled in their arms were almost a part of the rural Illinois landscape. They were a part of the accepted culture. Anyone who chastised them was being mean.

Now, I narrowed my eyes and furrowed my brow. I needed to make a close evaluation of the situation at the muskrat pond. I did not know whose door to knock on. One edge of the pond lay clearly within the bounds of the road's right-of-way. I could wade into the water without trespassing on anybody's land. There was no need at all to set foot into the corn field. I decided to chance it. If somebody objected they could tell me to pull my traps and leave.

As it turned out, there was never a problem. The area was isolated. I never saw another person. I would not have been surprised if the farmer was happy that I was stopping the muskrats from eating his corn.

I hastened to buy a trapping license. I stopped by Fleet Farm and bought a dozen #1 Victor Stoploss traps, and half a dozen Victor 110 Conibear body gripper traps. Both types of traps were small. They were an ideal size for trapping muskrats.

By counting the number of houses I estimated that there were about seventy-five muskrats living in that little pond. I had been taught when I was young that we should not try to trap everything, that we should leave about a third of the animals for "seed." Those animals would repopulate for the next season. I thought that if I could trap about fifty rats that would be enough.

Things went well. Opening day of the season I put on my hip boots and waded out to the houses. I set all of the dozen Stoploss traps. I set traps on top of the houses and baited them with chunks of apple. I found the fruit lying on the ground underneath a scraggily old apple tree on the edge of the airport. Someone must have planted it decades earlier then abandoned it when the land was purchased for an airport. Muskrats were attracted by the creamy flesh. Maybe it reminded them of cattails. I staked the traps in about two feet of water. When the trap snapped the muskrats would instinctively dive into the pond and drown.

I was out at the crack of dawn the following morning to check the traps. I was as excited as the twelve-year-old boy I had been when I had first begun a trap line. I did not know what to hope for. Maybe I would catch a couple of the rats; maybe none. The results were far beyond my expectations. I collected eight muskrat carcasses the first morning.

The rats were easy to skin. The soft and luxurious fur came off easily. I did the work in the basement. Jenifer and Chris watched in fascination. I gave them a lesson in anatomy. I opened up the carcasses to point out lungs and heart and liver. I stretched the hides on special metal frames and let them dry. Fur prices were high at the time, in the mid-1970s to the mid-1980s. There was a fur buyer in Alexandria who paid about six dollars for each muskrat pelt. And rather than wasting the meat, I donated the carcasses to a mink rancher. Mink love the taste of muskrat flesh.

The pond had frozen by the time I had trapped it out. There were fewer and fewer muskrats harvested each day. Finally, I moved on. I think I had trapped about forty rats. I had been so successful that I returned the next year, full of optimism. It had been a dry year with little rain. I was disappointed to find that there was not a drop of water in what the year before had been a little pond. As a consequence there were of course no muskrats.

That first year of trapping had rekindled the thrill I had felt when I had run a trap line in the seventh grade. To enhance the effect even more I had mailed off for a subscription to *Fur-Fish-Game* magazine. I poured through the periodical, searching in articles written by professional trappers on ways to hone my trapping skills.

That second year I moved on to a little patch of public land just north of Forada, a tiny farm town a dozen miles south of Alexandria. There were rat houses everywhere and, as had happened a year earlier, I could wade to houses before the water froze and walk on the ice later.

I remember a couple of times when Jenifer and Chris accompanied me as I ran that trap line by Forada. They were curious about everything. It was early in the season. They stayed on shore while I waded out to the muskrat houses.

Trapping muskrats after the water froze and the ice was thick enough to walk on meant taking a different approach. I could no longer set a trap on the top of houses. The rats swam under the ice to their underwater entrances. There were also smaller "feeder" houses where they could rest while they were feeding on cattails. It was easy to determine which houses were in active use. A trail of under-ice bubbles led to them.

The trick was to make a hole in the side of the house and set a baited trap inside. One had to carefully repack the hole after the trap was set. Otherwise the inside of the house could freeze along with the animals that lived there. It was in fact illegal to be so careless as to cause a rat house to freeze. A trapper could have his license pulled.

I also remember that a high school biology teacher lived across the street from us on Ridgeway Drive. He told me that he enjoyed trapping for mink. He used the little 110 Conibear traps like I had purchased at Fleet Farm. He said he set the traps in runways that wound their way through the weeds around marshes and lakes.

Well, the fur buyer was paying a lot more for mink pelts than he was for muskrats - twenty dollars as opposed to six dollars. I thought I would give it a try. I set my Conibears in the barely visible trails by my trap line in Forada. I had no luck at all. For one thing, I found no mink tracks, even when there was snow on the ground. Rumor had it that the old time trappers, who were quite skilled, would sneak out and trap all the mink shortly before the official trapping season had even opened. That did not sound entirely plausible but I had no way of disputing it.

I continued trapping through the 1983 season. (We moved in 1984.) I found another piece of swampy public land that was filled with muskrat houses. I read an article in *Fur-Fish-Game* magazine that explained how to build floats for trapping the rats. I placed traps onto boards about two feet long and baited them with chunks of apple. The rats would climb onto the board, the trap would snap, and the rats would dive into the water, where they would drown. It was an easy way to increase the number of sets I could make. I no longer had to rely solely on the rat houses themselves.

It felt good to be out with nature. I can remember driving up to that swampy area. It was filled with cattails and rat houses. I would get out of the car, smell the fresh air, and listen to pheasant roosters cackling among the cattails.

In 1952, when I had run my first trap line, fur buyers had paid $1.50 for a red fox pelt. The county had paid another $1.00 in bounty money. Now, in the 1970s and '80s the price had skyrocketed. Fox pelts were bringing in $50-$60 and trappers were concentrating on them.

I was walking in the Forada swamp one winter day when I came across a fox track clearly outlined in the snow. Hot Dog! Now I had a chance to make some big money. I bought a couple of larger traps, #1 1/2 long springs, and made dirt hole sets. The idea was to fool a fox into thinking a mouse had been buried there.

Well, I had no luck at all. I checked those traps every day for a month. No fox even approached my sets. Then one day I stumbled across a fox set another trapper had made. Perhaps that explained my lack of success. But I do remember how much I enjoyed the experience. I have a mental vision of one day when I was out. The temperature was ten below, there was a breeze, and I was bundled up in my Alaska parka and long johns. God, the air was bracing! It felt good just to be alive.

I had to smile when I thought about it. With the parka's hood snugged tight around my head, my view was limited to what I could see straight ahead of me. It was my window on the world. It reminded me of some of the religious and political nutcases we have to put up with. It is as if they have blinders on. They can only see what is directly in front of them and nothing to the side. They do not have the details, the broader picture, which would give them the whole story.

I kept intermittent trapping notes from 1973-1983, jotting down the temperature and the barometric pressure and the amount of clouds. I also described the sets I made and the number of animals I caught.

There was always a question associated with trapping. Protesters claimed it was cruel. Trappers argued that they were "harvesting" animals which would otherwise go to waste, that the animals would become overpopulated and die from starvation and disease. To my mind, as the years went by the situation pretty much resolved itself. Fur clothing was replaced by less expensive and easier to take care of man-made apparel. There is not much of a market for fur today but the cause has little to do with those who are opposed to trapping.

THE GREAT OUTDOORS

HUNTING

In Minnesota, I was looking forward to dining on some good pheasant meat. We would occasionally see some of the birds when we were driving the farm roads around Alexandria.

There was lots of public land in Minnesota. Local, county, state, and federal lands were set aside for recreational activity. There were a couple of areas where the pheasant hunting was particularly good. One was a patch of public land about twenty miles southwest of Alexandria. The other was farther southwest, near Ortonville, along the South Dakota border.

The thing I remember about that first patch was that one time I was walking in a flat field overgrown with weeds. It was a good place for pheasants to be hiding. Suddenly the sun was blotted out and a shadow passed over me. I looked up to see a huge piece of metal passing not more than 500 feet above my head. Then the roar of its engines hit and almost knocked me off my feet. It was an Air Force B-52 bomber on a low-level training mission. Holy cripes! I had heard about the missions but had never actually witnessed one. I remember hearing stories about farmers in North Dakota nearly getting knocked off their tractors by low-flying B-52s.

There was a technique to hunting the pheasants. Three or four of us would hunt as a group. Two would walk through a field while the other one or two would wait at the other end. The pheasants had a tendency to run rather than to fly. But when they reached the end of the cover and saw hunters waiting for them they would flush. Then a quick decision had to be made. Was it a rooster or a hen? Roosters were legal to shoot; hens were not. I had never been a good wing shot with my .12 gauge. I missed lots of shots.

When I was in the Air Force I had gone to France on leave. There were two items I had retained from the trip. One was a corkscrew for opening bottles of wine. It is still in our kitchen drawer today, in 2020, fifty-five years later. The other was a French cookbook. I thought we still had it but Louise said she got rid of it years ago. It was not in the best shape.

At any rate, the American way of handling meat seems to be to eat it or freeze it right away. I remembered seeing a side of beef hanging in a butcher's shop in Scotland. It had been hanging there for several days and had not seen the inside of a cooler. English meat tasted different. They claimed it had been "cured," or tenderized. I had not much cared for the taste of it. The English, for their part, claimed we Americans ate bloody meat.

I remembered that the French cookbook claimed that the best way to prepare pheasants for the dinner table was to hang the carcass by its neck or legs for several days in cool air. Some even claimed that it was better to keep them hanging until the flesh decomposed and the bird fell off the hook. "Yuk!" my wife and daughter just exclaimed in disgust, "Who wants to eat meat like that?" But I just now checked on the computer and the consensus was that game birds hung for several days tasted better, were more tender, and were more moist. I doubt if more than one in a hundred American outdoorsmen is familiar with this way of preparing wild game.

Ruffed grouse were a new game bird for me. I had never encountered them prior to living in Minnesota. They were a fun bird to hunt in the autumn but they were not easy to bring down. They would explode from the leaves that littered the forest floor and dodge around trees. It called for snap shooting. I had never been a good wing shot to begin with and this type of shooting really tested me. An added challenge was to find them after they had been shot. We tried to "mark" them closely. But they were so well camouflaged that it was difficult to find them among the leaves. Also, the grouse population rose and fell in about a ten-year cycle. They were abundant in some years and scarce in others. But like pheasants, they were a tasty bird to eat.

I remember that in southern Illinois in the 1950s and '60s we had never seen the tracks of whitetail deer. There were none. There were occasional hunters who would travel to Nebraska or Montana to hunt deer. I had tasted the venison once or twice and had not cared for it. It had a wild, "gamey" flavor that did not appeal to us farm folks who were used to eating fresh beef that had been fed on corn. One of my fellow workers at Flight Service had grown up on venison in Minnesota. He claimed that the gamier the meat tasted the better he liked it.

The only big game rifle I possessed was the Weatherby .300 magnum. I had shot a moose with it in Alaska. It was too much of a gun for deer but I did not want to buy something else.

The father-in-law of one of the Specialists had a cabin near Park Rapids. The specialist invited three or four of us to join him in a November deer hunt. I had not shot my rifle in a couple of years. I needed to "sight it in" to make sure that the 3 X 9 variable scope was still accurately adjusted. The specialist and I met at an abandoned gravel pit. I had my Weatherby; he had a 30-30. We set up a large bullseye paper target at a hundred yards and I fired three rounds. My rifle still shot accurately.

Then the other specialist tried his 30-30 with open sights. He could not hit anywhere on the large paper target at a hundred yards. We moved the target closer – to fifty yards. Still he entirely missed the target. We cut the distance to twenty-five yards. Now a couple of rounds penetrated the outer edges of the paper, nowhere near the bullseye. I had to laugh when he said that was good enough.

Well, a week or so later I was perched in the loft of an old abandoned barn, looking out over a nice meadow. The sun had gone down and there was barely enough light to see. A deer emerged and began to feed. I took careful aim with my scoped rifle. One shot was all it took. The deer dropped where it had stood. When we examined the small buck we determined that the rifle round had been so powerful that it had gone completely through him without fragmenting.

A couple of days later the other Specialist was perched on the limb of a small birch tree as the sun was just coming up. His seating was precarious and the tree swayed in the wind. A nice buck stepped out of the woods not twenty-five yards away. Our Specialist fired the 30-30 and dropped the buck with a single shot to the neck. It was a dandy shot. But our specialist had to admit, kind of sheepishly, that with the tree swaying and him clinging to the branches, he had been aiming behind the deer's shoulders and not for its neck!

That one little buck was the only deer I bagged in six or seven years of hunting. I returned to the abandoned barn the following year only to find it occupied by another party of hunters. In fact, the entire area seemed overrun by hunters. There seemed to be more hunters than whitetails. I remember returning home once after another fruitless season. I had not seen even one deer. Louise reported that while I was gone a nice buck had rubbed its horns on our deck.

One November three of us were reduced to sleeping in a tent for the entire five-day season. Oh my, after the sun went down at five P.M. there was not a damned thing to do. The tent was too small for us to even stand up. None of us were drinkers. Even so we went to a bar one evening just to get away from that damned tent. We listened to stories about poachers and game wardens.

One such tale was about a poacher who had three deer carcasses hidden away in a shed. The legal limit was one. Somebody, probably one of his neighbors, turned him in. A game warden drove to the farmhouse and approached the poacher. "I'll give you a choice. If you tell me where you have hidden the deer carcasses I will confiscate only your rifle, you will be fined, and your license will be suspended. But if you make me search for the deer I will do one more thing; I will confiscate your pickup truck as well." It was said that the poacher led the warden to the hidden venison. In the North Country a man's pickup truck means everything. It is his ultimate status symbol.

I grew to enjoy roaming those northern Minnesota woods. The stillness often was broken only by the roar of a distant chainsaw, or a farmer's yapping dog. At night we could listen to coyotes yodeling or a pair of barred owls hooting back and forth at each other. There was a freshness in the air, in wind soughing through pine trees, in the lakes and rivers, and in the cedar swamps. After the sun dipped below the horizon the darkness closed in incredibly fast. Being surrounded by tall trees at night can be almost claustrophobic if a person is not used to it. The patches of sky that are visible through birch and pine and maple twinkle with the light of a million stars.

I waxed ever more poetic in my mind. Northern Minnesota – forests and lakes and rivers – snow and mosquitos and wood ticks – dirt and gravel back roads – resorts and campgrounds and run-down motels. There were bait shops.

There were isolated taverns with double names – Bob and Betty's – Lou and Barbs – Mick and Elaine's.

Northern Minnesota - where logging and county jobs were the main sources of income – where family freezers were filled with fish and venison – where patriotism and the Bible and rugged individualism were not just words - where culture constricted and nature liberated – where reality seemed surreal.

Finally, so many hunters flooded the public hunting grounds that I was reduced to deer hunting on our forty acres of woods near Parkers Prairie. The advantage was that I could sleep in my own bed at night and have a hot meal waiting for me when I got home after dark. I could even stop by Deloris's house during the day for a hot cup of coffee.

There was plenty of deer sign. I had nailed some boards in a tree so that I could sit comfortably and watch over a nearby trail. I crept into the woods just before dawn on opening day. I could see my breath in the frigid air. I could hear rustling in the brush. It was likely that deer had heard me and were leaving. I climbed into my perch and waited. Shots rang out in the distance. The action had begun.

I was bundled in heavy winter clothing and I had a thermos of hot coffee. Nonetheless it was damned cold sitting in that tree. I began to shiver. I sat quietly for about an hour and a half. I saw no deer. Finally I climbed down to stretch my cramped muscles. It was then that the shaking began and I could not stop my teeth from chattering. It was the coldest I had ever been. I had hypothermia. I began walking so I would warm up.

It was my last deer hunt in Minnesota. The deer were there but I was not experienced enough to know how to hunt them. Plus, as the years went by it seemed that the number of hunters increased. They were everywhere. There seemed to be more hunters than deer. A person could not get away from them.

There was one last bit of hunting. In Illinois I had grown up hunting fox squirrels. Gray squirrels were abundant around Alexandria but nobody seemed interested in hunting them. I pretty much had the field to myself. I found a nice patch of oak woods I could sneak out to before dawn. The trees were on private property but I never ran across the owner.

Gray squirrels were a lot trickier to hunt with a .22 rifle than the fox squirrels I was used to. Fox squirrels had a tendency to freeze and try to hide. The grays would take off running through the trees. Plus the grays were a smaller target. Nonetheless, squirrel hunting brought back many pleasant memories of my childhood days. Once again I was sitting under a tree just before the sun popped above the horizon, listening to a squirrel gnaw away on an acorn. My heart thumped just as rapidly as it had when I was taking aim at a moose or a whitetail deer.

In that regard, there was a story in *Alaska* magazine. A trapper was holed up in his crude log cabin during a winter storm. He was kept awake at night by a mouse chewing on wood. He was determined to finish off the little varmint.

As he began his stalk he was surprised to find that his heart was thumping as wildly as it did when he was stalking a bear or a moose. There is something about the chase that excites men's blood. Perhaps it is in our genes, something we inherited from the thousands of years of hunting and gathering that our ancestors practiced.

There are many people who are opposed to hunting and trapping. I respect them for it but at the same time it is not the way I was raised. In the late 1940s and early 1950s I had learned to hunt and to fish in order to put food on the table. I had trapped so I could earn some money. Both purposes had seemed entirely legitimate. It must have been in the early 1980s, when I was in my forties, that I attempted to put my thoughts on paper. I still have the handwritten pages.

****

AN OUTDOORSMAN'S PHILOSOPHY

Twenty-five years ago I was a young pup roaming the fields and the woods of south-central Illinois. My life flowed with the seasons. Spring was a time for fishing. Summer meant blackberry picking, swimming, hunting woodchucks, and eating watermelons. Squirrel hunting was the main pastime in the fall, and winter meant trapping and rabbit hunting. It was a good and a full life, a life that I look back on with pleasure.

Then came college, the Air Force, and getting started with career and family. The fishing rods and the guns were often put aside. Those were the years of reaching maturity and assuming responsibility. When I took to the outdoors again I was a far different person than during my youth. There was still pleasure in the feel of the outdoors but I became more selective in what I enjoyed doing. Squirrel and duck hunting had mostly lost out in the transition. Neither my wife nor my children enjoyed eating them. Pheasants and grouse became more of the table fare. Trapping was limited because there was little time for it. Deer hunting became the one big event of the year

It was during the preparation for one of these annual deer hunting trips that a situation arose which baffled and confused me. I was asked by a non-hunter what pleasure I got from shooting a deer. It seemed like a naïve question. Hunting, fishing, trapping were to me as natural as cherry trees in blossom or evening breezes. I was amazed when I could not think of a ready response.

I asked my hunting partners the same question and received the same baffled response from them. We agreed that while none of us actually enjoyed killing a deer, we did enjoy hunting them, and that going after deer with a camera rather than a gun would not be nearly as enjoyable.

In the past few years more and more people seem to be opposed to hunting and trapping, mainly on the grounds that these activities impose unnecessary suffering on our animal populations. I have read and listened to arguments both pro and con, but have not yet been able to resolve the issue to my own satisfaction.

Hunters take to the woods for a variety of reasons. One deer hunter that I heard of faithfully bought new hunting clothes each fall, drove to the deer camp, set his gun in a corner, and became the camp cook. He never took his gun out of its case, yet each year he returned with a deer someone else had shot for him. Cooking and the camaraderie of a deer camp were more pleasurable to him than the actual hunting.

I have seen pictures of hunters standing in great rooms full of animal trophies from all over the world. I have difficulty in understanding the value of this type of hunting. Hunting for food, for fur, or even for a bounty is one thing, but killing an animal so that it can be stuffed and put on display is something else.

The hunter who is strictly out for trophies is too much involved with himself to have any real feeling for the world of nature. He is the hunter who will leave his office and fly to Alaska on Friday, shoot a caribou on Saturday, fly back home on Sunday, report back to work on Monday, and have the caribou's head mounted for all to see in his home or office. He will have shot a caribou but he knows nothing about the caribou. He is also the type of hunter who would pay huge sums of money to acquire a polar bear rug or the head of an elephant, not for his own use, but so that others may admire him.

Those who kill for records or to acquire "one of each species" are also not primarily interested in hunting but in satisfying some personal ego requirement. This is the area where competition seems to be the prime motivator. I shot a bigger deer than you did, therefore, I am a better hunter than you are.

I am not entirely against keeping records. If a hunter downs a huge moose or a fisherman nets a trophy musky when their primary intent was to enjoy the great outdoors and perhaps put some meat on the table, getting into the record books becomes an added reward. But, to me, the value of an animal does not lie in the size of its horns or its weight.

Then there is the "once a year" hunter. Each fall he makes the annual trek. Often he is overweight and out of condition. He drinks beer with the boys and suffers in the woods. He becomes lost. He becomes the victim of another hunter's bullet. He cannot distinguish clearly between a spike buck and a doe. He does not sense when a weather front is moving in nor can he determine directions by the sun or the stars. Half the venison he carries home will end up in the garbage. He numbers in the tens of thousands.

The slob hunter is the bane of all legitimate outdoorsmen. He is the mortal enemy of the anti-hunters. He litters and destroys. He shoots to kill on sight. It is a tiny minority, but embedded in his ranks are those who hunt for the sheer thrill of killing, who will shoot an animal and leave it to rot.

Outdoorsmen advance a number of reasons for the legitimacy of their sport. Population control is a concept often used, the idea being that if a certain proportion of the game population is not "harvested" each year it will increase to a point where the environment cannot support it. Then the excess population will be culled through disease and through starvation. It is more humane, so the argument goes, for the animals to die a quick death from a bullet. Nature, we are told, has a much harsher answer to population control than does the hunter.

It is also argued that animals are a renewable resource. Thus the meat and skins obtained by population control would be lost if nature were left to run its course. I have a feeling that mankind would somehow survive with the protein from domestic animals, fish, and certain plants without ever killing another wild animal. And the carcasses of dead animals are not wasted by nature. Whatever in not consumed by carrion eventually returns to the soil.

There are obviously areas where animal populations and human activities come into direct conflict. The developer cares little about nesting sites for ducks, the rancher does not want coyotes killing his livestock, and the farmer does not want deer eating his corn. It is a matter of economic "necessity."

There will always be a conflict among humans, plants, and animals for space and for nourishment. We obviously cannot kill off every plant and animal that gets in our way. To do so would be to virtually destroy our planet. Every particle of matter in our world and in our universe fits into a niche. There is a scheme to things, a delicate balance that is constantly shifting back and forth. It is a balance which we, for the most part, can see only the dimmest outline of.

We have learned that altering one part of the ecology can have disastrous effects on another part, can lead to more harm than good. All the chemicals that we spray into our environment do more damage every day than all the hunters do in a year.

****

Now that I am nearly eighty years old I no longer care much for hunting, though an occasional meal of pheasant or grouse would still taste good. I prefer using a camera rather than a gun for shooting deer. I buy a fishing license every year but seldom make use of it. The great outdoors has become a walk in the woods, driving the back roads with binoculars and bird book in hand, or watching the birds at our backyard feeders. They are more sedate yet still pleasing activities.

THE SEARCH FOR MYSELF

In Alexandria I had most of what I had spent many years longing for – I had a family. I had a soulmate and two adorable children. Still, the rotating shift work kept me physically and emotionally drained. I slept badly and I had nightmares. Ten years after the fact I had not resolved my earlier failed marriage; it still haunted me. It had left an emotional scar that had never completely healed. I needed to make an effort to figure things out.

The failed marriage had knocked me on my rear. I had been shocked by the degree of mental illness my former wife had managed to keep hidden from me. I had been traumatized by the sense of betrayal. It had been like a death in the family. My sense of self had been diminished. I was confused. I had trouble figuring out what was real and what was imagined, what was safe and what was threatening.

But so what? Betrayal had happened to other people and they had gotten over it. They had moved on with their lives. Why couldn't I? Was I being too maudlin? Was I wallowing in self-pity? Little did I know that it would take years to work it out, to regain confidence in myself, to fully accept who I was, to learn about something that came to be called Post Traumatic Stress Disorder (PTSD).

I later learned that one of the indicators of trauma and of PTSD is when a person relives a situation over and over without being able to resolve it. That is what had happened to me. I could not get the failed marriage out of my mind.

I wanted to believe that the betrayal I felt was not that much outside the norm, that for some reason I could not understand I was making too much of it. At the same time I kept the details to myself. I did not want any of my family or friends to learn how I had been so easily duped. Looking back, that was not a good sign. I had not acknowledged the effect the trauma had had on me and, therefore, I had not given myself a chance to heal.

The reader has likely arrived at the same conclusion as I have, that most of us do not have the self-confidence, the courage, to totally be ourselves. We are social animals and we want to fit in, to get along. We often question and criticize ourselves more than others do. I had screwed up big time with that first marriage. Acceptance or forgiveness was not just a switch I could flip.

When we are young we naively assume that life will eventually explain itself. We have no way of knowing how difficult the struggle will be. In the grand order of the universe are we humans even significant enough to say we have a purpose? If our Earth were destroyed today wouldn't the universe go on without us? I wrote a poem about it. It is included in my book of poetry *A Moment Passed By*.

YOU ASK, OLD FRIEND

You ask, old friend
How life has fared for me
Well it has not turned out at all
The way I had hoped it would be
When I had first thought about it
From the vantage point of youth.

Then I had naively assumed
That after my hair had turned full gray
Having by then experienced
Most of what life could throw my way
Would come a certain calmness
A certain resigned acceptance.

Instead I find that in my latter years
I have become more fearful
Ever more post-traumatical
Worrying that what went wrong before
Could go wrong again
Could perhaps be even worse
And I the weaker to deal with it.

Now as my end grows ever nearer
And ghostly memories crowd upon me
A feeling of dread overpowers my soul
And I cry tearless tears, internal tears
Anticipating echoes from the past
Anticipating future heartache.

The poem came out a bit gloomier than I would have liked. Nonetheless, the reader can get the idea. For most people life can at times be one hell of a struggle.

I remembered a time when I was in the Air Force, stationed in Sacramento, California. I had become embittered and down on myself because of the failed marriage. The world had looked bleak and I had been in a dark mood. I had read Norman Vincent Peale's *The Power of Positive Thinking* and it had changed my attitude. A person could dwell on a negative past or he could purposely choose to push pessimistic thoughts aside and go on with life. It had not been a final answer but it had helped. And it had confirmed for me that a person can in fact do something to improve his or her emotional well-being.

It was April of 1977 when I received a long, hand-written letter from my buddy, Mike Smith. Mike and I had become fast friends when we were both living in Anchorage. I had spent many happy times with Mike, his wife Arlene, and their son, Steve. Mike and I had both been struggling, trying to figure out what the hell to do with our lives, trying to put them into some kind of order. I was failing as a real estate salesman; Mike was an unhappy government investigator. He had come to our real estate office looking for a house to buy. It did not take long for him to see through me. We had known each other for about a month when he told me – "You're no salesman. It's obvious you are not happy with your job." His insight may have been a reflection of his own frustration with working for the government.

I had moved to Nome to begin my career as an Air Traffic Control Specialist. Mike and I had kept in contact. Mike had flown to Nome to attend the wedding when Louise and I were married. I had deeply appreciated his being there. He had been a friend when I was in desperate need of a friend. Then Louise and I had moved to Minnesota and started a family. In the letter, Mike said he had grown ever more dissatisfied with government work and finally had quit. He had moved the family to the Kenai Peninsula, south of Anchorage, and built a home from scratch. His son had helped with the work and the two had bonded closely. They'd sold the house for a large profit and moved to the Spokane, Washington, area, where Mike's job had been eliminated. Now he was thinking of going back to work as a government investigator. He was tired of moving around. He wanted to settle down.

I have reread the letter just now, in March of 2020, forty-three years after it was written. It tugs at my heart. Mike tries to find a way to adequately express how lost he feels. Christ, how both Mike and I had been struggling! We had been wanderers in the game of life. We had been like brothers. Perhaps both of us eventually learned that we do not sail through life in a straight line, that we tack this way and that, depending on the winds of chance, depending on the winds of change. I lost track of Mike years ago.

I have written in the past how there have been long dead people who, now that I have some idea who I am, I would like to have a long conversation with, with their spirits or their ghosts or whatever. My grandfather on my mother's side is one. My Chesterfield mentor, Myron Nixon, is another. There are more – the Chesterfield doctor, the writer, Mark Twain, and others. It is possible that Mike Smith is still alive. Oh, if we could spend a couple of hours on the telephone! I could tell him about my life: Mike could tell me about his. But how many Mike Smiths are there in the world? How would Louise and I even begin to search for our Mike Smith?

I might be that both Mike and I, having now reached old age, feel kind of a sense of rejuvenation now that we have stopped trying so hard, now that we have finally accepted who we are and what we have done with our lives. Who knows? I am only speculating about Mike's thoughts on it.

At the time, though, in the 1970s, and in Alexandria, I had to wonder what was different about me. Why had I felt a strong need to explore the world when I was in the Air Force, while everyone around me had chosen to stay at home? Why did I now bury my face in academic books while those around me showed no interest? It did not make me feel better or superior to them, only different.

I had long been concerned that there were people and groups who felt that their voices should be the only ones heard, that the rest of us should remain silent. But, damn it, my voice or your voice or anybody's voice is just as valid as theirs. Great thinkers, religious and sectarian, have throughout human history defended our right to doubt, to question, to oppose, to do our own independent thinking. I certainly did not count myself among that elite group of thinkers but I too, like everyone else, should have a voice.

I felt that as much as many of us may be limited, as much as we still had to learn, we were valid human beings who had rights. Nobody, king or emperor, president or autocrat, priest or preacher, or any extremist of any sort had a right to dominate or to control us, to speak for us without our permission. There is no need for us to give ourselves over to any cult, any extremist group, or any divinity.

Nighttime at Flight Service, when the pilots had retired, and the radios and telephones were silent, was a good time to sit quietly with a cup of coffee and a cigarette, and to ponder. I felt like the odd man out. Who the hell was I anyway? I was the only one in Alexandria Flight Service with a college education. And I most certainly was the only agnostic. There was no one I could entirely relate to among the other Specialists, or to most of the people in the community. That did not make me better than them; it only made me different. Nobody was much interested in discussing history or psychology or photography or science, or the books I read. Social isolation, then, was a part of the problem. I knew that it had been shown to contribute to depression.

God, I must have reviewed my life a thousand times, trying to make some sense of it. I thought of my father and the influence he'd had on me. He'd had the maturity of a sixteen-year-old. He had not known how to navigate his way through life. He had depended on others to help him. I had inherited some of that from him. I had felt more comfortable being a follower rather than a leader. He had been unsophisticated and honest. He had not known how to use people, to cheat or to steal. I had loved him.

There had been other good people in my life. There had been Myron Nixon, a WWII veteran and my childhood mentor. There had been teachers who had encouraged my love of learning. I had never fully understood, and I did not even now, what they had seen in me. Was that what I was searching for now? It had not been something I had been able to internalize. I had not felt all that good about myself.

Part of it may have been that I had seemed more interested in learning than many of the other children, that I was somehow different. Maybe these people had seen some potential in me and they had wanted to encourage it. Some had told me that I was the "nicest boy." Maybe character had something to do with it. Perhaps honesty and decency and a sense of empathy had mattered to them. I wondered, though, whether they had been able to discern my lack of self-esteem, of self-confidence?

I thought back to 1968, when I had left the Air Force after almost six years of service. There was a feeling that I had not done enough. I had served only one temporary combat tour. I could have stayed on and served at least one more, maybe two. But I had grown so weary of living out of a suitcase, so tired of being alone. Now there was a feeling that I was not doing enough with my education, that I was not doing the best I could. WE ARE BORN, WE DO THE BEST WE CAN. But I could not find a suitable way out of it. I was not interested in FAA management. The years passed. I had a family to support. That part of it made things worthwhile.

I looked around me. An excessive form of religion was all the rage in Alexandria. Many people with emotional struggles had turned to it. They had apparently felt put down, ignored, out of the main stream. I did not trust this fanatical form of belief. It went too far. It brought back dark memories of what I had taken as a form of bullying and abuse by a fire-eating, Bible-thumping evangelistic preacher in my pre-teen years. I had sensed even then that there was something psychologically unhealthy about it. It had seemed to me that the Rev's goal was not to help people grow but only to *diminish* them, to keep them ignorant and suspicious, to reduce their potential. I suspected that many people who relied on religion had not resolved their problems at all, that for the most part the personal issues that had bothered them still lay submerged somewhere in their psyches, that religion had covered up their problems rather than solving them.

I remember the time that neighbors down the street on Ridgeway Drive invited Louise and me to their house to share an evening meal. It was so depressing. We walked into their living room and were smothered with religious clutter. It was almost claustrophobic. Religious pictures were hung on every wall. There was nary a watercolor or a landscape. There were no travel posters that spoke of distant lands, no hint at all of an outside world. Cards with biblical quotations were strewn everywhere. An open Bible was prominently displayed. The radio played Christian music.

It was suffocating. The air inside the house felt thin. I was tempted to ask them to open a window and let in some fresh air. It was as if everything in their lives had been diminished to that dark and chilly room. I looked longingly at the door, my mind racing for a way out. I could not in all decency simply abandon them without some sort of explanation. Could I fib my way out? Did that sudden chill indicate a return of the pneumonia I had recently recovered from? Could I suddenly come down with a blinding migraine headache? My ability to worm my way out of tough situations failed me when I needed it most.

There was nothing to distract them from their religious obsession. The room was focused entirely on these two people. It seemed as though it was more about *them* than anything else. It was as if they had sucked all the life out of Life itself. The couple looked at us with evaluative eyes, making sure we took note of everything. Surely we would be impressed with the depth of their devotion. Surely we could see how special they were. It seemed incredibly childish.

I do not recall that we were ever invited to their house again, nor did we invite them to ours. They likely sensed that we were not impressed by their childish nonsense. We could not wait to get away from them. We had nothing in common. What they had done had been too much. It had at the same time been both stifling and overwhelming. How could they even breathe in such a closed environment? The fact that it was perfectly acceptable behavior in Alexandria was more than distressing. It was downright depressing.

That experience and others convinced me there could be an addictive element to extreme religion, that once some people were hooked on it they could not get through a day without it. There was also an element of hypersuggestibility, similar to that of hypnosis. I wanted none of it. I did not want to trade one problem for another. Nor did I want to give up my individuality in order to join a group. My individuality was the only thing I had that truly defined me. I wanted answers, as I had since I was young, that made sense, that added up.

I had been a reader all my life. It had been a way to learn, to expand my horizons. History and biographies and psychology, science and creative writing, had given me some understanding of the workings of humanity, and thus of myself. Now I turned to reading again in an expanded search for myself. What was real and what was fictional? I sensed it was important to try to figure it out.

That is not to say that fact is the ideal and fiction has little value. Myth and drama – stories – help us explore our own feelings, help to heal the traumatic events in our lives. They can lead, as the ancient Greeks discovered, to *catharsis*, to the release of repressed emotions.

Books lead us into both the known and the unknown, into the past and the present and the future. Most important of all, so far as I was concerned, books can lead us out of ignorance and into diverse views – if we allow them. It bothered me when parents or patriots or religious people censored what students were allowed to read, who thought that some books and some ideas were dangerous, that they needed to be suppressed.

Eric Hoffer's *The True Believer* opened my eyes to the world of the extremist. Hoffer was a man of the people, a longshoreman, self-educated and an avid reader, a moral and social philosopher. He pictured True Believers as frustrated, discontented, and guilt-ridden people who tried to enhance their own lives and reshape the world in their own image by joining a mass movement, whether it was the Commies or the Nazis, fanatical Christians or Muslims. Hoffer said True Believers were almost interchangeable, that they could move from one group to another and respond to the same kind of indoctrination techniques that were common to all mass movements.

The goal of mass movements, or of any extremist group, is not merely to prevent us from being independent, but to insure that we will always be dependent, on the cause, or the leader, or the god. The ideal is for us to become so obsessed, so addicted, that we cannot get through a day without our beliefs.

Of particular importance to me was the idea that in the minds of extremists there were only two kinds of people – their friends and their enemies. We were either with them or we were against them. There was no middle ground. In fact, extremists portrayed those in the middle as weak and cowardly. Holy crap – I heard this same contention most recently from Rush Limbaugh, a right-wing radio commentator! What an idiot! There was little doubt in my mind that he and his listeners were too unschooled to realize that he was pushing the same argument that Adolf Hitler and Josef Stalin had used. Fanatics on both the far right and the far left have more in common with each other than they do with moderates in the center.

Moderation, then, the middle ground, became a key for me - independence from both sides. I knew that philosophers had long advocated it. The best way to deal with extremists, whether they are far to the right or far to the left, is to tell both sides to go to hell. There are hardly ever only two options in life. More often than not there is a third or a fourth choice.

I looked around at some of the religious extremists I was working with. It seemed like being around the Rev all over again. It was not only as if they wanted to sanctify their own lack of education, to make a virtue of it, but that they wanted to turn knowledge itself into an evil. It was as if a person could know more than what was good for him, that what he was exposed to should be censored by childish and ignorant True Believers.

Their self-understanding was limited. It had not been obtained through a study of human psychology or meditation or any kind of deep thought. It had been handed down to them by others who claimed to have done the thinking for them. There was nothing original about it, nothing that accounted for individual identities. It was all group thought.

For some reason, Hoffer's analysis of True Believers reminded me of Henry David Thoreau's observation that "Most men lead lives of quiet desperation and go to the grave with the song still in them." It also reminded me of a couple of lines from poet T.S. Eliot's *The Love Song of J. Alfred Prufrock* – "I should have been a pair of ragged claws – Scuttling across the floors of silent seas." The life of the extremist was filled with desperation. I did not want to be one of them

I had an undergraduate degree in psychology but that did not qualify me to counsel anyone, probably including myself. Still, psychology was a subject that had held my interest for many years. What made humans tick, and in particular, what made me tick? I was interested in the human story, not just now, but throughout history. Psychology was a field of study that had had its problems, that was constantly evolving. I stumbled across a book - *Psychotherapy: The Hazardous Cure*. The author was Dr. Dorothy Tennov. My paperback copy had been published in 1976. The topic immediately piqued my interest. I remembered one psychology course I had struggled with in college.

It was a class in early childhood development and it had leaned heavily on Sigmund Freud's theory of childhood development. Freud surmised that during the phallic stage of childhood development, ages 3-6, boys developed an Oedipal complex, that is, they wanted a sexual relationship with their mother and wanted to do away with their fathers. The theory was based on an old Greek drama, *Oedipus Rex*, written by Sophocles. I had read the play in high school. In the tragic drama, Oedipus unknowingly kills his father and marries his mother.

I remembered shaking my head in wonder at the absurdity of such a theory. It had seemed more the product of someone's creative mind than anything related to reality, more related to fiction than to observable fact. It seemed to me that Freud's conceptualization of an Oedipal complex was as mythical, as much of a story, as the original play by Sophocles. Those were the days, too, when mothers and women in general were blamed for many psychological problems their children suffered. I had differed with the professor and she had given me a low grade, a D.

Now Dr. Tennov's research appeared to confirm much of the suspicions I had had about Freud. She explained that there was no scientific evidence to prove the existence of an id, an ego, or a superego, the three fundamental structures of the human mind that Freud had posited. Further, she suggested that if ten psychoanalysts evaluated a patient, using Freud's methods, it was likely there would be ten different diagnoses. In other words, the diagnoses were subjective rather than objective.

Supporters of psychoanalysis claimed there was *"clinical"* evidence, which consisted mostly of "insights" and "intuitions," to support Freud's theories, but again, the so-called evidence was mostly open to subjective interpretation. Clinical evidence was simply not the same as *empirical* evidence. To me, psychoanalysis had all the earmarks of a belief system, a pseudo-religion, rather than a legitimate scientific discipline. One had to more or less "believe" in the theories, to accept them based on a few facts and a lot of faith.

I was especially interested in Dr. Tennov's assertion that probably more people had been harmed by psychoanalysis than had been helped. She also claimed that the cure rate for those dealing with anxiety and depression was the same for both treated and untreated patients. In other words, in these two areas, which I was mostly concerned with, things eventually worked themselves out on their own, without any professional intervention. It may be that in some cases the adage that "time heals everything" really works. Perhaps in my case it was a matter of maturing, of growing.

Freud had gotten things started - give him credit for that. Prior to him there had been talk of being possessed by demons or being influenced by the moon (thus the word "lunatic"). He has been lauded as one of the most influential and authoritative thinkers of the twentieth century. Today, in 2020, though, Freud has fallen completely out of favor among academics.

I doubt that many of the old clinical studies are much referred to in psychotherapy anymore. They are mostly looked upon as a hodgepodge of gobbledygook and *je ne sais quoi*. They are filled with words that seem intended more to impress us with the analyst's high intellectual level and faith in his interpretation than anything to do with reality. The more original and the more esoteric the insight, and the more creative the interpretation, the better. What the hell, in many ways psychotherapy may have been no more effective than reading tea leaves or burning sage. It was vague and it was subjective. Subjects needed to <u>believe</u> and psychoanalysts were to be looked upon as high priests. In college I had leaned towards physiological psychology. I had thought that exploring the electrochemical functions in the brain could be a way forward.

That was sixty years ago. Psychological counseling has come a long way since then. It is not perfect but it has changed for the better. Many state mental institutions have been shuttered or have released their patients into the general population. More patients are treated with medications and with cognitive behavioral therapy, which enables them to function more or less normally in society.

Okay, so psychotherapy did not look like the way to go. What other means were there to help me through this life crisis, to help me understand myself? I continued my search for something that made sense, that added up.

I cast about for other clues. *Passages: Predictable Crises of Adult Life* by author Gail Sheehy was published in 1976. The author theorized that there were stages all of us transition through on the journey into adulthood, that each life crisis offers an opportunity for inner change, for growth, that we are a different person after we have gone through a crisis than we were before, that we are better equipped to deal with future problems.

The book opened a new window of understanding for me. What I had gone through in my failed marriage was almost normal in life's journey. Everyone struggles - with relationships, with frustrations, with inner questions, with fear, with health. Life is not a matter of avoiding pain and betrayal – that is impossible. It is more a matter of living through them with courage and integrity, of reaching back inside to re-examine the self, of adapting to change, of accepting and adjusting to the new normal. Struggles could be used to grow rather than to diminish the sense of self. Sheehy's book was not a final answer for me but it was a help. It was another piece of the puzzle.

I needed to remember, too, that even though I often questioned my own emotional maturity, Louise, my soul-mate, was of the opinion that I was one of the more adult men she had ever met. Oh my, what did that say about the emotional level of other men? I assumed Louise was thinking mostly about my affection for her and our children, and my honesty. She knew she could trust me.

So there were authors I could study, people who had attempted to make sense of life. In my search for myself I turned next to philosophy, or, rather, to a particular ancient Greek stoic philosopher by the name of Epictetus. In his *Discourses* Epictetus argued for the development of self-control and fortitude as a means to overcome negative emotions. He posited that the only way to happiness was to stop worrying about things which are beyond the power of our will, that all external events are beyond our control, that we should accept calmly or dispassionately whatever happens.

Okay, I was pretty sure I was never going to be that calm or dispassionate. But it was something to think about. We humans do fuss about things beyond our control. We do invent "worse case scenarios" where we are afraid that disaster is going to happen. We do try to "carry the world on our shoulders." Recognizing this flaw in ourselves is a positive means of reducing stress. My copy of Epictetus is heavily highlighted and underlined.

Years later I had a casual conversation with a psychiatrist. I mentioned Epictetus and his stoicism. The psychiatrist felt that philosophy offered a long and difficult path to an understanding of a person's problems. I don't know – he could be correct. But in my opinion a truly effective self-exploration, whether it is based in psychology or philosophy, involves years of hard work rather than an epiphany which instantly explains everything. It is a process rather than the instant cure a religious conversion offers.

I have kept searching these past fifty years or so, searching for what makes sense, for what adds up. My reading has taken me across a wide landscape. Religion was another topic that, in Alexandria in particular, was a source of stress. I remember that in Alexandria I was much taken by the poetry of John Milton, especially his *Paradise Lost*, an epic poem that had been published in1667. It is a retelling of the Biblical story of the Garden of Eden and the Fall of Man. I was no student of poetry but for some reason the blank verse appealed to me. *Paradise Lost* also reinforced my conviction that the Garden of Eden was a Hebrew creation *story*, that it was fiction and not fact.

Winter traffic was slow at Alexandria flight Service. We filled in the slack times by visiting, or especially in my case, by reading. I had my head buried in a book one day. It was *The Evolution of Man and Society* by C. D. Darlington. The author was described as a scientific historian. He explored the development of humanity and societies as an interplay between genetics and environment, much like physical evolution in that it was a series of trial and errors, of successes and failures, of slow and agonizing progress. Holy crap! There was nobody in my social circles, other than me, who was even interested in such a subject. They would have turned up their noses or even laughed at me. But it was a part of my search for myself.

Here was the kind of environment I was working in. One of the other Specialists looked at the title, saw the word "evolution," and was visibly upset. "That doesn't go against the Bible, does it?" he asked me. How was a person to explain it? Evolution is a perfectly acceptable term. There was a gap that was likely impossible to bridge between his emotional response to the word and other's more pragmatic understanding of it.

This is probably as good a time as any to talk about the theory of evolution, whereby small variations in biology are passed from one generation to the next and enable a species to adapt to environmental changes. It is a scientific concept with mountains of data to support it. But as with anything in science, it is a work in progress. It is constantly being honed and fine-tuned as more evidence is collected. Evangelists hate it. They want it taken out of public education. They'd like to substitute in its place a Hebrew creation story involving a garden, a scantily clad man and woman, a tree, and a snake. It makes no sense.

I remember when I was a youngster looking up in awe at a sky filled with stars. I wondered what it all meant and how I fit into it. Religion did not have much to say about it, about the relationship between man and nature, between man and the cosmos. Religion seemed obsessed, instead, with sin and salvation. It was not until I was a junior in college that I learned anything about evolution. Then the relationship between man and the universe became clearer. The same kind of atoms that made up the stars were also in my body. The same atoms were also in rocks and eagles and plant life. There was a relationship, a brotherhood of sorts, among all living and non-living entities.

In that regard, Native American religious beliefs link man to nature and to the universe. The Incas and the Aztecs and the Cahokians aligned their cities to celestial bodies – to phases of the sun and the moon. The moon governed the seasons and the planting of crops. There was Father Sun and Mother Earth. It is somewhat ironic that their religious beliefs are held to be "primitive" while our Western religions are thought to be more "sophisticated." It may be that so-called primitive religions are more attuned to reality, to the extent that they focus more on nature than on sin. I have found nature to be incredibly soothing. It levels the emotions. It thrills the senses.

The Mind in the Making by James Harvey Robinson further cemented my own predilection for wanting things to make sense, to add up. Robinson valued the scientific method in the accumulation of knowledge. He had written his book in the early 1920s, when the social sciences had been in their infancy. He felt that science could be used as much to research the human mind as it had been in exploring physics and chemistry and mathematics. He thought that the Greek's use of skepticism had been significant in the development of human thought, *that scientific doubt, not faith, was the beginning of wisdom, that holy books and the "wisdom of the ages" produced a kind of mental brain fog.*

Hot dog! Here was a man who had something to teach me. I read on. Robinson held that in the West, in particular, there were people who believed there were classical religious and philosophical texts that had pronounced the last word on various subjects, that there was nothing new to be learned or discovered. That was certainly how many people in Alexandria felt about the Bible. They thought it foolish or even dangerous to question their holy book.

I had been exposed to the mechanics of the scientific method while doing psychological research in college. I had found it a reasonable and rational means for the accumulation of knowledge. It is a method of research whereby a problem is identified, relevant data is gathered, a hypothesis is formulated from the data, and the hypothesis is empirically tested. It involves careful observation, the application of rigorous skepticism to what is observed, and the repetition of results.

Of course the scientific method cannot be used to answer all our questions. It does not explain the purpose of our existence or the basis of morality or the meaning of beauty. But it does provide a better understanding of what is reality and what is fiction, and it does provide for the _accumulation of knowledge_, which in my opinion is one of mankind's greatest and most lasting accomplishments.

There are numerous examples where science has proven religious beliefs to be wrong. Evolution comes to mind, as does the belief that the sun revolves around the earth rather than the opposite. But are there proven instances where religion has proven science to be wrong? I can think of no examples.

I wanted to try to understand more about religion in general, and especially about the religious extremism which surrounded me. *The Seduction Of The Spirit, The Use and Misuse of People's Religion* was a 1973 book written by Harvey Cox, a professor at the Harvard Divinity School, a minister and a theologian. Cox viewed religion as a form of <u>story</u> <u>telling</u>, that humans have an innate need for a story to live by. Rites and myths and customs provide an individual or a group with a meaningful picture of the whole.

In Cox's opinion, all religions have three things in common. (1) They tell us where we came from and where we went wrong. (2) They tell us we can be saved or liberated. (3) They tell us what we need to do to be saved, how to get from our fallen condition to a state of grace.

I thought about it – so many different religions with so much in common, and yet they hated each other. How many people had suffered and died because one group worshipped one god and another group worshipped another god? Even people who worshipped the same god hated and killed each other. It didn't make sense. It didn't add up. Could it be that all humanity suffered from the same streak of madness? There was more that I needed to learn. In future years I would speculate as to whether there was a self-serving aspect to religions, a narcissistic element.

I was fascinated by a different kind of book. The title was - *Alive: The Story of the Andes Survivors*, by Piers Paul Read. In 1972, a Uruguayan rugby team, along with friends and families, had crashed high in the Andes Mountains. They were not rescued until seventy-two days later. Sixteen of the forty-five survived the sub-zero temperatures by resorting to cannibalism. They had used razor blades and broken glass to cut thin strips from the frozen cadavers

I had long assumed that cannibalism was the lowest form of brute savagery, that it was the ultimate taboo in just about every modern culture. I had read about the Donner Party, a group of pioneers who had become stranded in the Sierra Nevada Mountains in the winter of 1846-1847. An early blizzard had dropped several feet of snow. They'd roasted and consumed corpses in order to survive.

In respect to the Donner Party, I remember thinking that I would die before I would consent to eating the flesh of another human. *Alive* provided an entirely different perspective. Some of those who had survived the crash but had later perished had *given permission* to use their bodies for food. Some of the survivors had felt guilty. They were certain that the families of those who had perished would look down on them. That proved not to be the case at all. The families understood.

It was another book which opened my eyes to a different way of looking at things. What I had accepted as a universal taboo had not turned out to be the case at all. Cannibalism was acceptable in some extreme circumstances.

There was some light reading that I did just for the enjoyment of it, to take a break from the stress of daily life, even if only for an hour or two on an evening or a mid-watch when there was nothing else going on. It helped to pass the time. I pored through just about everything Louis L'Amour had written. The author was quite a storyteller of American frontier life, of gunslingers and rustlers and lawmen. His main characters, the Sackett family in particular, were rugged individualists who were willing to fight for what they thought was right. It was simple and easy reading. It was relaxing and therapeutic.

At times there was a bit more depth to L'Amour's writing. He did pen some historical fiction. I no longer remember the title or when I read it, it may have been years later, but I recall one paperback L'Amour wrote about Marco Polo's travels to China. The book seemed well-researched. I felt as though I knew a lot more about Marco Polo after I finished reading the book than I had before. History was one of my favorite topics anyway.

For some reason I have had in my mind that I did not really begin writing until I was in my early sixties. It was then that I ran across a copy of Walt Whitman's *Leaves of Grass* and was motivated to try my hand at poetry. I was in my seventies before I set out to leave an autobiographical record for my grandchildren.

But reality has proven otherwise. Among the collection of volumes I have saved are five 8 1/2 X 11 notebooks filled with my scribblings. I began the first one in 1973 and marked it Volume I. It is 160 pages of mostly my thoughts laced with a few excerpts from my reading. Volume II covers the years from 1983 to 1991 and is another 130 pages long. I talk a lot about religion and personal development and the state of our society.

The very first entry, in 1973, was as follows:

"The ideal is independence. Both independence and dependence create problems. When we are independent we are responsible for our own security. We risk losing what we have. Being dependent on someone else offers some security, but it is often a hazardous security at best. And being dependent necessarily means we lose our independence, our freedom of action and thought, and, often, our self-identity. We have to mold ourselves to a particular subservient role."

The final entry in July of 1991 read like this:

"When Americans were polled on the sleaziest jobs, drug dealer was rated No.1. TV evangelist was No. 3. Prostitute was 4. Car salesman was 8. Wall Street executive was 12. Motion picture star was 18. Prison guard was 20,"

Then, in about 1979, I began a second series of notebooks. These developed into three volumes and a total of about 900 pages of handwritten notes. They are titled "Things I Have Read: Books, Articles, and Clippings." Excerpts from the readings are interlaced with personal comments.

I recalled a story I had heard from one of my college classmates. It was about the American author James Jones, whom my classmate had played tennis with. Jones's mentor had encouraged him to improve his own writing style by transcribing the works of famous authors. Now I spent many enjoyable hours when I was alone on evening or mid-watches copying passages from books and newspapers and magazines I was reading. They were a part of the search for myself.

I began with a short excerpt from "Buddenbrooks," written by Thomas Mann, one of my favorite authors. Oh, I could only fantasize about being as accomplished a writer as Mann was. The words flow. The thought are kernels of insights and of wisdom. Some of the other readings in Volume I included *Lady Chatterly's Lover*, *The Psychology of Speaking In Tongues*, "Scientists question mind-body separation," and *Vietnam*. Volume II included, among others, *The Strange Tactics of Extremism*, a newspaper article on self-help hypnosis, *Custer Died for Your Sins*, *The Good War* by Studs Terkel, and *Harvest Poems* by Carl Sandburg. *The Spanish Inquisition* filled the last fifty pages of Volume II and spilled into Volume III. The final forty pages of Volume III were excerpts from *How I found Freedom in an Unfree World*, where Harry Browne talks about how to avoid Identity Traps that rob us of our individuality.

There were themes that ran through all the readings and all the personal comments – the use of reason to figure things out, the dangers involved in extremism, the struggle to maintain our individuality.

I had written in Volume I of *We Are Born* about the legend of Cherokee blood in our family. I had also written about finding arrowheads and pieces of pottery when I was growing up in Illinois. That background and the continued exposure to Native American history and customs in Illinois and the Dakotas had sparked an interest in further research about my possible Native American heritage. I have about 200 pages, in two notebooks, of information I gathered. I began the informal research in about 1983 and it has continued off and on to this day, 2020. I will talk more about it in my final volume.

Oh my, the search for myself eventually took decades. I was in my sixties before things finally came together. Even so, it is unlikely that I will ever have the total answer, that maybe 75% is the most I can hope for. That is okay, though, that is the story of humanity. But I can testify that it is a fine feeling, a contented feeling, after all the years of searching, to finally accept, and to even endorse oneself.

Throughout it all I have managed to hold on to my basic sense of values and to my individuality. The doubt that had sometimes plagued me had more to do with my failure to read reality correctly than with anything else. I have come to the conclusion that there is likely not a hidden sacred meaning to life, that, like grains of sand on a wide beach, we are a very tiny and mostly unimportant part of a vast universe, that when we die our atoms return to the earth and nothing more, that it is unlikely there is such a thing as an afterlife, that WE ARE BORN, WE DO THE BEST WE CAN, THEN WE PASS ON.

PARADISE MISSING

John Milton, in his *Paradise Lost*, may have had his own poetic thoughts on religion but he was a Believer. There were other Believers who condemned him for his interpretation of the Fall of Man. I had my own thoughts and I was a non-believer. I placed my faith in reason, in trying to make things "add up." There was little doubt that the many True Believers in Alexandria would have condemned me. It did not make for a pleasant social environment for either of us but I was not about to surrender my soul just to please them or anybody else.

I have long worried that friends and family may view my thoughts on religion as arrogant and uncaring, perhaps even addled. I would not be surprised if they shake their heads in pity. Nevertheless, I feel a need to say my piece. I have promised my grandchildren and their grandchildren to be open and honest about myself, so that they can have an idea of who I am when they look at a picture of me.

I want to say this before we get too involved. If someone were to approach me and give me a choice between the following two options: (1) Let us get rid of religion and we will allow you to live, or (2) Keep religion and we will have to kill you - my choice would be to die. Freedom of religion is too precious to give up. Of course freedom of religion must include the right to worship any god or no god at all. And freedom of religion does not mean the right to harass or to persecute anyone. There is no doubt in my mind that people can live honorable, decent, meaningful, and moral lives with or without religion, that they can contribute to humanity.

It is obvious that I have a problem with much of religion, as I do with much of politics. They are too divisive and they have a long history of self-serving greed and hypocrisy and violence. I wonder how any billions of lives could have been spared, how much suffering could have been avoided, if religion and politics had never been a part of human history. Our Earth is soaked with the blood of victims and their bones lay scattered everywhere. But does that mean I have a problem with all Believers? Of course not. There are good people almost everywhere. At the core of all things human, it is the goodness that counts, not the beliefs.

There are religious people who are tolerant enough to accept non-believers and people of other faiths. Then there are those followers who view all others outside their own beliefs as infidels, as threats. It is these people with whom I have a problem. They are out to save not only themselves but the entire world. They make things miserable by continuously stirring the pot, by harassing the rest of us. If we could, we'd prefer not even to associate with them.

There are too many people out there who do not seem to understand that it is the person who counts, not their beliefs. If a person is a bigoted and ignorant jackass before he finds religion or joins a political cause, the chances are that he will remain a bigoted and ignorant jackass thereafter. His beliefs do not change a thing. Too many people use their beliefs to avoid dealing realistically with their personal problems. Different people approach religion from widely different perspectives, some with confidence in themselves, some with bruised egos, and some with serious emotional problems.

I have said that I am an agnostic. Perhaps I should try to explain what agnosticism means to me. If we look back in history we can see that humanity at one time or another has worshipped hundreds, if not thousands, of gods and goddesses. Why? What was their origin? It is obvious that the role of divinities was to explain the unknowable. Where did we come from? What is our purpose in life? What happens when we die? Why do people act the way they do? Why do floods destroy our crops? What causes a solar eclipse? When primitive men did not have answers they invented ones out of their rich imaginations, and they invented the gods to go along with them.

Today most of the old gods are long since dead. Science has killed off many of them. Much of the workings of the universe and of human behavior are no longer such a mystery, though there obviously is still much to learn. Who knows the limit of our universe? Our long ago ancestors believed heaven was located just above a layer of stars which topped the earth like icing on a cake. Where is heaven located today, when we know that the stars are scattered over millions of light years of space?

I have spent years thinking about religion, from high school on. I have tried to fathom it, to make sense of it. For me, there are still legitimate questions for which we have no answers. My mind is not as settled as are the minds of Believers. I make a distinction, too, between *knowing* and *believing*. Knowing is being able to observe, to measure, to touch, to deduce unequivocally through logic, to accept through *a priori* knowledge. Believing is a *feeling* of knowing something. Thus a Believer may say that he knows a god exits when what he is saying in reality is that he has a strong belief. There is of course nothing wrong with that. It is just a matter of definition. And as an agnostic I can say that I believe there is no way yet for humanity to be able to prove or disprove the existence of a divinity or divinities. To me that is reality. It makes sense. It adds up.

To extremists, though, beliefs have a tendency to become more powerful than facts. Facts are dry and uninspiring; beliefs are emotionally compelling.

I do not lay claim to superiority. I do not *feel* superior. That is not it at all. What I am talking about is the conviction of myself and others that reason rather than *blind belief* is the way to go, that questions and doubts lead to progress, that the accumulation of knowledge is one of mankind's most lasting and meaningful achievements.

The absolute truths that extremists cling to are so much easier, so much less work, so much simpler, than the difficult and messy task of sorting through mountains of evidence to find a common thread. It is so much more difficult to doubt and to ask questions, to be always skeptical about what we know. Someone has already done the thinking for Believers so that they do not need to make the effort. Someone or some holy book already has the answers. In my case, though, I am too stubborn and too much of an individualist to allow someone to do my thinking for me. That is my responsibility and my responsibility alone. To my mind our sense of "truth," of reality, is constantly evolving as we accumulate ever more knowledge.

I want to make another point. I have my own way of thinking and others have theirs. What I am trying to do is to make some sense of my own life. It is the responsibility of others to figure out things on their own.

The True Believers who Hoffer talks about in his book scare the hell out of me. They seem a kind of socially tolerated insanity. Their ultimate goal is to take over, to seize power, to control the rest of us, to force themselves and their extremist beliefs on us. They want to rule the government and the courts, the schools and the news media. I am ever mindful that when the Nazis took over, and when Communist tanks rolled into Eastern Europe, the first place they headed for were the radio stations and the newspaper offices. They had to control the news.

It is of course utterly biased to think that all extremists are alike, but it seems to me that too many of them are utterly lacking in a broad-based education. They seem to have no background or even a basic interest in history or philosophy, in physics or chemistry, the social sciences or classic literature, or anything else beyond their limited field of experience. It is as if they do not have the mental capacity to entertain large ideas or anything the least bit abstract. They seem terrified of questioning or doubting accepted beliefs. They are akin to the self-serving and self-glorifying provincials that Sinclair Lewis found in Sauk Centre. What is it, then, that they think entitles them to a controlling voice in human affairs? A voice, yes, most certainly - but that they should be in charge, no way. They think it is their beliefs and their beliefs alone that qualify them, that elevates them above the rest of us.

As to the question of True Believers being "special," being among the "chosen few," well, let's think about that. Everyone wants to feel good about themselves. It is a natural impulse. But is there a need to feel "special," to be somehow better or superior to others? In my mind I am better than some; not as good as others. There may be something different or unique about me but that is true of everyone. WE ARE BORN, WE DO THE BEST WE CAN, THEN WE PASS ON – how does that make any of us more special than someone else? It only makes us human.

It was not the lack of education *per se* that bothered me the most. Hell, I was no genius myself. I was smarter than some people but dumber than others. That was not what mattered – it was the *willful ignorance*, the self-serving ignorance that got to me. It was their belief that they had *common sense*, and that somehow made them better, more qualified, than all the doctors and professors, all the school teachers and psychologists, all the lawyers and scientists. What the hell did those arrogant intellectuals really know anyway? They, even with all their learning, knew no more than any of us. It reminded me of the Rev's rantings when I was young. He had made himself special in his own eyes by devaluing anything intellectual.

There are people out there, many people, who are so much smarter, so much more talented than I could ever hope to be. Thank goodness for it! I love it! It means that mankind's accumulation of knowledge will continue. It means hope and optimism. For good people knowledge is a wonderful thing. For True Believers it is something sinful and dangerous.

Believers may not understand much about a given subject but, by god, to their way of thinking that does not disqualify them from having an opinion about it, uninformed as it may be. Alcoholism, atomic energy, archeology, whatever the subject, they feel compelled to say something. Four simple words – "I do not know" – are simply foreign to them, much less needing to say – "I am not qualified enough to have an opinion." It is as if they are <u>expected</u> to have an opinion, that their beliefs automatically qualify them, that it does not matter what they say so long as they say something.

But on the other side of it, they become sullen if they are asked to provide evidence to support their opinions. They want nothing to do with facts. Perhaps that explains it. Perhaps we are not talking about opinions so much as we are talking about self-serving beliefs.

Many people think that the value of education is not so much in learning what we do know as it is in learning what we do <u>not</u> know. My god, there's so much out there, so many fields of study, so much accumulated knowledge. Yet surely what mankind has learned thus far is little more than the tip of the iceberg.

The ultimate appeal of an extremist belief system had struck home with full force a few years earlier. It was 1965 and I was in the Air Force, stationed on Cape Cod, Massachusetts. I was at a luncheon with a group of middle-aged German immigrants. They had lived in Germany during WWII. I asked them, out of curiosity, what they thought about Adolf Hitler. I expected they would strongly condemn him. I was stunned when the answer was: "Oh he was not so bad, people just did not understand him." Holy crap! If Hitler was not an evil monster then how could we ever define evil? He had caused the death of millions of innocent people, all in an effort to prove how great he and the German people were. The "Master Race" - my ass. How could otherwise sane and civilized people delude themselves into believing such extravagant nonsense? How could they become such barbarians, such animals, such sub-humans? It was frightening.

One of the True Believers, the Chosen Few, who worked at Alexandria Flight Service bragged about being invited by the public high school coach to give the athletes a talk on the evils of homosexuality. Really? What the hell did he know about the complex psychological problems associated with being homosexual? He barely had a high school education himself. He was not qualified to counsel anyone on the subject. To him counseling meant talking about his brand of religion and what it meant to be a sinner. I was concerned that if one or more of the boys were struggling with their sexual identity our True Believer would only have encouraged them to feel like crap about themselves instead of offering help. How many people throughout history have committed suicide as a result of being harassed and persecuted by extremists, by being told that they are evil? It was disgusting that such a poorly qualified person would be invited into our public education system to voice his bigoted and ignorant opinions.

I looked more closely at this Believer. He seemed reluctant to reveal much about himself. It was as if he wanted to keep his inner problems a secret, though he inferred on occasion that he had been raised in a dysfunctional family. I had the strong feeling that he was using religion to cover up some unresolved psychological issues. Religion had not solved his problems, it had only buried them somewhere deeper in his psyche. It had left him somehow incomplete as an individual. Religion can help good people get through difficult times. So can psychology. So can meditation. So can education.

Our True Believer had no business inserting himself into other people's lives. Did he ever consider the possibility that he could be harming them? Of course not. It is unlikely he ever thought of it. It was all about him and the possibility of heaping praise and glory upon himself.

There was another time when this Believer and a cohort confronted me. They knew that I had a college education and they knew that my wife was a teacher. "Those who can – do. Those who cannot – teach," they recited in unison as a way of downgrading Louise and me, of downgrading education in general, and exalting themselves.

It was as if it was they, the doers, who should be getting the attention and the praise, and not those who were better educated. It was childishly self-serving. I shook my head in disbelief. How petty, how small, can some people be? It is said that great minds think alike. What is not as often mentioned is that so do simple minds.

I knew these two. They barely had a high school education. They knew nothing about science or history or art, nothing about education itself. They were barely one step beyond illiteracy. And yet in some insane and odd way they felt they were qualified to tell the rest of us how to live our lives, to define what was good and what was evil. In some self-serving way they felt they were superior to those with an education.

Had they turned against a broad-based education because they had been poor students themselves? If they had been lost in a history or a math class were they compensating for it now by claiming history and math were not important, indeed, that education itself was not important? I suspected it may have been the cause.

I don't know, in the search for myself I seemed to be looking for my *place* in society, in history, in the world, in the universe. Where did I belong? What was I even qualified for? Zealots seemed not to be plagued with such a problem. They joined a cause or a church or a political party and their *place* was dictated for them. There was no need for them to figure it out on their own.

We were surrounded by True believers in Alexandria. They appeared to look at Louise and me with suspicious eyes. We were strangers, maybe with dangerous ideas. I was agnostic and she was a Catholic, a worshipper of that "dirty old Pope," as one woman phrased it. We were not one of them. We had not lived in Alexandria all our lives.

Moral decay was one of the cornerstones of their concerns. They felt that humanity in general was going to hell. That belief had been a cornerstone of their brand of religion for centuries. But I soon discovered that their own definition of morality was pretty damned flexible, that it could be twisted and turned so as to benefit themselves. There was the contractor who had dug the basement for our new house, who had quoted Bible verses then cheated on his taxes. One of my fellow Flight Service Specialists was especially devout. But it did not bother his conscience in the least to use our government copying machine and our government ink and paper to crank out hundreds of pamphlets for his poverty-stricken church when no one was looking. He made no attempt to pay. It was out-and-out stealing.

This was the same specialist I overheard conversing with his pastor. They were talking about the evils of drinking and how religious conversion was a cure-all. The pastor seemed to look around himself with hateful and suspicious eyes, searching for evil. Then he made a statement that floored me. He said that when wine was mentioned in the Bible they were not really talking about wine, they were talking about grape juice. What! It was one of the dumbest things I had ever heard. This was a man who thought he could tell the rest of us how to live, who could counsel and pass judgement on us, who could bless us? How could that be? Was the universe that much out of kilter? I could only shake my head in disbelief.

Believers seemed quick to forgive sin when the sinner was one of their own. Remember Jimmy Swaggart? He was a TV evangelist who twice was picked up in the company of a prostitute. Oh my, I remember how the tears flowed when he publicly announced his transgressions. He sobbed and blubbered – "Oh, Lord, how I have sinned!" His followers felt sorry for him. I heard one woman who pronounced that Swaggart was wrestling with *deep sin*, as opposed to ordinary sin. Really? Where had she gotten such a crazy idea? Surely someone must have invented the concept. Apparently Swaggart is still in business today, in 2020, but in a much diminished role.

Then there were Jim and Tammy Bakker, two other TV evangelists and their PTL Club (Praise The Lord – how childish and corny). The Bakkers were buffoons and charlatans. For god's sake they raked in so much money that even their dog's house was air conditioned! Jim was convicted of fraud and sent to prison.

I came to realize over the years that there was a *narcissistic* element, an excessive self-glorification, to fanatics. Their vanity and self-indulgence are never-ending. They will do almost anything to feel good about themselves, to cover up their frustration and their low self-esteem. They blame the world, not themselves, for their failures. They can see the world only through their own eyes or the filter of their beliefs, or their holy cause, which form a barrier between themselves and reality. They are unable to empathize with the rest of us and they cannot tolerate criticism. Their wants, their desires, their needs come first.

It seems that one answer to severe criticism or emotional abuse when one is young is to compensate for it by becoming narcissistic, to change ones feelings of self-worth from one of inferiority to one of superiority, and to strongly resist any form of criticism. Narcissists have a "savior" complex. They believe they know more than the rest of us. They think they know how to save us.

Extremists and nationalists like to think of themselves as being at the center, as being the best. The Germans and the Japanese held themselves to be a superior race. Look at where it got them. Commies and capitalists believe their economic systems are superior to all others. True Believers and evangelists believe the world revolves around them and their divinity. It is more than absurd; it is dangerous and it is insane. It threatens the rest of us.

Most extremists will not admit to being extreme. They think that what they are doing is important, that they have access to special inside information the rest of us are unaware of. The more absurd an idea is the more it becomes a test of their "faith." Thus we have read in history books how some believers flagellated themselves into a bloody mess in an attempt to rid themselves of doubt. As far as U.S. politics are concerned, today, in 2020, there is something called the "deep state," a secret government that runs everything within the legitimately elected government, though no one can cite specific examples. But True Believers feel they are somehow being persecuted as a result.

Let's face it, extremists, be they political or religious, deal in threats and fear mongering and wildly exaggerated claims. Their currency of choice is hatred and bigotry and distrust. Intolerance becomes a virtue. There is always the belief that some ideas are dangerous and need to be suppressed. History books and education must be cleansed of them. Fanatics must identify an enemy they are struggling against. After all, how can a person be a hero if he does not have an enemy to conquer? It does not matter much whether the enemy is real or imagined, though fictional enemies are easier to deal with. They provide a foil for fictional victories.

It may be that True Believers feel that somehow they deserve a *bigger* life, one more meaningful. Perhaps they want the world to give them more attention.

There are desperate people in the world, impatient to put some meaning into their otherwise unfulfilled lives, so anxious for recognition that they will do almost anything. I remember the time when there was a traffic accident at a major intersection. The police had not yet arrived. The traffic was snarled. I watched as a man jumped into action and began directing traffic. It quickly became obvious he had no idea what the hell he was doing. The traffic jam got even worse. Irate drivers were yelling and blasting their horns. But the man had a big smile on his face. "Look at me," he seemed to be saying, "I'm a hero." It was absurd. He was attempting to play a role for which he was not qualified. All he accomplished was to make a fool and a failure of himself.

Our True Believer in Alexandria made other wild and unconfirmed assertions. He claimed that when Darwin was on his deathbed he had recanted his theory of evolution. It was a rumor that had been circulated for many years by church groups but proven false by reliable sources. To my mind it was another example of how True Believers can forego morality and spin untruths when it is to their benefit.

It is apparent that True Believers are searching for a meaning in life, just as most of us are. "We Are Born, We Do the Best We Can, Then We Pass On" is a philosophy that is not good enough for them. It does not make them special, only human. It does not make them feel superior to the rest of mankind.

There was something wrong with all of it. There was more to life than being self-serving. I am who I am. I am not the best and not the worst, not the brightest and not the dumbest. I am no more special than anyone else and they are no more special than me. What happens to me is my personal responsibility, not somebody else's. And I sure as hell am not one of the "chosen few." What a horrible, self-serving, narcissistic idea! It has led to all kinds of evil. Yet it seems at the core of extremist belief systems.

There is no perfect dogma, no perfect ideology, no perfect political system, no perfect religion, no perfect economic theory, no perfect group, no perfect person. There never has been and there never will be. There are no chosen few – we are all in this together.

There is a joy in doubt, in not knowing. Life would be extraordinarily dull if we had all the answers. We do not know what new thing we will learn tomorrow, let alone a year or a century into the future. It could change everything we think about science or religion or philosophy. It could change what we know about the universe itself, or what we know about ourselves. There is always more to learn. Thank goodness for that.

EPILOGUE

When Louise and I look back at the thirteen years we lived in Alexandria we both agree on one thing – we never felt as though we fit it. Those who had lived in Alexandria all their lives praised it as being a friendly community. Maybe it was for them. But if Louise and I met somebody new they often looked at us with suspicious eyes. Who are you? What church do you go to? Louise said that even after thirteen years none of the cashiers in the grocery store seemed to recognize her. I compared this to the time when I stopped a man on a street in downtown Montgomery, Alabama, to ask him for directions. We ended up talking for an hour. He wanted to know all about me. He was interested. I would expect a similar reception in Minneapolis or Milwaukee or any large city. City dwellers seem more open minded, more tolerant of diversity, less provincial than those who live in small, rural towns.

In the city, one's life hinges around meeting and getting along with strangers, both in business and in personal dealings. Small town life seems more to revolve around people known since elementary school and greeted in church every Sunday morning.

When we moved away from Alexandria I did not exchange Christmas cards with anyone other than a couple of neighbors, and with Deloris Blashack, the lady who had owned the forty acres of woods. Louise corresponded with two or three of the teachers she had worked with.

It was Easter break in the spring of 1984 when we set out on another family adventure. We booked a flight from Minneapolis to Disney World in Orlando, Florida. It proved to be our most enjoyable trip ever. Oh my, was I ever impressed when the huge Boeing 747 leaped off the runway at Minneapolis. There must have been 350 passengers. The pilot pointed the nose in about a forty-five-degree climb and we seemed to have power to spare. It took only a few minutes to climb to 37,000 feet. I compared that to the old Constellations I had navigated while I was in the Air Force twenty years earlier. We had staggered into the air with a crew of twenty. It had sometimes taken us half an hour to climb to 15,000 feet.

We landed in sunshine and spent a week exploring the area. Disney World was a unique experience, especially for Jenifer and Chris. Did I ever get sunburned! I think the rides terrified me more than they did the children. We drove to Tampa and spent a few hours at the beach. Then we visited Cypress Gardens. We watched a water ski show and viewed the many unique and colorful plants and animals.

We spent one of our last days touring the Kennedy space Center at Cape Canaveral. I was surprised to find alligators roaming the grounds. Jenifer was fascinated by the nearby ocean. She loved the sight and the sound and the smell.

The Space Center gave me a sinking feeling that I was not doing the best I could with my life, with my education. Sending men to the moon and exploring space was a mission far beyond and far more meaningful than being a lowly Flight Service Specialist. Holy crap! - I would have swept the floors and emptied the waste cans just to be a part of something like that. My own career seemed puny in comparison.

I remember the day we departed Orlando. The temperature was in the low seventies. Flowers were blooming. The children took one last dip in the motel's swimming pool. When we landed in Minneapolis we had to wade through snow to get to our car. Then we drove 140 miles of slippery highways to get back to Alexandria. Florida had given us a new look at the world. We'd had enough of cold weather. It was time to think about moving farther south.

Over the years I had sometimes thought about transferring to a larger Flight Service facility. It would have meant a higher pay grade and more money. Then I would remember the horrible work environment the Specialists at Anchorage Flight Service had bitterly complained about. They had said that the station Chief was little more than a dictator. Management was all over the Specialists, monitoring their every move. I did not think I would function well in that kind of micromanaged work environment. Still, the idea of moving had remained in the back of my mind. Perhaps other large facilities did not have as poor a reputation as Anchorage.

I had been assigned to Minneapolis Flight Service several times for short periods of training. There were management problems there as well. I crossed it off my list of possibilities.

The St. Louis Flight Service Station had the advantage of being near my home town of Wood River, Illinois. It would also of course be farther south and in a warmer climate than Minnesota. When I was home on vacation I hopped in the car and drove over to visit them. I walked through the door and it seemed as if I could almost cut the tension with a knife. A short tour of the facility confirmed my suspicions. Specialists had someone looking over their shoulders at all times. The work environment was suffocating.

I telephoned St. Louis Flight Service as my family was preparing for the long drive back to Minnesota. I wanted to get an up-to-date briefing on what the weather was like. I pretended to be a pilot. The Specialist on the other end of the line was crabby and gave a very poor briefing. He spent part of the time talking about expected bad weather in Ohio, which was nowhere near my route. I surmised that he had a supervisor looking over his shoulder and was forced to brief by the book rather than being professional. He was likely embarrassed to be talking about weather in Ohio when it so obviously was not pertinent.

In this regard one would assume that a larger facility would be more professional than a smaller one, that they would have a wider variety of pilots to deal with. But it was not uncommon for Alexandria Flight Service to receive long-distance telephone calls from pilots flying from St. Louis or Kansas City or Omaha to Alexandria. These were mostly people who had summer homes in our area. They found that they could receive a better, more professional, less bullshit briefing from us than from their larger home stations. The difference was that in Alexandria we were not micromanaged. We received less pay but were given more of an opportunity to be the professionals we wanted to be.

Then, beginning in the late 1970s and early 1980s, the Federal Aviation Administration (FAA) formulated a plan to modernize the Flight Service system. Much of our equipment was old and outdated. We were still using teletype machines rather than computers. The FAA's plan was roughly to consolidate the three or four existing Flight Service Stations in each state into one large Automated Flight Service Station (AFSS), using the latest in computer technology.

To make the plan more economically appealing to the taxpayers, communities in each state were invited to bid on the new facilities. The communities were encouraged to offer monetary and other incentives, such as paying to construct the new facilities, in exchange for sixty or seventy higher paying jobs. The process turned out to be less than perfect.

In Minnesota, Fergus Falls and Brainerd and a couple of other communities spent a fair amount of time, money, and effort to put together a nice package. But the little community of Princeton was selected. They had offered the most financial incentives. Little did the FAA know, though many of us at the lower level suspected it, but the main financial backer for Princeton was a pilot and an assumed drug dealer by the name of Casey. We had met Casey on several occasions in the Flight Service at Alexandria. He was young and handsome and very personable. His girlfriend was taking flying lessons from Harold Chandler. Whether Casey was able to fulfill all the promises he made to the FAA before the Feds hauled him off to prison is something I do not know. But I suspect he fell far short. I suspect the FAA and the taxpayers got screwed.

In late July of 1984, Louise and Jenifer and I drove to Green Bay, Wisconsin. Our son, Chris, was a pitcher on his Little League baseball team and his coach needed him to remain behind in Alexandria. I had been selected to work for a week during the annual Experimental Aircraft Association (EAA) air show held at Oshkosh. The airshow routinely drew between 600,000 and 800,000 spectators. Pilots arrived from all fifty states and several foreign countries. Antique and home-built little bug smashers were everywhere. Huge military airplanes flew in. Aircraft and equipment manufacturers had their latest products on display. There was a magnificent air show each afternoon of the week-long event.

Green Bay Flight Service was the hub station for the fly in. Business was balls to the wall for most of the seven days. Green Bay recruited about a dozen specialists from nearby Flight Services to help them through the busy week.

I had applied for one of the temporary positions and had been selected. I had an ulterior motive in mind. Green Bay had been selected as the site for the new AFSS that would cover all of Wisconsin and the Upper Peninsula of Michigan. The week in Green Bay would give Louise and me an excellent opportunity to check things out, to decide if Green Bay would be a good place for the two of us to live and to raise our children.

I worked the airshow and we returned home to Alexandria. The following month, August of 1984, Green Bay Flight

Service advertised an opening for a Specialist. I bid on the job and got it. I was scheduled to report for duty at the end of October. We would be leaving Alexandria for a new adventure in Green Bay.

There were still a couple of projects I needed to take care of before we had our house on Ridgeway Drive ready to sell. I had not gotten around to finishing the master bathroom. Now I concluded that. And the driveway was still gravel rather than being paved. I hired a contractor to take care of it.

We put the house on the market by the first part of September. It did not give us much of a window before we would have to move in late October. I had made a rough appraisal on my own. I figured we had about $43,000 in construction expenses plus about an equal amount in sweat equity. $89,900 seemed like a reasonable place to start. We could negotiate down from there if we found a willing buyer. I would have accepted an offer of $85,000. I placed an ad in the local newspaper.

We soon discovered there was a glut of houses waiting to be sold. If I remember correctly there were about 300 in our little town of 7,000. I don't recall that we received even a single response to our newspaper ad. Finally, with only a few days remaining before we moved, we in desperation rented the house to a young preacher and his wife. They had been recommended by friends. No lease was signed. The agreement was that if the house was sold the renters would have to move.

There was a backup plan. The FAA had agreed to buy the house if we were forced to move and unable to sell it on our own. That is what we finally had to do. The property was appraised for $77,500. The appraiser felt it had not sold because it was overpriced and there was an oversupply. It was about $7,000 or $8,000 less than what we had hoped for but we had no choice but to accept the deal and move on. We wanted to build another house in Green Bay.

As an afterword, in the summer of 1993 Louise and I stopped by the Alexandria airport. We wanted to see how things had changed. The old Flight Service building where I had spent many hours pacing the floor in worry over bad weather and overdue aircraft, and many sleepless nights working mid-watches, had been torn down and hauled away. Its duties had been transferred to the Princeton AFSS. The now empty space left a hollow feeling in the pit of my stomach. It felt as though thirteen years of memories, of my life, had been hauled off to the dump.

A new and more modern Airport Operations building had been erected next door. One of our old Flight Service Specialists had a part-time job there. It was Joe, who I had talked about on pages 177-178. Now he was doing nothing more than taking weather observations. After the preliminary greetings were over we started in, telling one story after another – remember the time when this had happened and the time when so-and-so had done that? I reminded Joe about the Tweet Tweet story when Chris and I had been playing hockey. Once again he roared with laughter. The years slipped by and the memories seemed as though they had taken place only yesterday.

There was still a single FAA electronic technician stationed at Alexandria. When I had first arrived, twenty-two years earlier, there had been three. Now the navigational aids were monitored remotely. There was little need for someone to actually spend time at the sites. The sole survivor was Bill, the same man who had helped wire our new home when it was under construction. I asked Bill what he did now that there was little need for an electronics technician. "I mostly hide," he responded with a chuckle. He explained that he was near retirement age, that he did not want to move, and that he did not want FAA management to find out that he actually worked only a few hours a week. Louise and I had to laugh. Bill and his family had been some of the good people in Alexandria.

Louise and I got into our car and drove away, heading west for Dickinson and a visit with her family. I did not realize it then but it was the last time I was ever to sit foot on the Alexandria airport.

The country had not stood still in the thirteen years we had lived in Minnesota. I will mention only a few of the highlights. In February of 1973 we watched on television as American Prisoners of War returned home from North Vietnam. A peace accord had been signed between the U.S. and North Vietnam. The ragged airmen stepped off the airplanes and saluted the American flag. I had to wonder if I had listened to some of their mayday calls as they had been shot down over North Vietnam. In 1968, I had been a navigator on an Air Force radar plane flying over Laos and the Gulf of Tonkin. We had monitored bombing runs over Hanoi.

I have kept a newspaper in my box of mementos. It is the Friday, August 9, 1974 issue of the *St. Paul Pioneer Press*. The headline blares – **Nixon Resigns**. The nation had suffered through two years of the Watergate scandal, where Republican operatives under Nixon's approval had burglarized Democratic National Committee headquarters in Washington, D.C. Nixon resigned before he could be impeached for obstruction of justice and abuse of power.

There are television images which stick in a person's mind. I remember Nixon proclaiming in one TV appearance that "Your President is not a crook." Of course he was and he had tried to cover it up. There were also rumors that Nixon had an "enemies list," names of those politicians and well-known people who opposed him. It was no way to run our country.

The Vietnam War had finally staggered to an end when the city of Saigon fell to North Vietnamese troops on April 30, 1975. We watched news reports in horror as South Vietnamese citizens clung to helicopters that were evacuating them to offshore U.S. Navy ships. The first U.S. soldiers had been killed in Vietnam in 1959. A little over 58,000 had eventually perished. A total of more than one point three million lives had been lost.

The early 1980s saw Iran release fifty-two American hostages held in Tehran for 444 days. A deranged man attempted to assassinate President Ronal Reagan. The AIDS virus made its appearance. Sandra Day O'Connor became the first female Justice on the Supreme Court. Maya Lin's Vietnam War Memorial was established in Washington, DC. The first artificial heart was implanted.

Of course there was much, much more going on, in our country and in the world. There were always violent conflicts where people were being displaced and killed. Our social environment was changing in response to rapidly evolving technology. Humanity continued to move forward, to accumulate ever more knowledge.

It is Saturday, April 11, 2020, as I sit at the computer and type my story. I am winding up the first draft of this latest book. It will probably be another two or three months before it will be ready for publication. It will be part of the legacy I will leave behind for my grandchildren and their grandchildren.

The sun is shining. I can see through the office window that the pond across the street is finally free of ice. The walleyes have begun to spawn in the Oconto River. Gray squirrels are in the back lawn, using their noses to locate the acorns they buried last fall. There are a few places in deep shade where the last of the winter snow has not yet melted. In the woods the red maple trees have begun to bud. The temperature in northeast Wisconsin is forecast to be in the high fifties today and in the thirties and low forties next week. Snow is forecast for Monday.

Monday is expected to be significant for an entirely different reason. It is the day when the coronavirus pandemic, COVID-19, is expected to peak in Wisconsin. Nationwide, there have been more than half a million cases reported thus far and 20,000 deaths. Worldwide, there have been at least 100,000 deaths. Louise and Jenifer and I have been mostly housebound for the past month, fearing for our lives. We leave the house only to buy groceries or to pick up medications. We practice social distancing, keeping at least six feet apart when we are in public, and we wear the cloth face masks which Louise has made. Our daughter, Jenifer, has lived with us the past decade. She has been unable to work due to medical issues. Both her immune system and mine are compromised due to Type II diabetes and other health problems. We are fairly certain that if we contract the virus it will kill us. Louise has Parkinson's, a neurological disease. Her immune system is not bothered by the disorder but age could be a factor. She is seventy-two.

I have told my grandchildren that we are living through historic times with this coronavirus pandemic, that it is something they will talk to their grandchildren about. When the crisis first hit people rushed to the stores to stock up on toilet paper. It seems like such an unusual issue to be worried about. Will we suffer horribly if we cannot wipe our butts? I am trying to figure out what it says about our society.

At this point there is only guesswork as to the long-term economic and social changes that the pandemic may bring about. Here at the local level, though, life goes on. Even with the window closed I can hear our three wonderful little neighbor girls playing in the street. It is the sound of the future. It is the sound of life itself. The older we get the more we realize how meaningful and important love is in the story of humanity. It may be that someday those three will stumble across my books and remember the old grandpa who used to live across the street from them.

Being housebound has given me more of an opportunity to work on this book. It is a daily project though I cannot toil for more than three or four hours without getting tired. The threat of dying has motivated me to push on while I still have time.

If I have the time and the energy to write Volume V of this rather lengthy autobiography, on the more than three decades in Wisconsin, then I will feel as though I can relax a bit. I will have accomplished my main goal – a story for my grandchildren and their grandchildren. Anything beyond that, a book on the value of doubt and a book on outdoor photography, will be icing on the cake.

I have been retired now for twenty-two years. I will be eighty years old in another five weeks. It has been pleasurable to enjoy the fruits of my labor. I sit in my lounge chair and look out the family room window at the block wall I built around our house fifteen years ago. Now I am too old to even attempt such a large project. I can see the grass I sowed and the shrubs I planted.

Of course it is not just about me. Louise's work is everywhere inside the house. She has been the interior decorator. I cannot walk into any room without seeing her reflected in it. And, after many years of struggle when we were first married, we are financially comfortable with our government retirement checks.

I cannot think of Louise and our children and grandchildren without getting a warm glow. They have made everything meaningful – especially Louise. She rescued me when I was at a low point in my life. She has been a steady and loyal and loving soulmate for fifty years. She has made my life's journey worthwhile.

COPIES OF THIS BOOK AND OTHERS WRITTEN BY THE AUTHOR MAY BE OBTAINED THROUGH AMAZON.

Made in the USA
Columbia, SC
10 July 2020